**Captivity Beyond Prisons**

# Captivity Beyond Prisons

## Criminalization Experiences of Latina (Im)migrants

MARTHA D. ESCOBAR

University of Texas Press ◆ *Austin*

Requests for permission to reproduce material from this work should be sent to:
 Permissions
 University of Texas Press
 P.O. Box 7819
 Austin, TX 78713-7819
 http://utpress.utexas.edu/index.php/rp-form

♾ The paper used in this book meets the minimum requirements of ANSI/
NISO Z39.48-1992 (R1997) (Permanence of Paper).

**Library of Congress Cataloging-in-Publication Data**
Escobar, Martha D., author.
 Captivity beyond prisons : criminalization experiences of Latina
(im)migrants / Martha D. Escobar. — First edition.
  pages  cm
 Includes bibliographical references and index.
 ISBN 978-1-4773-0816-5 (cloth : alk. paper) — ISBN 978-1-4773-0901-8
(pbk. : alk. paper) — ISBN 978-1-4773-0829-5 (library e-book) —
ISBN 978-1-4773-0830-1 (non-library e-book)
 1. Women immigrants—United States—Social conditions.  2. Hispanic
American women—United States—Social conditions.  3. Women illegal
aliens—United States—Social conditions.  4. Emigration and immigration—
Social aspects.  5. Emigration and immigration—Women—United States.
6. Immigrants—Government policy—United States.  7. Emigration and
immigration law—United States.  I. Title.
 JV6347.E73  2016
 365′.4308968073—dc23
                                                        2015035742

doi:10.7560/308165

*Para Sandra, donde quiera que te encuentres . . .*
For Sandra, wherever you may find yourself . . .

# Contents

# Acknowledgments

It is difficult to acknowledge everyone who provided me support, especially when it takes an entire community to sustain us through such endeavors. Some will be mentioned by name and others will remain anonymous, but I am eternally grateful to everyone who, in one way or another, made this work possible.

Editors Theresa May and Kerry Webb were very supportive and made what seemed an insurmountable undertaking viable. I also appreciate the insightful feedback and comments of the reviewers who engaged this project in meaningful ways.

Institutional support was fundamental. The Center for US-Mexican Studies at the University of California, San Diego provided me with the time, space, and intellectual inspiration to conduct research. My current academic home, California State University, Northridge, was also instrumental. In addition to support from the Chicana/o Studies Department, the College of Humanities Research Fellowship provided me with invaluable time to dedicate myself to this work.

I am indebted to Justice Now, Critical Resistance, California Coalition for Women Prisoners, Instituto Madre Assunta, and A New Way of Life for opening their doors to me and for their work against gendered and racialized violence.

I am also grateful to the many people at the University of California, Riverside, who continue to offer me their friendship and support. The list is too long to mention everyone by name, but I want to especially thank Alfredo Figueroa, Veronica Ortega, and Estella Acuña. They continue to inspire me every day and serve as reminders of why we do what we do.

This book would not have been possible without the mentorship of several amazing scholars to whom I will always be indebted. Lisa Sun-Hee Park unreservedly supported me, challenged me to be a better scholar, and modeled what a good mentor should be. I know I would not be where I am without her guidance. Natalia Molina also offered critical insight for this project and has been vital to my academic development. David Pellow was always encouraging and directed my thinking in new and complicated ways. A remarkable educator, he significantly influenced my pedagogy. David Gutierrez's openness to pushing the boundaries provided a fresh outlook and motivated me to take some risks in my own work. There is no way to overstate the impact that Dylan Rodríguez has had on my academic and personal life. He saw many of us through difficult times and has supported me in so many ways since my undergraduate years. His influence is apparent throughout this work. Finally, Setsu Shigematsu's commitment to social justice and her conversations with me on the need to ground ourselves in feminist praxis greatly inspired my research.

This has been a difficult journey, and I know that it would have been even harder without many of the amazing people who struggled with and supported me. I am eternally grateful to Xamuel Bañales, Long Bui, Gabriela Cazares, Myrna García, Rebecca J. Kinney, Angela Kong, Stevie Ruiz, and Angelica Yañez, great friends and colleagues whose words and solidarity have helped sustain me over the years. I thank Myrna García, Rebecca J. Kinney, and Stevie Ruiz for providing important feedback on parts of this project. Jodie Lawston's work, insight, and friendship also made her a valued companion in this journey.

I feel fortunate to be able to call CSU Northridge home. David Rodriguez, former chair of the Chicana/o Studies Department, helped guide me from the very beginning. Mary Pardo has been incredibly supportive and offered important feedback for this project. I would like to express my gratitude to everyone in the department, not only for the warm welcome, but also for their commitment to creating a more livable world. The list of people and their individual contributions is too long to enumerate, but I do want to recognize a few in particular. I am grateful to Francisco Tamayo and Alicia Ivonne Estrada for motivating me to continue writing even in moments when I thought I could not and for always being my companions in this struggle. Marta López-Garza provided such important spaces for me to build community and carry out some of my work. Ana Sánchez-Muñoz and Yarma Velázquez-Vargas provided important advice when I needed it and constantly make me smile. Through their energy, words, and dedication, Rudy Acuña,

Christina Ayala-Alcantar, Jorge García, Ramon García, Gabriel Gutié-rrez, Rosa RiVera-Furumoto, and Juana Mora have made my time at CSUN invaluable. Also, I appreciate Cynthia Martinez, José Rosas, and Rosa Salamanca, students who not only assisted me with this project, but also kept me grounded by sharing their experiences and dedicating themselves to creating change.

This work illustrates the importance of working through boundaries. The following acknowledgments need to be written across languages.

Le doy las más sinceras gracias a mi familia, quienes me apoyaron a través de este largo camino. Me dieron consejos cuando los necesité, me ayudaron a entender el mundo un poco mejor, y supieron comprender cuando no pude estar con ellas/ellos. Gabriela, mi hermana, sus palabras y cuidados han sido un recordatorio de la importancia de echarle ganas. Alberto, mi pareja, le agradezco ser la persona que es y siempre ser atento, tanto conmigo como con todas las personas a su alrededor. Ahora compartimos a nuestro hijo Omar, quien nos inspira aun más a tratar de vivir una vida más justa. Finalmente, quiero agradecerles a las mujeres y compañeras que compartieron sus historias, sus vidas, sus pensamientos, y sus energías conmigo. Fue un privilegio ser parte de sus vidas, por mucho o por poco tiempo. Estaré siempre en deuda con ustedes. ¡Gracias!

# Abbreviations

| | |
|---|---|
| AEDPA | Antiterrorism and Effective Death Penalty Act (1996) |
| ASFA | Adoption and Safe Families Act (1997) |
| AdSeg | administrative segregation |
| ANWOL | A New Way of Life |
| BNDD | Bureau of Narcotics and Dangerous Drugs |
| Casa | Casa del Migrante |
| CCWF | Central California Women's Facility |
| CCWP | California Coalition for Women Prisoners |
| CDC | California Department of Corrections |
| CDCR | California Department of Corrections and Rehabilitation |
| CIW | California Institution for Women |
| COINTELPRO | Counter Intelligence Program |
| CR | Critical Resistance |
| DACA | Deferred Action for Childhood Arrivals |
| DAPA | Deferred Action for Parents of Americans and Lawful Permanent Residents |
| DEA | Drug Enforcement Agency |
| DIF | Desarrollo Integral de la Familia |
| DHS | Department of Homeland Security |
| H.R. 4437 | Border Protection, Antiterrorism, and Illegal Immigration Control Act (2005) |
| ICE | Immigration and Customs Enforcement |
| IIRIRA | Illegal Immigration Reform and Immigrant Responsibility Act (1996) |
| INA | Immigration and Nationality Act (1965) |

| INM | Instituto Nacional de Migración |
|---|---|
| INS | Immigration and Naturalization Services |
| Instituto | Instituto Madre Assunta |
| IRCA | Immigration Reform and Control Act (1986) |
| LEAA | Law Enforcement Assistance Administration |
| LEAD | Leadership, Education, Action, and Dialogue |
| LIC | Low Intensity Conflict |
| LPC | Likely to become a Public Charge |
| LSPC | Legal Services for Prisoners with Children |
| NIYA | National Immigration Youth Alliance |
| NLRA | National Labor Relations Act (1935) |
| NLRB | National Labor Relations Board |
| PEP | Priority Enforcement Program |
| PIC | Prison Industrial Complex |
| Prop. 9 | Criminal Justice System, Victims' Rights, Parole (California) (2008) |
| Prop. 21 | Gang Violence and Juvenile Crime Prevention Initiative (California) (2001) |
| Prop. 187 | Save Our State (SOS) ballot initiative (California) (1994) |
| PRWORA | Personal Responsibility and Work Opportunity Reconciliation Act (Welfare Reform Act) (1996) |
| Realignment | California Assembly Bills (A.B.) 109 and 117 (Public Safety Realignment) |
| S. 744 | Border Security, Economic Opportunity, and Immigration Modernization Act (2013) |
| S.B. 1070 | Support Our Law Enforcement and Safe Neighborhoods Act (Arizona) (2010) |
| S.B. 1135 | Prison Sterilization Prohibition (California) (2014) |
| SNY | Sensitive Needs Yard |
| USCIS | United States Citizenship and Immigration Services |
| VAWA | Violence Against Women Act (1994) |
| VSP | Valley State Prison |
| VSPW | Valley State Prison for Women |
| VTVPA | Victims of Trafficking and Violence Protection Act (2000) |

**Captivity Beyond Prisons**

# Shifting the Conversation from (Im)migrant Rights to Abolition

The US (im)migrant rights movement erupted in 2006 in the wake of the passage of the Border Protection, Antiterrorism, and Illegal Immigrant Control Act (H.R. 4437). The movement initially signaled the possibility of imagining means of social belonging outside territorial legal citizenship.[1] It asserted that *all* (im)migrants, regardless of legal status, deserve social and economic justice. It also demanded legalization for *all* 11 to 12 million undocumented (im)migrants.

However, these re-imagining possibilities were rapidly undermined as the movement shifted attention toward pragmatic endeavors in order to effect justice for (im)migrants. Predictably, the domain of *all* (im)migrants tightened, returning to the bad/good (im)migrant dichotomy that polices the boundaries of US citizenship. The focus of most sectors of the (im)migrant rights movement shifted toward re-defining the "good" (im)migrant category in attempts to expand the number of people who could potentially qualify for legalization and eventual citizenship. Yet these organizing strategies neglected to take into account the ways in which (im)migration policy performs as racialized population control, inherently tied to and dependent on binaries that construct particular (im)migrants as perpetually outside of belonging.[2] In other words, racialized governance constructs particular (im)migrants as expendable under hegemonic governing logic.

Since the 1990s, the United States has witnessed tremendous expansion in the numbers of imprisoned (im)migrants, specifically Latinas/os. Consequently, the number of deportations has also increased. Under existing (im)migration law, a felony conviction for an aggravated felony almost automatically results in an (im)migrant's deportation to his or her country of origin and permanent barring from the United States. The outcome is the same whether the (im)migrant is documented or undocumented prior to conviction, highlighting how prisons function as sites where legality is unmade since imprisoned legal residents are deported and permanently banned from returning.[3] The vast majority of people deported under the category of "criminal alien" are racialized as non-white, with Mexicans making up the largest number (Simanski 2014).

In addition, (im)migrants who appear unable to care for themselves are often designated as "likely to become a public charge." This designation limits their ability to legalize their status. The gendered impact of this category is evident in its application, as underscored by the exclusion of poor women, women racialized as non-white, and/or women of childbearing age (Fujiwara 2008, 122–124; Luibhéid 2002, xx; Park 2001 and 2011). As the (im)migrant rights movement strives to expand the boundaries of US citizenship, it simultaneously reinforces the expendability, and thus violability, of people labeled as "bad" (im)migrants. This includes the imprisoned, women, and gender nonconforming individuals. What results from this impulse to be pragmatic is the reinforcement of hegemonic narratives and structures. Myths such as those that portray this country as a land of (im)migrants and extol the American Dream regard the United States as exceptional—a land of opportunity that people around the globe are eager to reach. Advocates of (im)migrant rights often draw on these myths to make claims on the state on behalf of (im)migrants.[4] Such myths construct (im)migration as individual actions and serve to erase the role of the United States in (re)producing authorized and unauthorized (im)migration.[5]

The limitations of the dominant (im)migrant rights framework materialized on November 20, 2014, with President Barack Obama's executive action on (im)migration. In his speech, Obama rhetorically drew from this framework to substantiate his actions. Both the speech and the executive action reinforced the bad/good (im)migrant dichotomy. Obama stated:

> Even as we are a nation of immigrants, we're also a nation of laws. Undocumented workers broke our immigration laws, and I believe that they must be held accountable, especially those who may be dangerous. That's why over the past six years deportations of criminals are up 80 percent, and that's why we're going to keep focusing enforcement resources on actual threats to our security. Felons, not families. Criminals, not children. Gang members, not a mom who's working hard to provide for her kids. We'll prioritize, just like law enforcement does every day. (Office of the Press Secretary 2014a)

The president constructed explicit dichotomies—felons/families, criminals/children, gang members/hard-working mothers. These dichotomies assume that these categories are mutually exclusive; that "felons" are not part of families, that "criminals" are not children, that "gang members" are not hard-working parents. These false dichotomies have been in part reinforced by the ideological work carried out by the dominant (im)migrant rights advocates with intent to provide some level of protection for (im)migrants. Up to 5 million people will potentially benefit from the executive action, including temporary relief from deportation and access to legal work permits. Still, as the above excerpt from the speech demonstrates, the action requires sacrifices from ineligible (im)migrants. These include increased border enforcement (and the inevitable violence that accompanies these practices) and the continued use of the logics of criminality and dependency to maintain levels of exclusions and deportations.[6] Given the vast number of people who are excluded from Obama's executive action and the fact that this is temporary relief, (im)migrant justice continues to be a salient social and political issue. From this moment forward, people invested in the issue of (im)migration and (im)migrant justice, especially in relation to (im)-migrants excluded from President Obama's executive action, should reflect on the ideological frameworks used to advocate for transformative changes.

To speak to the bad/good (im)migrant conundrum in which the (im)migrant rights movement seems to be locked, I look toward the prison abolition movement. Unlike (im)migrant rights, this movement strives to deconstruct binaries of deserving versus undeserving, instead struggling to bring about freedom for *everyone*. Its productiveness is located in the fact that it refuses to give up on people legally conceptualized as criminal, which marks them as expendable and violable. Once they are legally classified as "criminal aliens," (im)migrants are marked for removal from the nation-state and permanently banned from returning. Thus, I argue that their criminalization renders them legally irrecuperable. Incarcerated US citizens also experience certain levels of irrecuperability. For example, several US states have implemented legislation that permanently disenfranchises people convicted of a felony (Manza and Uggen 2006).[7] The prison abolition movement takes on the labor of imagining ways of social belonging that depart from relying on existing binaries. As opposed to rendering individuals worthy or unworthy of belonging, the movement draws attention to the fact that the same opportunities do not exist for everyone to thrive, considering instead the structural changes needed to socially reach the point where prisons' obsoleteness becomes common sense.[8]

Furthermore, the prison abolition movement provides an understanding of criminalization and imprisonment as performing fundamental ideological and material labor for modern governance. In other words, this movement conceptualizes imprisonment as a constituting logic of US society in that imprisonment becomes the answer to perceived social crises (Gilmore 1998 and 2007; Rodríguez 2006). Rather than locating criminality in individuals and as poor choices made, the prison abolition movement examines the ways in which crime is socially constructed and politically deployed to advance particular interests.[9] Doing so shifts the lens away from the irrecuperability of particular bodies and toward carceral statecrafting projects that organize and regulate the relationship between the state and civil society.

A discussion of imprisoned (im)migrant women is essential to generating a dialogue between the (im)migrant rights movement and the prison abolition movement. The latter's insistence that society understand the United States as a fundamentally carceral society, which organizes itself by capturing and warehousing undesirable and surplus bodies, directs us to see the violability of (im)migrants and their families as natural extensions of the experiences of imprisoned (im)migrant women. Put differently, the punitive actions lived by (im)migrants have a long trajectory in US prisons. The detention and separation of families have been made possible because the ideological and material groundwork necessary for this moment was already produced in relation to the bodies of people in prison.

In turn, the experiences of imprisoned (im)migrant women point the prison abolition movement toward the centrality of (im)migrants in the expansion of the carceral society beyond the territorial boundaries of the US nation-state. Part of the state's function is to engage in statecrafting projects that produce exploitable workers. With the increasing translation of the status of undocumented to "criminal," a project in part organized through the criminalization of (im)migrant women's reproduction, (im)migrant bodies are transformed into raw material for the global expansion of a carceral society. The US-Mexico border is a space that makes this production a possibility by first rendering bodies "illegal." Centering the experiences of imprisoned (im)migrant women reveals the dialectical relationship between the national and transnational, linking the ways in which the US carceral society constitutes and is constituted in relation to the rest of the world.

## The Social Productiveness of Racialized and Gendered (Il)legalization and Criminalization

The central purpose of this study is to provide an understanding of the criminalization of Latina (im)migrants. In other words, how are Latina (im)migrants criminalized and what purpose does this serve? Also, what are the implications and possibilities of centering their experiences in the (im)migrant rights movement?

To address these questions, I examine the experiences of jailed, imprisoned, detained, and deported Latina (im)migrants. I argue for their centrality in both the (im)migrant rights and prison abolition movements. Their irrecuperability is made viable because their origins are outside the US nation-state and their entrance is consigned to the realm of (il)legality since the dominant imagination equates the figure of the (im)migrant to that of the "illegal." In my analysis, I bridge what is occurring with (im)migrants—criminalization, imprisonment, detention, deportation, and family separation—to the larger history of imprisonment in the United States. In particular, I demonstrate how the processes of racialization of Blacks inform the racialization of Latina/o (im)migrants and mark this process as fundamentally gendered. The analysis demonstrates how the merging of criminality and state dependency that occurs in relation to Black motherhood gets re-mapped onto Latina (im)migrants. The ideological construction of (im)migrant women as dependent and as reproducers of criminality makes them logical targets of interpersonal and state violence.

My analysis is largely informed by two main bodies of literature. The first focuses on the social construction of (il)legality, which considers the productive labor that making "legal" and "illegal" (im)migrant bodies performs for US nation-building. The second body of literature, critical prison studies, examines the political deployment of criminality and explores prisons as sites of hierarchical local and global social organization. This work is not solely interested in the materiality of prisons, but it seeks to understand how the social meaning produced through prisons extends beyond their physical walls. In other words, critical prison studies consider how the logic of carcerality participates in the organization of society. By connecting these literatures, I not only reinforce the arguments that (il)legality and criminality are essential constituting logics of racialized, gendered, and classed US formation, but also underline the importance that (im)migrant women assume in the deployment of these logics.

In the late nineteenth and early twentieth centuries, racialized (il)le-
gality (the making and unmaking of "legal" and "illegal" immigrants
that is informed by racial ideas) assumed a significant role in modern
US governance. Processes of racialized (il)legalization were initially developed in relation to Asian (im)migrants and later extended to others.
Particularly significant was the Immigration Act of 1924, which implemented (im)migration quotas for the Eastern Hemisphere intended
to restrict further (im)migration of groups considered racially undesirable. This law served to solidify the national identity as white and joined
whiteness to Europeans (Ngai 2004). That same year, the Border Patrol
was established, which contributed to instituting the socio-legal concept
of the "illegal alien."[10] The production of "illegal aliens" maintained
a national social hierarchy based on white supremacy and privilege.[11]
Ngai (2004) describes "illegal aliens" as "impossible subjects," individuals who are a social reality but a legal impossibility. Although they
are desired for various types of labor and they live, develop relations,
and lead social lives in the United States, they represent a legal impossibility because they are outside the scope of legal citizenship. Racialized (il)legalization is a mechanism used by the state to affect the racial
make-up of the United States while balancing the economic desires of
the nation. Thus, there is nothing natural or essential about (il)legality
or related categories, such as "illegal aliens." These are socio-legal constructions that are productive in modern governance (Lytle-Hernández
2010, 9–10; Molina 2014, 95; Ngai 2004).

With the increased exclusion of Asians, Mexican (im)migrants became vital for the US labor market. As (im)migration restrictions focused on Mexicans, the "Mexican (im)migrant" identity congealed with
the category of "illegal alien" (Lytle-Hernández, 17; Molina, 21; Ngai,
7). The racialization of Mexican (im)migrants as "illegal aliens" made
it easier to create and sustain these workers as flexible and cheap labor
(Chavez 2007; De Genova 2002, 2013a, 2013b). Being undocumented
generates fear of deportation, which is a central tool used to discipline
(im)migrants, especially workers. Thus, state practices of (il)legalization,
of designating bodies as "illegal," produce capital value for the nation
and its citizens. In this sense, the law is an active agent in producing unequal relations that center on constructing exploitable bodies (Chang
2000; Chavez 2007; De Genova 2002, 2013a, 2013b; De Genova and
Peutz 2010; Gardner 2010; Rodriguez and Paredes 2013; Willen 2010).
The vulnerability of undocumented Mexican (im)migrants extends to
other bodies that are racially signified as "Mexican."

The disciplining of (im)migrant workers continues through neoliberal ideologies of personal responsibility. In contemporary neoliberal labor arrangements, undocumented (im)migrants are "ideal neoliberal workers." Their social positionality renders these workers exploitable, but, despite their exploitation, they are not supposed to access social welfare. In other words, ideal neoliberal workers need to labor and are "willing" to perform this labor at very low costs, but also "decide" not to access social welfare to ameliorate their situation because doing so ideologically implies dependency and thus a lack of rationality on their part. Historically, the ideal (im)migrant laborer was defined as the sojourning male who traveled to the United States to labor temporarily and later returned to his country of origin. In this sense, undocumented (im)migrant labor functions as the ideal labor arrangement because the United States reaps the benefits without contributing to its reproduction (Wilson 2000). Thus, rather than exclude (im)migrants, the state endeavors to differentially include them within conditions of vulnerability.[12] Although made expendable, undocumented (im)migrant workers are central to the production of wealth in neoliberal conditions that require substantial labor market flexibility (Dreher 2007; Fernández-Kelly and Massey 2007). This understanding of undocumented (im)migration demonstrates (il)legality as an essential social US condition.

However, even if legally present, the condition of deportability makes (im)migrants vulnerable and exploitable (De Genova and Peutz 2010; Molina 2014). For example, despite the fact that guest worker programs usually include a minimum level of security and benefits for (im)migrant workers, structurally, these arrangements often provide significant power to the employers that leaves (im)migrant workers vulnerable to poor working conditions and low wages (Gardner 2010; Hahamovitch 2003). Employers can confiscate guest workers' legal documents, including visas and passports, and threaten them with deportation. Thus, although these workers are legally present, the condition of deportability, which is structured by states and existing labor relations, serves a similar function as (il)legality in ensuring their exploitability.

While the neoliberal state engages in furthering capitalist interests through processes of (il)legalization and creating conditions of deportability, it must also create national legitimacy by appearing to control (im)migration, particularly unauthorized (im)migration. Part of the statecrafting in which many nation-states engage includes the actual exclusion and removal of (im)migrants, as prominently reflected in the post-9/11 moment and the more recent economic recession, both signified as moments of national "crisis." A central mechanism used to address various crises is the deployment of notions of crime. Constructing criminality is a productive tool in managing and governing (im)migration (Dowling and Inda 2013; Gonzales 2014; Stumpf 2006). Criminalizing (im)migrant bodies and behaviors serves to discipline (im)migrants while simultaneously providing a mechanism for their exclusion. Once they are legally marked as "criminal aliens," they are not only deportable, but also permanently irrecuperable. Once removed, they cannot return and if they do, they face potential re-incarceration. This exemplifies one way in which prisons are productive sites for US governance that allow for the management of different populations. However, before engaging in a discussion on the ways in which US carceral logic is useful in the governing and management of (im)migrants, I first provide a discussion of historical changes in definitions of US citizenship, especially in relation to the labor market. This discussion provides the context for understanding the centrality of racialized processes of (il)legalization and criminalization in modern US governance.

From its very foundation, the US social contract was fundamentally a racialized, gendered, and classed contract. In the United States, citizenship, the binding relationship between the individual and the state, is exclusionary (Glenn 2002; Mills 1999; Pateman 1988). Feminist scholar Evelyn Nakano Glenn (2002) discusses the historical creation of US citizenship as founded on two governing dichotomies, *dependent-independent* and *public-private* (18–23). Glenn explains how dependency was imputed onto Black slaves and how this was later fundamental to defining US citizenship against Blacks. American revolutionaries attempted to define voluntary citizenship against British subjecthood, which was perceived as innate and immutable. In contrast, US citizenship was defined as voluntary and consenting. However, "consent required independence, not only in terms of having property, but also in terms of personal freedom" (22), something enslaved Blacks inherently lacked. Glenn also demonstrates how US citizenship was defined within white masculinity. Notions of women as irrational (driven by emotions) and dependent on their husbands or other family patriarchs, as well as their association with sexuality and motherhood, served to ideologically confine them to the private realm, mark them as dependent, and thus exclude them from substantive citizenship (23). Rather than an aberration of US liberal democracy, patriarchal white supremacist racism is foundational to this project.

US citizenship underwent significant transformations during the twentieth century. In the post–World War II era, the Keynesian welfare state concerned itself with interrogating the effects of the capitalist market economy on citizens' lives and redistribution. This in a sense held the market accountable for the inequality it participated in producing. However, communities of color were systematically excluded from policies of redistribution. Social policies, including de facto and de jure segregation, ensured that these redistributive policies disproportionately benefited whites.

Within neoliberalism, states are engaged in statecrafting projects in which agents empowered to represent the state implement public policies that fundamentally develop and re-order the relationship between the state and civil society (Malloy 1991, 4, cited in Jayasuriya 2006, 32). This is done in order to further expand privatization, as well as deregulation and labor market flexibility. These practices redefine citizenship within the boundaries of the economic market. To put it in the words of political scientist Kanishka Jayasuriya, the regime of citizenship has been altered from a relationship between the state and civil society in which citizenship is defined through the notion of rights to a regime of citizenship "organized through the language and practices of contractualism" (2006, 152) that equates social inclusion with participation in the market economy. The institutionalization of neoliberalism performs the labor of depoliticizing citizenship. The responsibility of the state to citizens shifts from managing the redistribution of wealth to ensuring participation in the labor market.[13] While this conceptualization of the relationship between neoliberalism and citizenship is on target, the ways in which notions of race and gender are fundamental to statecrafting projects also merit further reflection. This includes the Keynesian postwar welfare state period and the contemporary neoliberal United States that presents itself as a post-racial society.[14]

The retreat of the US Keynesian welfare state and the shift toward a competition state occurred precisely as the impacts of the Civil Rights Movement and the various social movements of the 1950s, 1960s, and 1970s were felt throughout society. During this time, the number of people accessing public resources increased, partially because de jure and de facto exclusion had prevented many non-white bodies from accessing these resources. Black women's reproduction functioned as the center of public anxiety over state dependency and was explicitly marked for state intervention (Katz 1989; Roberts 1997; Neubeck and Cazenave 2001; Handler 2002). National social issues, particularly state dependency and criminality, were ascribed to Black women (Collins 1999;

Jordan-Zachery 2009; Roberts 1997 and 2002). Following this logic, the state implemented policies to address these domestic "problems," using as its central tools the retrenchment of the welfare state and the intense buildup of the criminal legal system, which developed into the largest existing prison regime.

The criminalization of Latina/o (im)migrants must be considered within this history, especially with respect to the imprisonment of (im)-migrant women. Changes in the enforcement of (im)migration laws have resulted in making Latinas/os the largest ethno-racial group in the federal prison system (Lopez and Light 2009; Light, Lopez, and Gonzalez-Barrera 2013). Recognizing the significance Black motherhood assumed in the criminalization of Blacks forces us to focus on Latina (im)migrant motherhood in order to understand the criminalization of Latina/o (im)migrants. In other words, if linking state dependency and criminality as ideologically taking place in relation to the reproductive bodies of Black women was central for reorganizing the relationship of Blacks to civil society, and if similar discourse is deployed against the reproductive bodies of Latina (im)migrants, we must consider the extent to which this discourse provides the rationale for the criminalization of (im)migrants in general. The shift from the welfare to the competition state and from social to market citizenship highlights issues of race and gender.[15] When changes in the state signaled a potential shift for non-white families to benefit from a certain level of social protection, changes that were created largely by making claims through citizenship, society witnessed significant state reorganization. It is when the welfare state is compelled to address the needs of communities of color, when the potential for women of color to experience state-sanctioned domesticity develops, that welfare is criminalized and the shift from "welfare to work" takes place (Fujiwara 2008, 33).

The criminalization of welfare corresponds to the moment when Blacks as workers are made expendable, largely due to their ability to make citizenship claims to the state, including demands for better living and working conditions. In turn, undocumented (im)migrants are made into ideal neoliberal laborers through their undocumented and thus flexible status. Understanding how the merging of state dependency and criminality in relation to the bodies of Black women informed the US shift toward market citizenship, which facilitated the advancement of neoliberal governance, provides insight into the criminalization of Latina (im)migrant women as a means to separate their productive labor from their reproductive capabilities. Latina (im)migrant women then serve their neoliberal purpose as laborers and conclude this purpose when they assume the identity of mother. Thus, recognizing the re-mapping of criminality and state dependency onto (im)migrant women provides deeper understanding into the ways that imprisonment serves as a response to the (im)migration "problem" that (im)migrant women ideologically represent. Latina (im)migrant women are largely constructed outside the ideal neoliberal laborer identity because their ability to have children presents permanent settlement, which reduces their value as flexible laborers. Racializing (im)migrant women as dependent and criminal participates in the neoliberal project of producing exploitable laboring bodies by separating their productive from their reproductive labors.[16]

Even prior to assuming significance as laborers, (im)migrant women's bodies served as political sites where the nation-state reproduced itself. Their position as mothers contributes to their permanent outsider status since they are conceptualized as too culturally and racially different to contribute to the US citizenry. Their sexualities are constructed as racialized national threats. The border has served as a significant site for the control of women's sexualities, and thus, the racialized constitution of the nation. For example, Luibhéid (2002) highlights the border as a site where meaning is made through the construction of sexual identities and the enforcement of heteronormativity. Other works (Luibhéid and Cantú 2005; Canaday 2011; Cantú 2009) expand the analysis of how (im)migration control participates in constructing racialized, gendered, and classed sexualities and oppressive sexual norms. In essence, these works demonstrate how the US nation-state constructs itself as heteropatriarchal and white supremacist through (im)migration control, and how (im)migrant bodies, particularly women and gender nonconforming individuals, are central sites where this ideological labor takes place. The re-mapping of dependency and criminality onto (im)migrant women's reproductive bodies rationalized punitive policies and practices against Latina (im)migrants and their communities. Racialized and gendered (im)migration enforcement serves to contain and, in the case of incarceration and deportation, dispose of the "threat." This directs our attention to the significance of incarceration as a mechanism for (im)migration control.

Critical prison studies as a field has expanded since the mid-1990s, making invaluable interjections in our understanding of the ways in which society racially organizes itself through the criminalization of people of color (Alexander 2010; Davis 2003; Gilmore 1998 and 2007;

Rodríguez 2006; James 2000 and 2007; Parenti 1999; Richie 2012). In part, the productiveness of these works stems from the generative national discussion they helped to establish on the use of incarceration as a "solution" to America's "race problem." They are partially responsible for bringing to the forefront of academic and activist circles the notion of prison abolition as a visionary possibility.

Scholars such as Jael Silliman and Anannya Bhattacharjee (2002), Angela Harris (2011), Beth Richie (2012), and Julia Sudbury (2005) have greatly contributed to this discussion by privileging gender and sexuality and demonstrating how controlling and disciplining women and gender non-conforming bodies serve as fundamental features of imprisonment that achieve the goal of racial reorganization. These works are also significant in that they highlight the role of individuals and the state in perpetuating violence against women of color and gender non-conforming individuals.

Sudbury's work is especially helpful in thinking about (im)migrant women's criminalization. Her edited compilation centers on women's imprisonment globally and highlights how gendered incarceration operates as a global phenomenon connected to "colonialism, global capitalism, neoliberalism, and militarism" (xi). Sudbury maintains that "both the fabric of the prison and the people caged within it are shaped by global factors, from free trade agreements and neoliberal restructuring to multinational expansion" (xii). This collection reveals women's (im)-migration and imprisonment as fundamentally connected processes. (Im)migrant imprisonment works/behaves as a local-national response to the global-transnational phenomenon of (im)migration, designating (im)migrant women's bodies as sites through which the national and transnational are negotiated and constituted.

Bridging the scholarship on the social construction of (im)migrant (il)legality and the social construction of criminality binds the policing and incarceration that (im)migrants currently encounter to a longer history of US captivity.[17] Central to this critical integration are the works of scholars such as David Manuel Hernández (2008) and Dylan Rodríguez (2008) who dislodge the contemporary anti-(im)migrant moment from exceptionality. Instead, they consider detention and incarceration as historically fundamental in the racial organization of US society. Nationalist voices use exceptionalist discourses to construct the post-9/11 period as a markedly different era in which a new social crisis (terrorism) threatens the nation. At the same time, voices for (im)migrant justice characterize the contemporary targeting of (im)migrant communities as distinctively unique, in part because of the unprecedented blurring between civil and criminalized activities.[18] By displacing exceptionalist discourses, these works reveal the racialized organizational labor performed by the policing and incarceration of target populations, nationally and globally. The analysis furthers the argument that human captivity is constitutive of US social formation as a racialized global neoliberal power.

By focusing on the criminalization of (im)migrant women, I do not simply join the efforts to displace an exceptionalist understanding of the contemporary anti-(im)migrant moment. I also seek to draw from existing scholarship on (im)migrant women's experiences and advance a critical feminist conceptualization of US captivity that accounts for the centrality of (im)migrant women's bodies in maintaining US global dominance.

The irrecuperability of (im)migrant women in prison is crystallized for them through their captivity. Their status as (im)migrants, regardless of their official legal standing, consigns them to the conceptual space of (il)legality that influences their experiences. Ideologically, their imprisonment serves to confirm their "inherent criminality" and thus irrecuperability. Socially and legally, they are foreclosed from all possibilities of belonging in the United States.

In reinforcing the bad/good (im)migrant dichotomy, the (im)migrant rights movement participates in the ideological production of imprisoned (im)migrant women's irrecuperability. This is the case regardless of how well intentioned and/or expanded the category of "good" (im)migrant becomes. As subjects outside of belonging, and thus outside of rights and protection, these women are not only expendable, but also violable. In essence, and although unintended, the (im)migrant rights movement participates in passing judgment over persons' deservingness. Consequently, the line between innocent and criminal denotes the point that defines which (im)migrant families deserve to be kept intact and which ones can be separated, who can remain in the nation and who can be deported, and whose bodies deserve protection and whose merit violation. In response, the prison abolition movement's resolve to organize around *all or none*—its refusal to leave anyone behind—provides direction for the (im)migrant rights movement and presents possibilities for collaborative work across movements.

Building on the prison abolition movement's critique that crime is socially constructed and politically deployed to organize the relationship between civil society and the state provides an understanding of the ways in which (il)legality is elemental to social organization, particularly with respect to contemporary racial neoliberal labor arrangements. As a result of many civil rights struggles that forced federal legislative intervention, the exploitability of workers can no longer be achieved through explicitly racist policies, such as "separate but equal." If worker exploitation secures capitalists' accumulation of wealth, and if this is inherently a racial project in the United States, how has this accumulation endured, given changes in federal law that prohibit racial discrimination? The racialized (il)legalization of (im)migrants secures their flexibility and enables accumulation (Calavita 1992; De Genova 2002; Hernández 2008; Menjívar and Kanstroom 2014).[19]

Coming to terms with the fact that (il)legality is constitutive of the United States leaves entities invested in (im)migrant justice with two main choices. One, they can continue trying to expand the "good" (im)migrant category, using dominant narratives to make claims on the state for the inclusion of a limited number of undocumented (im)migrants. Or, two, they can take on the task of deconstructing the binary of deserving and undeserving, essentially recuperable and irrecuperable (im)migrants.

The first option necessitates practices of social valuing that are fundamentally relational and violent since ascribing value necessitates the devaluation of (an)other (Cacho 2012). Most often, devaluation occurs against already vulnerable and legally unprotected people (17). As noted above, President Obama's executive action on (im)migration, which is greatly informed by the dominant (im)migrant rights framework, serves to enforce the good/bad (im)migrant binary. While some will benefit, we must ask what sacrifices will be required of "bad" (im)migrants?

The second option calls for re-engaging the task of imagining means of belonging outside the confines of legal citizenship. Deconstructing binaries of deserving and undeservingness requires an understanding of the socio-structural factors involved in (im)migrants' criminalization. Scholars largely attribute the origins of the current criminalization of (im)migrants in the United States to the passing of the 1986 federal Immigration Reform and Control Act (IRCA). IRCA contributed both to the militarization of the border and to the increased presence of (im)-migrants in the United States. The fact that IRCA provided amnesty to more than 2 million people and allowed for family reunification contributed to the increase (Cornelius and Bustamante 1989, 165; Dunn 1996, 159; Massey, Durand, and Malone 2002). IRCA was particularly significant to the criminalization that (im)migrants endure. However, what is lost in this narrative is how the development of the criminalization of Blacks rooted in the 1960s, which merged state dependency and criminality and led to the development of the largest prison regime in the world, provided the founding logic for the criminalization of (im)migrants within neoliberalism.

## Feminist Abolition

In this study, I employ a feminist abolitionist framework to analyze the criminalization of Latina (im)migrants. Prison abolitionist scholars maintain that mass criminalization and incarceration are a continuation of the racialized relationship of subjugation established during slavery. Thus, the purpose of abolitionist efforts is to continue the struggle of creating real democracy and radical freedom. In using the term "radical freedom," I draw from feminist prison abolitionist scholars such as Angela Y. Davis (2003 and 2012) and Joy James (2005), who maintain that freedom is not a thing that is granted by an external entity, particularly the state. Rather, it is the process of collective struggle to create real democracy. I term it *radical* freedom to signify it as a process that aims to get to the root of social problems, including mass displacement (local, national, and international), poverty, state violence, and vulnerability to premature death. These abolitionist insights inform my analysis.

However, this must be an explicitly feminist abolitionist framework because anti-criminalization and anti-incarceration understandings can often erase or exclude the ways in which these forms of subjugations are sexualized and gendered by primarily focusing on heterosexual men's experiences.[20] Instead, a feminist abolitionist framework demands that we focus on the ways in which women and gender non-conforming individuals are affected. Specifically, we need to analyze and address the ways in which interpersonal and state forms of violence work in tandem to shape the lives and experiences of women and gender non-conforming individuals (Harris 2011; INCITE! Women of Color Against Violence 2006; Richie 1995 and 2012; Sudbury 2005). Thus, engaging in radical freedom necessitates challenging all forms of oppression simultaneously.

Central to these efforts is the refusal to leave anyone behind. In this sense, it is a refusal to engage in politics of human valuing.[21] Instead, a structural analysis of power relations is emphasized. This leads to one of the most productive aspects of a feminist abolitionist framework, which is to demand that we imagine the unimaginable. This framework asks, "What does a world without prisons look like?" However, what is really at the heart of this question is, "What does a world look like where someone's freedom and life are not contingent on (an)other's immobilization and death?" And after imagining the unimaginable, this framework necessitates the question, "How do we create such a world?"

## A Map of the Methodological Journey

This project developed from a 2004 internship with Justice Now, a prison abolitionist advocacy organization in Oakland, California. During the first couple of weeks, interns received training on methods for conducting advocacy for imprisoned women. I engaged in advocacy work centered on issues of health care and parental rights termination. This entailed gathering case information from files, visiting with the individuals, and then discussing possible methods of advocacy for these individuals with the organization staff. The work included making phone calls, writing letters, and conducting research.

I was assigned to provide advocacy for several women in Central California Women's Facility (CCWF) in Chowchilla, California, approximately one hundred and sixty miles southeast of San Francisco. January 2012 figures show the Chowchilla population numbering 17,817, of which 6,058, or 34 percent, were people in prison.[22] In part, this is due to the fact that, until January 2013, Chowchilla was home to the two largest women's prisons in the world, Valley State Prison for Women (VSPW) and CCWF, which are across the street from each other.[23]

During my ten-week internship, I learned a great deal from the experiences of imprisoned women. However, what consumed much of my time and energy were issues of parental rights terminations. Five of the cases entailed monolingual Spanish speakers who faced the termination of their parental rights. All five had children in the foster care system and were scheduled for deportation at the end of their sentence; four were sentenced on drug-related charges. The pattern in their cases was overwhelming. For all five women, placing their children with friends or family was a problem, given the requirements implemented by child welfare policies. In all the cases, the lack of English proficiency prevented them from obtaining adequate social and legal support to maintain their parental rights. With the exception of one of the families, the women received little to no support from the children's fathers.

These facts demonstrate how losing their children was characteristic of larger structural challenges. While I was unable to create any substantive changes for this group of (im)migrants and their families, I continued learning what structured their lives, and I turn to these initial five stories to guide this project. Thus, the essence of my study comes from learning from the experiences of this group of incarcerated (im)migrant women.

Their stories led me to the *Los Angeles Times* as Juana's case was widely publicized in this newspaper. Her story received significant attention because of its horrific nature, including the fact that two of her children were killed by their father. Although these news articles do not appear in this study, largely because returning to this story is incredibly difficult emotionally, my research made me aware of the role and investment of the media in representing (im)migrants. As a result, this led to a discourse analysis of the gendered representation of (im)migrants in the *Los Angeles Times.* In particular, I was interested in examining how the separation of families caused by parents' deportations was addressed by this newspaper. The analysis revealed how the hegemonic narrative of (im)migration as locked in a bad/good (im)migrant binary reinforced gendered racial boundaries and how the media participates in this process.

Advocating for (im)migrant women in prison in 2004 informed my desire to keep learning from these women's experiences. In May 2008, I joined the California Coalition for Women Prisoners (CCWP), a prison abolitionist organization. I immediately became involved in their Compañeras Project, a component of the organization dedicated to working with Latina (im)migrant women. The project's coordinator, Xiomara, organized bi-monthly visits of CCWP volunteers with an initial group of fifteen (im)migrant women at VSPW. My research consisted of prison visits, case files, and letter correspondence gathered through my involvement with the project. The experience of being part of the Compañeras Project allowed me to focus on their stories, but, more than that, it informed my understanding of advocacy work within prison abolition and of the difficulties implementing an abolitionist vision. I intimately learned how even within prison abolition, an apparently radical space, relationships of power can be reinforced. I expand on this discussion in chapter 5.

Before contacting Xiomara, I had difficulty finding organizations that worked with (im)migrant women in prison. Thus, I decided to reach out to (im)migrant shelters in Tijuana, Mexico, to contact (im)migrant women who had been imprisoned in the United States, then deported. Sister Orilla Travesini, the director of Instituto Madre Assunta (Instituto), an (im)migrant women's shelter in Tijuana, and Mary Galvan, the shelter's social worker, agreed to allow me to conduct my research. I visited the shelter every Thursday for more than six months, conducting ethnographic research with (im)migrant women. I met several women who had been imprisoned in the United States. However, it was through learning the stories of (im)migrant women in general that I realized how connected their lives were to those of imprisoned (im)migrant women. Therefore, I decided to include their stories in this study and show these connections, especially with respect to racialized and gendered forms of violence.

During one of my visits to the shelter, I met Esther, an (im)migrant woman deported after being imprisoned in California for five years. She left Instituto to go to another (im)migrant women's shelter in Tijuana, Casa Refugio Elvira. While in Tijuana, Esther and I remained in contact. After visiting the shelter, I would meet her for lunch or coffee after her workday. She became involved in the (im)migrant rights movement. Her daughter Elisa, who was ten when Esther was imprisoned and fifteen by the time her mother was deported, visited Esther in Tijuana. (Im)migrant rights activists enlisted them as representatives of (im)migrant families affected by separation. However, they were asked not to discuss Esther's imprisonment, so their story undertook various adaptations. The new accounts maintained that Esther was recently deported for being undocumented. This version, prompted by (im)migrant rights advocates, highlighted the limitations of the framework available to advocate for (im)migrant rights that attempted to expand the inclusion of "good" (im)migrants and unintentionally rationalized the violence of (im)migrants constructed as "bad." In addition to Esther and Elisa's narratives, my research also included media coverage of their story.

In addition to literature that addresses the limitations of the dominant frameworks employed by the (im)migrant rights movement (Gonzales 2014; Chávez 2013), my observations are drawn from my own involvement in the (im)migrant rights struggle. I have consistently attended events (marches, protests, meetings, and so forth), *attempted* to organize with (im)migrant rights advocacy organizations, supported and worked with students considered DREAMers, and I grew up in a mixed-status family that confronts issues of (im)migration on a continual basis. These experiences greatly inform this work, especially the critique of (im)migrant rights discourses addressed in chapter 2.

Drawing from feminist standpoint theory, I allowed the experiences of Latina (im)migrant women to guide my methods. Feminist standpoint theory posits knowledge as located and produced via individuals' everyday life experiences; it highlights how women's experiences differ not only from those of men,[24] but also from those of other women, depending on individuals' positionalities.[25] Before interning at Justice Now, I was unaware of how (im)migrant women's mothering was shaped by the development of the US prison regime. The desire to learn about what produced the many challenges they encounter led me into the space of their captivity—prison—and to the *Los Angeles Times*, to the Compañeras Project, to shelters in Tijuana, and to the many people I met along the way who provided insight into the criminalization of (im)migrant women. In order to follow their stories and examine the day-to-day practices that create some (im)migrant bodies as irrecuperable and make the violation of (im)migrant women and their communities possible, I traveled through many of the spaces that they navigated.

Particularly significant was learning how their experiences were structured at different levels and by various sources. To understand the patterns of violence that echoed through the many stories, I constantly had to shift the analytic lens from the private to the public and the local to the national and transnational in order to reveal how one constitutes the other. This technique of tightening and broadening the lens of analysis, of shifting between the macro and the micro, allowed me to see how gendered processes of racialization are central to projects of nation-building that, in an era of globalization, rely on the policing of certain boundaries and the blurring of others. The analysis reveals that the discipline and violence lived by (im)migrant women and their communities are central aspects of modern governance.

In terms of confidentiality, I share specific information about the spaces where I conducted my research (Instituto, Justice Now, and CCWP) because they are so rare that it would be very simple to deduce their identities. I also believe that the anti-violence work conducted in these spaces merits recognition. However, I maintain individuals' anonymity by excluding identifying information as much as possible and using pseudonyms throughout. In cases where individuals' identities were more vulnerable, I discussed with them the possibility of excluding their narratives. Consistently, the response was that the political significance of this work outweighed the possible risks. Thus, we jointly decided to include their experiences.

## A Note on Terminology and Style

The book centers on the experiences of Latina/o (im)migrants in general and Latinas in particular. Thus, unless otherwise stated, the use of the term "(im)migrant" reflects the focus on Latina/o (im)migrants.

It is difficult to make use of the generalizing term "Latinas." This term erases tremendous differences of class, ethnicity and race, national origin, region, (im)migration experiences, and language, to name a few. However, since this study centers on a particular group—criminalized Latina (im)migrants—there are some overarching commonalities that warrant the use of this term. The people represented here are overwhelmingly poor, predominantly from Mexico but also from Central American countries; most are monolingual Spanish speakers; and the vast majority (im)migrated or attempted to (im)migrate as adults. These commonalities intersect with racialized hegemonic ideas that equate "undocumented" and "illegal" with brown bodies, and specifically bodies that "look Mexican." Structurally, these commonalities, along with the racialization of (im)migration, make these individuals vulnerable *as a group*, and thus I make use of the term "Latinas." Given that the majority of the women I encountered in this study are of Mexican origin, their experiences are more visible.

Throughout I employ a politicized language that explicates the criminalization of Latina (im)migrants. Processes of racialized criminalization make particular bodies vulnerable to different forms of violence. I draw my definition of violence from INCITE! Women of Color Against Violence (2006). Their definition encompasses interpersonal violence (including sexual and domestic) and state violence (including police brutality, militarism, attacks on immigrants and Indian treaty rights, the proliferation of prisons, economic neo-colonialism, and violence from the medical industry). INCITE! maintains that these forms of violence are co-constitutive, meaning that they develop relationally and make each other possible. Central to making bodies vulnerable to these material forms of violence is the ideological (cultural) labor that constructs and naturalizes social inequalities. Thus, in defining violence, I also include the ideological labor that naturalizes unequal power relations.

The formation of ideas is key to the construction and organization of our social realities. Concepts that are central to the criminalization of Latina (im)migrants include "illegal" (both as a noun and adjective) and "illegal alien(s)"; "crime" and "criminal"; "public charge" and "dependent"; and "good" and "bad" (im)migrants. Here I remind the reader that there is nothing essential or inherent about these concepts, which is why I problematize them by placing them in quotations. Rather, they are ideas created and deployed to further specific interests. Thus, throughout I emphasize that these are concepts operationalized in power negotiations and struggles.

The exploration of the criminalization of Latina (im)migrants furthers the project of connecting the (im)migrant rights and prison abolition movements. Central to this discussion are working definitions of the (im)migrant rights movement and the prison abolition movement. While I acknowledge that there are various viewpoints within the struggle to bring about justice for (im)migrants, there are voices and narratives that dominate the national scene and have greatly affected (im)migrant rights mobilizations.[26] Throughout I refer to this assemblage as the "(im)migrant rights movement," the overarching goal of which is (im)migration reform in order to create a path to legalization for undocumented (im)migrants. A similar dynamic of diverging perspectives characterizes the prison abolition movement. However, like the (im)migrant rights movement, in part, what makes this a social movement is a common ideological goal. In the case of prison abolition, the unifying vision is ending the use of incarceration by creating changes in society and addressing the root causes of social inequities. Although, as discussed in chapter 5, the strategies employed by this movement can often lead to their appropriation by the state and further entrenchment of prisons, the vision remains abolitionist.

(Im)migration is a fundamental concept interrogated throughout the study. Nicholas De Genova (2002) critiques the concept of "immigration" as unidirectional. "Immigration" assumes a linear movement from one country to the next and in the context of the United States serves to reinforce American exceptionalism (420–421). The assumption of this framework is that people (im)migrate from their country of origin to make use of the opportunities available in the United States. Instead, De Genova complicates this reading and argues that people's movements and reasons for moving are much more complex, and thus, the notion of "migration" (instead of immigration) proves more useful because it accounts for nonlinear movements. This includes (im)migrants' returns to their countries of origin and migration within the United States, and, in its place, allows for an array of (im)migration accounts. I make use of "(im)migrant" and "(im)migration," rather than "migrant" or "migration," because this does not only account for De Genova's critique, but also acknowledges that for some, their (im)migration *is* compulsorily unidirectional since they cannot leave the territorial boundaries of the US nation-state without the risk of never being able to reenter.

Throughout I also employ the term "criminal legal system," rather than "criminal justice system," to signify the actual lack of justice marginalized communities find in this space.[27]

Another term that requires defining is "Black," which I use instead of African American for several reasons. As noted above, the neoliberal shift depoliticizes citizenship, and the term "African American" participates in this process. "African American" characterizes bodies as originating in another geographical space, but eventually assuming an identity of American. It follows the narrative of (im)migration and assumes the possible inclusion of African-marked bodies into the United States. The term "Black," however, is rooted in the social movements of the late 1960s and 1970s and was embraced and deployed not only to note pride in a particular history and heritage, but also to indicate the relationship between Blacks and the United States for what it is: a racialized relationship of power. Therefore, continuing the work of displacing the linear narrative of (im)migration and explicitly noting the ways that society is racially organized, I use the term "Black" throughout this study.

The nature of the ethnographic aspect of the research, predominantly conducted with monolingual Spanish speakers, resulted in significant translations throughout the book. This is especially the case in the last four chapters and the conclusion. Unless otherwise noted, all translations are my own.

### Chapter Previews

Chapter 1 provides the socio-historical context of the book. It demonstrates the interconnectedness between the development of the US prison regime as a response to Black rebelliousness and the various forms of captivity and immobilization that (im)migrant communities face today. By providing a relational analysis between Black and (im)migrant motherhoods, I show that imprisonment and other forms of state containment serve as strategies to control the reproduction of women of color. I argue that this needs to be conceptualized as a form of racialized warfare that participates in the production of a flexible neoliberal labor force.

Chapter 2 considers some of the strategies used by the (im)migrant rights movement and demonstrates how efforts to decriminalize (im)-migrants can result in devaluing others, specifically Blacks. I show how this movement makes use of already existing definitions of "good" and "bad" (im)migrants to advocate for (im)migrant rights and underscore the limitations of organizing along this binary. More specifically, I reveal some of the ways in which strategies employed by the (im)migrant rights movement contribute to the creation of gendered and racialized irrecuperability. I argue that these strategies work against the efforts of the prison abolition movement, which seeks to unstabilize boundaries of deservingness. I call for us to consider the connections between the particular criminalization of (im)migrants and the general criminalization of people of color and poor people in the United States by radically engaging and rethinking notions of inclusion.

In chapter 3, I shift the discussion from the role of the dominant (im)migrant rights framework in reinforcing relationships of power and I consider the ways in which state violence blends with interpersonal violence to discipline and punish (im)migrant women. I contribute to existing scholarship that argues that racial and heteropatriarchal efforts to control the bodies of women of color construct the private as public and the public as private. This makes personal relationships complicit in state efforts to police racial boundaries while simultaneously enlisting the state to perform the labor of domesticating (im)migrant women.

Chapter 4 examines Mexico's conflicting relationship with (im)migrants. While the Mexican government institutes some means for the protection of (im)migrants, this protection is organized by ideas of heteronormativity. In other words, by examining the experiences of (im)migrant women in Colonia Postal, a predominantly (im)migrant space in Tijuana where Instituto Madre Assunta and Casa del Migrante[28] are located, I demonstrate how local police participate in the gendered criminalization of (im)migrants as they discipline (im)migrant women into femininity and punish women who, through acts of (im)migration and their physical appearance, perform or embody masculinity.

The analysis also reveals a relationship of collaboration between Mexican and US authorities in relation to (im)migration control. I argue that Mexico's punitive response to (im)migrants, in part related to the increased policing of (im)migrants, makes the Mexican state a participant in the racialization of (im)migrants as "criminals." Mexico's criminalization of (im)migrants further naturalizes violence against (im)migrant bodies. Ultimately, the analysis illustrates that bodies marked by transnational expressions of criminalization are made violable across national borders. In other words, the labor that criminalization performs in making (im)migrant women irrecuperable remains with them even in their country of origin where they are further policed and targeted. I also consider (im)migrants' responses to their gendered criminalization and highlight how some are able to draw from dominant tropes of heteronormativity to guard others from state violence.

Having highlighted various actors involved in processes of criminalization, I shift the analytic lens one more time in chapter 5. In this case, I look toward the prison abolition movement and in particular, my experiences as an advocate and activist during an internship with Justice Now and volunteer work with CCWP. I draw from the work of Joy James (2005), who points to the differentiation between emancipation and freedom. James argues that emancipation is something that is given by the dominant while freedom stands as something that is created or taken by captives and potential captives who are negatively affected by these dominant relations. I consider some of the ways that the advocacy work of the prison abolition movement, under the charge of bringing relief to people in prison, is often emancipatory and can result in (re)producing relationships of power that work against people in prison.

I conclude the book with an exploration of the productiveness that an abolitionist vision presents to the struggle of (im)migrant justice. I reinforce the argument that if those of us who are concerned with social inequalities are serious about working toward justice for (im)migrants and ending the violence to which (im)migrant women and their communities are subjected, we must extend abolitionist visions to the realm of (im)migration control. Simply expanding inclusion into the nation of a number of (im)migrants will not address the roots of (im)migration and the violence often associated with it.

## CHAPTER 1

# Understanding the Roots of Latina (Im)migrants' Captivity

Incarceration is a constitutive logic of US social formation in that technologies of physical immobilization and annihilation have proven central to the makeup of the United States (Alexander 2010; Davis 2003; Gilmore 2007; Rodríguez 2006). To understand the societal role of prisons, Rodríguez (2006) advances the concept of the prison regime, which he defines as "a dynamic state-mediated practice of domination and control, rather than as a reified 'institution' or 'apparatus.'" It is worthwhile to cite Rodríguez at length:

> The prison regime has become an indispensable element of American statecraft, simultaneously a cornerstone of its militarized (local and global) ascendancy and spectacle of its extracted (or coerced) authority over targeted publics. *The specificity of the prison regime as a production of state power is its rigorous and extravagant marshaling of technologies of violence, domination, and subjection otherwise reserved for deployment in sites of declared (extradomestic) war or martial law* (emphasis in original). (44)

Prisons are spaces where history is written by and through the bodies of captives, where society re-orders itself and power is made tangible. According to professor of geography and leading prison abolition activist Ruth Wilson Gilmore (1998 and 2007), prisons have become the predominant *fix* for and central response to most forms of deviancy, often constructed as forms of crisis (e.g., criminality, terrorism, and undocumented (im)migration). Prisons are state spatial responses to socio-political crises that are in part organized by the state. The fact that the United States leads in incarceration numbers worldwide, exceeding 2 million people in prison at the turn of the century, speaks to Gilmore's argument.

California's history reveals significant changes in incarceration trends. For example, between 1852 and 1984, a total of 132 years, California built twelve prisons. In contrast, in the eleven years between 1985 and 1996, the state built sixteen additional prisons (Dyer 2000, 158). Currently, the California Department of Corrections and Rehabilitation (CDCR) has thirty-four adult institutions and three youth facilities. These facts highlight the significance that prisons have assumed in California and mark the 1980s and 1990s as an especially significant era in terms of incarceration.

The dramatic increase in the number of women in California prisons reflects the greater reliance on incarceration. In 1976, California imprisoned a total of 1,124 women (California Department of Corrections 1997), in contrast to 11,416 in 2007 (California Department of Corrections and Rehabilitation 2008b).[1] This represents a 915 percent increase over the course of three decades.[2] During this same time, the incarceration of Latinas tended to parallel their overall representation in California's demographic population.[3] The significant racial discrepancy largely centered on the massive incarceration of Black women and the under-representation of white women.[4] In addition to the significance of race is the mass criminalization and incarceration of women in general.

Rather than increased crime rates, the drastic incarceration of women highlights the prison regime's power in (re)organizing society as reflected by the ways that crime has shifted and has been redefined over time.[5] Most prominently, changes in the economy and the welfare state, combined with penal policies, such as the war on drugs, have increasingly targeted women, extensively augmenting their numbers in prison.[6] Such a growth in incarceration has, in turn, had significant negative effects on their families and communities. In this way, imprisonment not only serves as a response to perceived social problems, such as poverty, but also participates in their production.

(Im)migrant criminalization functions as an expansion of the prison regime. For example, of the 171,085 people held by the CDCR in September 2008, 19,008 had (or potentially had) an (im)migration hold (California Department of Corrections and Rehabilitation 2008a).[7] This means that approximately 11 percent of those detained in CDCR custody were (im)migrants facing deportation. The most recent available numbers reveal an increase: of 132,645 people held in May 2013,

17,963, or 13.5 percent, had an (im)migration hold (California Department of Corrections and Rehabilitation 2013). This represents a 2.5 percent increase in five years in the number of (im)migrants with immigration holds. While information on the demographics in terms of gender is not readily made available, it is clear that (im)migrants are increasingly targeted for containment.

A consideration of federal incarceration reveals patterns similar to those in California. For example, in 1992, immigration-related criminalized activities accounted for 5 percent of federal convictions. By 2012, this had increased to 30 percent. The impact of the state's criminalization of (im)migrants is also reflected in the citizenship status of people in federal prisons. In 1992, non-citizens accounted for 22 percent, and by 2012, they made up 46 percent. The racialized criminalization of (im)migration is underscored in the racial composition of federal incarceration. In 1992, Latinas/os made up 23 percent. By 2012, this had increased to 48 percent, making Latinas/os the largest ethno-racial group in federal prisons (Light, Lopez, and Gonzalez-Barrera 2013).

The trend of (im)migrant incarceration must be considered within the role of the US prison regime because prisons regulate society and control populations. As sites designed for social isolation, prisons serve to curtail the reproduction of captive bodies.[8] Given that the majority of people in prison are poor people of color, population control then targets these particular classed and racialized bodies. Consequently, (im)migrant women's imprisonment performs as a reproductive control strategy by restraining their ability to have children while at the same time participating in the separation of mothers from their children.

In this chapter, I offer a relational analysis of the gendered racialization of Black women and Latina (im)migrants. By considering this dynamic, I provide the contextualization needed to understand (im)migrant women's criminalization in relation to the history of captivity lived by Blacks in the United States, the group most affected by incarceration. The gendered and racialized discursive tools created by neoconservatives during the 1960s and 1970s functioned as a response to Blacks' rebelliousness. These discursive tools proved useful in later years as the presence of undocumented (im)migrants, particularly Latinas, prompted public concern. Neoconservative and neoliberal projects found constructs grounded in state dependency, such as the "welfare queen" (a term that merged state dependency and criminality onto the bodies of Black mothers), particularly productive.

John Marquez's work (2012) is valuable in considering the centrality of race in neoliberal statecrafting projects, including the criminalization of Black women and Latina (im)migrants. Marquez discusses scholarly critiques of border militarization as a contemporary strategy for labor exploitation, which he terms the "neoliberal entrapment model" (475). He challenges the assumption that anti-(im)migrant mobilizations and border militarization are simply tools for economic exploitation and introduces the theory of the *racial state of expendability*. Marquez's theory asserts that, rather than neoliberal capitalist exploitation, the death and violence endured by Latina/o (im)migrants are rooted in much longer histories of racialization that have origins in European modernity, as well as being specific to the development of Latinidad in relation to the US borderlands (476).[9] He focuses on the role of racial ideas in processes of life devaluation, "or expendability and legal impunity," and argues that "[this] is not a mere consequence of or a tool for broader plans for economic exploitation. By contrast, expendability represents a base or foundational effect of power through which plans for economic exploitation can be and have been instantiated" (476). Marquez's theory privileges a racial analysis and argues that class relations draw from racial knowledge to carry out economic exploitation. In the case of Black women and Latina (im)migrants, the racialized expendability of Black women gets re-mapped onto Latina (im)migrants, and neoliberal projects draw from such expendability to produce wealth via exploitation.

The central argument advanced in this chapter is that incarceration participates in a racialized neoliberal arrangement, where the capturing and warehousing of brown (im)migrant bodies result in the reinforcement of a flexible labor market where Latina/o (im)migrants perform as ideal neoliberal laborers—flexible workers with minimal rights. I reinforce Marquez's theory of *racial state of expendability* and argue that the representation of Latina/o (im)migrants as ideal neoliberal laborers is made possible by their racialized constructions as foreign and "illegal."[10] Undocumented (im)migrants are the archetype of neoliberal laborers because their vulnerable legal status secures their flexibility while, at the same time, it hinders their ability to safeguard rights. Through mothering, which implies permanent settlement, (im)migrant women threaten this racialized neoliberal arrangement. Their labor is considered necessary, but their non-white racialization signifies them as culturally and morally inferior and undesirable mothers of future citizens.[11] As a result, their imprisonment performs the work of constructing them as irrecuperable since it results in their deportation and permanently bans them from future entrance into the United States. This reinforces their value as neoliberal workers and their violability when they defy this role. The physical deportation and permanent exclusion of criminalized (im)migrants serve to rid the United States of bodies categorized as racial neoliberal *excess*.[12]

Additionally, as highlighted by my analysis, (im)migration enforcement functions as an expansion of the prison regime. This is underscored in the increase in numbers of people in (im)migration detention. For example, in 1990, an average daily population of 6,532 (im)-migrants were detained. By 2000, this number had increased to 19,244 and by 2010, the daily average population detained was 29,676 (American Civil Liberties Union). During the fiscal year 2011, the average number of (im)migrants in detention was 33,330 (Immigration and Customs Enforcement 2011). These numbers show how the criminalization of (im)migrants expands the carceral capacity of the state.

## Road Map

In this chapter, I consider the legacies of chattel slavery, which are central in establishing racial relations where non-white bodies are subjected to various forms of control and violence for the benefit of white life. I draw parallels among slavery, current carcerality, and the US labor market and provide a relational analysis between the experiences of Blacks and Latina/o (im)migrants. The analysis underscores the significance of slavery in fashioning contemporary (im)migrant lives within neoliberalism. Furthermore, emphasis is placed on the significance that controlling the sexuality and reproduction of women of color assumes in this process. My attempt to provide an understanding of US criminalization in relation to Blacks and its impact on Latina/o (im)migrants is, in part, my anticipation of arguments that maintain Latinas/os as having explicitly different histories and experiences of criminalization.[13] I am familiar with arguments that contend that analyzing the experiences of Latinas/os through the experiences of Blacks reinforces a Black/white binary that erases the particular histories of Latinas/os. My contention is that criminality in the United States developed in direct relationship to Blackness, and anti-Black logics have informed the criminal legal system throughout history (including westward expansion and the conquest of Mexican territories), all the way to the present moment. Thus, I argue that we cannot understand Latina/o (im)migrant criminalization without this relational and comparative analysis.

After considering the legacies of slavery, I discuss the formation of the logic of law and order during the late 1960s and 1970s and how this development was rooted in attempts to discipline rebellious communities of color, particularly Blacks (Parenti 1999; James 2007). The analysis illustrates how the expansion of the US prison regime is directly correlated with policing racialized relationships of power.

I continue the discussion by considering how part of this racial reordering depended on cultural constructions of Black motherhood as undeserving through the rhetoric of state dependency (Collins 2000, 86–88; Gilens 2000; Roberts 1997; Seccombe 2010), which was ideologically merged with criminality (Collins 2000, 87). This merging, in turn, gets re-mapped onto (im)migrant women's bodies, especially during the 1990s. These transformations took place with the neoliberal shift of the early 1970s, which signaled changes in labor relations in the United States.

I then focus on the expansion of the war on drugs at the border, which was central to the criminalization of (im)migrants. The war on drugs is an amalgamation of social policy initially waged mainly in urban Black spaces (Alexander 2010; Bush-Baskette 1998; Lusane 1991). The analysis highlights its usefulness in interpreting the US-Mexico border as a space of criminality (Dunn 1996), as well as the role of both the United States and Mexico in this production. In this context, border militarization proves essential in organizing a bi-national relationship that privileges the movement of goods and capital and aims to regulate the exploitability of bodies by racially categorizing them as either "legal" or "illegal."

Through the Immigration Reform and Control and Act (IRCA) of 1986, I link the war on drugs to the criminalization of (im)migrant women. IRCA is indicated as exceptionally important in border militarization—in part, because it expanded the war on drugs to the border. However, it simultaneously contributed to the increased (im)migration of women through family reunification policies, which generated increased concerns over (im)migrant settlement and their use of public resources (Hondagneu-Sotelo 1994, 26; Mattingly 1997, 50). In other words, IRCA served to ideologically join border militarization and women's (im)migration, which was marked by gendered notions of state dependency.

Finally, I conclude by arguing that the criminalization of (im)migrants—in particular, women—needs to be understood in relation to the history of captivity of Blacks in the United States. This relational analysis enables us to see how (il)legalization, criminalization, and captivity are constituting logics of the US nation-state.

## Legacies of Slavery and the Consequences for Latina/o (Im)migrants

The US nation-building project was, and continues to be, made possible through the creation of technologies of control designed and targeted toward non-white bodies. Central to colonialism in the Americas was the development of physical, juridical, spiritual/religious, social, and economic forms of constraints that were directed at indigenous and African people for the gain of Europeans. This colonial logic continued throughout the making and re-making of the United States and currently manifests itself in practices of mass incarceration, detention, and labor arrangements. In this section, I focus on chattel slavery in what became the United States and demonstrate how the legacies of this slavery continue to have an effect on the present moment, including (im)-migrants' experiences in both the labor market and various forms of captivity.

Slavery was central to the development of early Western capitalism. In *The Slave Ship: A Human History* (2008), historian Marcus Rediker notes that the primitive accumulation of capital was made possible only through force, conquest, enslavement, and murder of non-white bodies, specifically African and indigenous people.[14] In doing so, Rediker disrupts the narrative of slavery as pre-capitalist and demonstrates its critical importance in the development of the capitalist world market (42–43). The analysis thus centers on race as a fundamental ideology constructed and deployed in the development of early capitalism.

Rediker traces the transformation of the slave ship and its many different functions: as an instrument of war (9, 270); as a factory that transformed humans into commodities for the world market (44–45); as a space where racial meaning was created (10); and as a traveling prison (44–45, 60–61). In this sense, the slave ship served as a prison during times when the modern prison had not yet been created (45). His comparison of the slave ship to prisons is insightful in considering the connections between slavery and contemporary criminalization. Today, prisons serve as central sites where wars are waged (war on drugs, war on crime, war on terrorism). They also serve capitalist interests in that they do not only commodify bodies, as is underscored by the private prison industry, but also function as warehouses for bodies constructed as racial neoliberal *excess*. Finally, prisons are spaces where racial meaning is constructed. Examples include the neoconservative narratives that attribute the massive captivity of people of color to these communities' deficient cultures.

Enslaved people were socially constructed as potential threats, and slave ship crews prepared themselves, for example, through barricade construction in case of an insurrection (70). Akin to prison architectural design in the present, the ship's design centered on its capacity to carry as many enslaved people as possible while also taking into account modes of controlling its captives. In addition, the creation and use of shackles, chains, and whips, among other technologies of control and torture, were central to the operations of slave ships (72). Systemic terror and violence were essential to the captains' and crews' endeavors to carry out their charge of human captivity (348).

Similarly, California's prisons,[15] Abu Ghraib, and Guantanamo[16] demonstrate how, although technologies of control changed with modernization, these sites of US captivity, at their core, employ systemic terror and violence for the purpose of controlling mostly non-white bodies for the benefit of the United States, a racially marked white nation-state. Rediker's analysis of the slave ship, coupled with the ideological and material parallels to contemporary US carcerality, highlight how, from its origins, the United States was a project enabled through intense violence against and control of bodies marked outside of whiteness. In a significant sense, violent captivity has always been central to the making of the United States.[17]

There are also important parallels between slavery and contemporary labor relations. The enslavement of Blacks fundamentally constituted the US labor market, and Latina/o (im)migrants' experiences are intrinsically connected to this history. In "Slavery as Immigration?" (2009), legal scholar Rhonda V. Magee asks what the implications are of understanding chattel slavery as a form of "forced migration immigration," as a "state-sponsored, pernicious system of immigration" (274). Magee considers the objectives, functions, and consequences of slavery and draws parallels to contemporary (im)migrant labor. She argues that the institutionalization of chattel slavery "inculcated the notion of a permanent, quasi-citizen-worker underclass, and privileged white ethnics under naturalization law" (276). Slavery was a system that distributed resources along racial lines; it enabled "the involuntary, forcible, virtually permanent transportation of people from one part of the globe to another" for the purpose of capital accumulation (278). Importantly, Magee highlights the role of the state in establishing and securing this racial order. For example, she cites Walter Berns, who observes that while the US Constitution never mentioned slavery, its provisions served to protect this institution. Using the language of migration, the Importation and Migration Clause maintained:

> The migration and importation of such persons as any of the states now existing shall think proper to admit, shall not be prohibited by Congress prior to the year one thousand eight hundred and eight, but a tax or duty may be imposed on such importation, not exceeding ten dollars for each person. (Article 1, Section 9 Clause 1)

While the term "slavery" is explicitly excluded, this clause allowed Congress to tax, but not prohibit, the importation of slaves, thereby providing constitutional protection to this racial institution. Thus, the expanded freedoms for whites brought about by the creation of the United States were dependent on the literal unfreedom of Blacks.[18]

Once slavery was transformed (rather than abolished) in 1865, the federal government began to regulate who entered the nation and under what conditions. This regulation was established in part because the United States desired cheapened labor in order to continue its westward expansion. However, the end of slavery limited the ability of white settlers to make use of Black bodies for this project. Consequently, the United States turned toward Asia, specifically China. The introduction of Chinese and other Asian (im)migrants enabled the development of the West. However, informed by racial knowledge developed in relationship to slavery and indigenous genocide, the presence of foreign bodies who culturally and racially appeared different created conflict and, in turn, influenced (im)migration policies. The first federal (im)migration law, the Page Law of 1875, barred the entrance of Asian women believed to be entering for "lewd and immoral purposes" (Luibhéid 2002, 2 and 31–32). This served to bar the (im)migration of Chinese women who were single and significantly limit the (im)migration of wives of Chinese laborers. Feminist scholar Eithne Luibhéid argues that this policy served to enforce a labor relationship where the United States accepted Asian (im)migrants as laborers, but denied them social membership by restricting their social reproduction. Such legislation drew from the logic of slavery that made Black bodies into non-citizens available for exploitation by white civil society.

Post-slavery federal (im)migration laws enabled the (im)migration of

non-white foreign bodies into the United States to labor and participate in creating wealth for the white nation. Thus, slavery and the experiences of Blacks must be central to conversations on (im)migration. As
Magee maintains, the failure to conceptualize the connections between
slavery and contemporary labor relations, particularly in relationship to
(im)migration, prevents us from grasping a central tenet of US labor relations: "the demand for ever more cheap and expendable labor, and the
standard racialization of, and racism against, that most expendable immigrant labor pool" (300).[19]

Another significant aspect of the institutionalization of slavery is
the racialized construction of gendered meaning. The creation of racial
meaning drew from existing ideas about gender while simultaneously
constructing new gendered knowledge that shaped social relations. Enslaved African women were made responsible for the social care of the
domestic sphere, often in both the slave owner's home and their own
home. At the same time, similar to enslaved men, they were forced to
labor outside the home (Davis 1981, 7; Morgan 2004).[20] Though expected to carry out the responsibilities assigned to women in the domestic sphere, they were denied the minimal patriarchal protection
that the ideology of femininity is supposed to afford women. As Davis
(1981) maintains, "In order to function as slave, the black woman had
to be annulled as woman, that is, as woman in her historical stance of
wardship under the entire male hierarchy. The sheer force of things rendered her equal to her man" (7). Furthermore, their reproduction, that
which socially characterizes women as distinct from men, was also separated from femininity. The commodification of their biological reproduction served to create wealth for slave owners at the same time that it
denied their identity as social mothers (Morgan 2004, 68). They were
denied the protection afforded by the ideology of femininity since they
were vulnerable to compulsory sexual violence, in part to further their
procreation. They were also denied social mothering since their children, who inherited the status of the mother, could be sold at the slave
owners' impulse. Thus, sexual control and domination were fundamental to ensuring racial subordination deemed necessary for the reproduction and prosperity of white life (Hartman 1997, 84). Black women's
bodies "functioned as a spatialized nexus of power and discourse, em-
bodying and resolving the sometimes-contradictory demands of white
supremacy, capitalism, and patriarchy" (Kaplan 2007, 115). The legacies
of slavery include society's ability to intervene in the most intimate parts
of the lives of women of color.[21]

The experiences of enslaved Black women reveal that gender and sexuality were central to the organization of slavery in particular and of the US labor market in general. To further whites' accumulation of wealth and enable their social prosperity, enslaved Black women were denied access to the benefits of hegemonic femininity, including social motherhood. The targeting of their sexuality, a central condition of slavery, continues to inform Black women's lives, and their homes and families, constructed as deviant, continue to be targets for state intervention. The racialized and gendered relations established during the creation of the United States continue to inform experiences, not only for Blacks, but also for society in general. The institution of slavery was fundamental in establishing a racialized labor market where non-white non-citizens or quasi-citizens are introduced to labor for the benefit of the (white) nation. As discussed, controlling Black women's sexuality and reproduction was essential to establishing this process.

Given that the group targeted to assume the lower strata of the labor market today is Latina/o (im)migrants, (im)migrant women's reproduction is also a site for intervention. The biological reproduction of enslaved Black women was desired and served capital's interest, but in the case of Latina (im)migrants, while their labor is desired, their biological reproduction is marked as a threat. Feminist sociologist Elena R. Gutiérrez (2008) examines the racialized targeting of Mexican American and Mexican (im)migrant women's reproduction. She notes how these women have historically been constructed as "hyper-fertile baby machines," an identity that informed social policy. Gutiérrez documents how, during the 1970s, responses to Mexican-origin women's perceived uncontrollable fertility included coerced and involuntary sterilizations.

Specific to California, Alexandra Minna Stern (2005) effectively argues that concerns over public health drew on racial logics to target Chicanas and Mexican (im)migrant women for sterilization. These practices officially ended in 1979. The significance of incarceration in (re)producing relationships of power by targeting women's reproduction is evident in California's practice of coercively sterilizing women in prison, which was addressed with the signing of S.B. 1135 by Governor Jerry Brown on September 25, 2014.[22] Since women of color make up the majority of women in California prisons, they are disproportionately targeted by these practices. Again, for poor women of color, their bodies are marked as sites for social and state intervention to further racialized white life, a dynamic that originated in the experiences of enslaved Black women.

The discussion thus far highlights how chattel slavery was central to the creation of the US nation-state, and specifically how this functioned as an arrangement in the labor market where non-white foreign bodies were introduced and exploited to meet the labor needs and desires of the United States. This agreement was made possible through violence and force against Black bodies. Furthermore, the state is very much implicated in organizing and maintaining a racialized labor market historically rooted in slavery. Finally, the discussion of slavery and its legacies also demonstrates that targeting the sexuality and reproduction of women of color is fundamental to US labor relations. My purpose in this discussion is not to equate the situation of undocumented (im)migrants with slavery. Rather, my objective is to establish the centrality of slavery in the creation of the US labor market and to note its impression in contemporary labor arrangements responsible for fundamentally affecting (im)migrants.

Currently, the labor market is guided by neoliberal ideologies and practices that create similar conditions that introduce non-white bodies for the purpose of producing wealth for the nation. Neoliberalism promotes political ideologies that emphasize economic growth for the private sector. Ideologically, neoliberalism opposes state intervention in the economic redistribution of wealth by stressing individual choice and responsibility. According to this logic, "success" or "failure" is a product of individuals' own making. The neoliberal state favors free market and trade and individual private property rights and maintains economic relations through the logic of the rule of law. According to David Harvey (2005), it is the state's responsibility to ensure neoliberal social organization, so the state "must therefore use its monopoly of the means of violence to preserve these freedoms at all costs" (64). A central objective of the neoliberal state is to maintain itself globally competitive, and it does so through internal reorganizations and new institutional arrangements (65).

One way that the neoliberal state makes itself competitive is through the production of exploitable labor. Until the 1960s, Blacks were essential to US labor relations because their exploitability was assured through racialized practices such as de jure segregation. In great part, post–World War II activism, coupled with the expansion of the economy and labor market, allowed Blacks to secure, for a brief moment, some mobility and economic gains (Collins 2000, 65–66; Marable 1999, 59–60). Federal policies such as the end of de jure segregation and the implementation of affirmative action somewhat improved Blacks' participation in the labor market. Social movements of the 1950s and 1960s informed these social transformations through citizenship claims. Historiographer Manning Marable (1999) notes that the capitalist crisis of the 1970s not only nullified, but also reversed these gains (60–61). Black feminist Patricia Hill Collins (2000) makes a similar argument, but provides an examination of the uneven incorporation of Black men and women. According to Collins, changes in the global political economy increasingly displaced Black men from manufacturing jobs, and for Black women, when they did find jobs, they tended to be part-time with low pay and few or no benefits (66).

The discussion highlights how advances made through the Civil Rights Movement, which largely centered claims on citizenship, are in part responsible for constructing Blacks as undesirable workers within a neoliberal economy because they were not exploitable in the same fashion as the pre-1960s era. The fact that racial discrimination was prohibited in the public sphere, including the labor market, made it difficult to exploit Blacks. Consequently, this constructed them as racial neoliberal *excess*, and prisons assumed a central role in managing this excess.[23]

Within the context where Blacks were constructed as neoliberal excess, undocumented (im)migrant labor assumed an essential function due to (im)migrants' limited abilities to make claims on the state and society.[24] The neoliberal trend of employing flexible foreign and (im)migrant labor is related to the fact that citizen labor is less exploitable. Citizens can make claims on the state that non-citizens, particularly undocumented (im)migrants, cannot. Therefore, state neoliberal policies that produce (im)migrant labor are the same policies that expel significant portions of citizen labor, which in the United States consists predominantly of Blacks (Collins 2000, 67).

## The Logic of Law and Order in Subduing Black Rebelliousness

As I illustrated in the previous section, the law delineates what is legally possible with the threat of force and serves as a significant tool in organizing society— including the labor market—along racial lines. Criminalization, as a legal technique, epitomizes the way in which law creates and reproduces relationships of power. In this section, I provide a reading of the law-and-order logic that has driven much of the social policy enacted since the late 1960s. I highlight the ways in which human captivity and warehousing has served as a *fix* to perceived social problems. I demonstrate that central to the origins of this logic is the need to control the rebelliousness of communities of color, especially Blacks as they are perceived to threaten the racial order of the United States.[25] In order to contextualize this critique, I refer to the abolition of slavery and the subsequent criminalization of Blacks by considering some of the ideological and material parallels to contemporary practices of incarceration.

Several authors trace the development of criminality in the United States and reveal how the notion of crime was directly developed in relation to Blacks. Historian Saidiya Hartman addresses the 1855 case of *Missouri v. Celia.* Celia was an enslaved woman who killed her owner to stop the sexual violence that she had endured for years since her purchase. Through the discussion, Hartman reveals the "law's selective recognition of slave humanity" (1997, 80). The status of enslaved Blacks denied them personhood and agency as their lives were legally defined by slave owners specifically and whites in general. However, the law recognized an enslaved person's intentionality and agency "only as it assumed the form of criminality" (80). In the case of Celia, she could neither give nor deny consent to her owner. However, in order to punish her for his killing, the court legally recognized Celia's agency. As Hartman explains:

> The slave was recognized as a reasoning subject who possessed intent and rationality solely in the context of criminal liability; ironically, the slave's will was acknowledged only as it was prohibited or punished. It was generally the slave's crimes that were on trial, not white offense and violation, which were enshrined as legitimate and thereby licensed, or obviously, the violence of the law, which in the effort to shift the locus of culpability is conceptualized here in terms of the crimes of the state. In positing the black as criminal, the state obfuscated its instrumental role in terror by projecting all culpability and wrongdoing onto the enslaved. (82)

Hartman's discussion of the experiences of enslaved Blacks demonstrates the historical development of criminality as specifically constructed in relation to Blacks and ascribed to their bodies.

This ascription continued in the post-Reconstruction era and still informs society's conceptualization of crime (Davis 2003; Lichtenstein 1996; Muhammad 2011). In *Black Reconstruction in America,* first published in 1935, W. E. B. DuBois demonstrated that the re-enslavement of Blacks was made possible through the re-definitions of crime that occurred with the establishment of Black codes (1995, 167–180). The criminalization of Blacks during the post-Reconstruction era served to meet the labor needs generated by the abolition of slavery and the development of industrial capitalism.[26] Along a similar vein, feminist scholar-activist Angela Y. Davis argues that an analogous relationship exists between the contemporary imprisonment of Blacks and profitability (2003, 68). While the labor of prisoners continues to yield some economic revenue, the major private profiting occurs through industries—such as construction, food, clothing, and health care—that service prisons to meet the needs of the more than 2 million people incarcerated.[27]

Another significant period in the criminalization of communities of color and specifically Blacks began during the 1960s.[28] The social movements that took place between the 1950s and early 1970s unsettled racial relations globally. Society responded with a reconfiguration of race by deploying cultural difference (Omi and Winant 1994; Bonilla-Silva 2001 and 2003; Alexander 2010).[29] Particularly significant in the United States were radical movements—such as the Black Power Movement, Chicano Movement, American Indian Movement, and the Asian American Movement—that negated the legitimacy of the United States and, rather than advocating for inclusion, called for a radical transformation.[30] The militant images of non-white bodies igniting entire cities between 1965 and 1968, protesting, engaging in civil disobedience, and defying agents of the state, all in the name of self-determination, threatened the racial order of the United States. The significance of these critiques lies largely in the fact that these movements constructed the United States as unredeemable because its very existence was predicated on the racial subjection of bodies racialized as non-white. Since the United States was conceptualized as an inherently white supremacist nation, inclusion necessarily signified participating in racial subjection. Instead, many members of these various rebellions advocated for the creation of alternatives. During the 1960s, society saw the deployment of the discourse of criminality, particularly against Blacks in urban communities, as a response to what was constructed as a national crisis of disorder and lawlessness (Alexander 2010; James 2007; Macek 2006; Parenti 1999).[31] Critical race theorist Denise Ferreira da Silva (2007) provides a genealogy of race and demonstrates that spaces inhabited by people of color are constructed as outside the law, and thus, violence is naturalized as indigenous to these spaces.[32] In efforts to reconfigure racial relationships of power, acts of self-determination, which offered a critique of structural white supremacy, were ideologically transformed into acts of criminality.

The threat of racial disorder mobilized state responses that reconstituted Blacks as criminal through the attachment of illicit drugs to urban spaces racialized as Black. Alexander (2010) historically contextualizes contemporary mass incarceration and makes significant connections to slavery and the Jim Crow era: "Like Jim Crow (and slavery), mass incarceration operates as a tightly networked system of laws, policies, customs, and institutions that operate collectively to ensure the subordinate state of a group defined largely by race" (13). In this sense, the category of "criminal" serves as a proxy for race and is specifically productive to criminalize Blacks.

Christian Parenti (1999) makes a similar argument. Parenti maps the historical development of the current US policing and prison regime. He demonstrates how the political crisis of the 1960s and 1970s, in part fueled by the economic crisis stemming from the costly Vietnam War, threatened to transform US power relations. According to Parenti, the domestic scene of rebellious turmoil, combined with the police's difficulty in controlling the domestic landscape, made it difficult to sell capitalism and liberal democracy to the rest of the world and establish the United States as a world superpower. The response was a re-fashioning of the police, the judicial system, and prisons. The deployment of the rhetoric of law and order enabled this re-fashioning.

The work of Hall, Critcher, Jefferson, Clarke, and Roberts (1978) provides insight into the significance of this type of discursive work to the larger order of policing. Using the British mugging panic of 1972 and 1973, the authors demonstrate how the state organizes society in part through the production of moral panics. What changed were not the activities associated with mugging, but rather, the authors note, the narrative produced for civil society in relation to these activities. British authorities and media drew from US law-and-order narratives that merged criminality and lawlessness with Black youth to construct *mugging* as a mounting threat.[33] The ideological construction of moral panics participates in securing state hegemony and allows the state to escalate repression. Hall et al. provide insight into the ideological work in which the state engages in order to further particular interests while simultaneously obscuring the root causes of social problems (vii).

Conceptualizing the ways in which the state deploys notions of crisis to reorganize society is productive in understanding the 1960s shift toward mass criminalization and incarceration. Due largely to the various social movements that threatened the social order, the United States shifted the focus from foreign to domestic threats, or the *enemies inside*. Parenti (1999) first locates this shift in the influence of Barry Goldwater's Republican presidential campaign in which he promised to restore law and order that had presumably been lost. In his 1964 presidential nomination speech, Goldwater stated, "Security from domestic violence, no less than from foreign aggression, is the most elementary and fundamental purpose of any government, and a government that cannot fulfill this purpose is one that cannot long command the loyalty of its citizens" (6). In the same speech, Goldwater linked crime to state dependency, foreshadowing the logic that would drive the criminalization of Blacks, and later Latina/o (im)migrants, in the following decades: "If it is entirely proper for the government to take away from some to give to others, then won't some be led to believe that they can rightfully take from anyone who has more than they?" (7)

Although Goldwater lost to Lyndon B. Johnson, his rhetoric won out. During Johnson's presidency, the initial groundwork for the policing and prison regimes was established. Particularly significant was the increased criminalization of drugs. In 1967, Johnson's administration created the Bureau of Narcotics and Dangerous Drugs (BNDD), precursor of the Drug Enforcement Agency (DEA) (6). He also proposed the legislation that created the Law Enforcement Assistance Administration (LEAA) to "strengthen ties between the federal government and local police" (6). During the next decade, the LEAA "spent billions of dollars in an effort to reshape, retool, and rationalize American policing" (6).[34] The ideological construction of domestic lawlessness as a moral panic provided the political power to expand the repressive nature of the state.

Richard Nixon followed Johnson in reinforcing the constructed crisis—the loss of law and order. Initially, Nixon found it difficult to deliver on his promise to restore law and order, since it became evident that crime control was the jurisdiction of state and local authorities. In 1970, borrowing from New York Governor Nelson Rockefeller's tough-on-crime policies used against drug users, Nixon and his administration, under the premise that drug control was the one area where the federal government could have a local effect, nationally merged the issues of drug use and crime. Parenti shows how Nixon and his administration used drug trafficking to rationalize the federal government's involvement in local policing. On June 17, 1971, Nixon spoke on the need to create a program for drug abuse prevention and control. In this speech, he declared a war on drugs, stating that "America's public enemy number one in the United States is drug abuse. In order to fight and defeat this enemy, it is necessary to wage a new, all-out offensive." Parenti cites Nixon's July 14, 1969, address to Congress:

> Within the last decade, the abuse of drugs has grown from essentially a local police problem into a serious national threat to the personal health and safety of millions of Americans. . . . A national awareness of the gravity of the situation is needed; a new urgency and concerted national policy are needed at the Federal level to begin to cope with this growing menace to the general welfare of the United States. (9)

It is significant that Daniel Patrick Moynihan, who wrote the now infamous 1965 federal report, *The Negro Family: The Case for National Action*, served as the Counselor to the President for Urban Affairs during Nixon's administration. According to political journalist Edward Jay Epstein (1977):

> Moynihan, concerned about the reports of heroin abuse in the ghettos, had persuaded the president that the State Department should do everything diplomatically possible to curtail opium production in foreign countries such as Turkey, and that the president should elevate the suppression of narcotics to an issue of national security policy. (77)

By this time, criminality was already fused to Black urban spaces and the bodies that resided there. Declaring the war on drugs, which activated the buildup of the criminal legal system, was thus a declaration of war on Black bodies (Lusane 1991; Bush-Baskette 1998) and simultaneously served as a mechanism for intervention in other countries.

Nixon's administration ideologically linked the rebelliousness occurring on the streets, especially in inner cities, with crime, deploying notions of Black criminality that drove the expansion of policing and prisons. Parenti quotes from a letter addressed to Eisenhower from Nixon: "I have found great audience response to this [law and order] theme in all parts of the country, including areas like New Hampshire where there is virtually no race problem and relatively little crime" (7). This statement profoundly speaks to the logic of criminalization that naturalized Black lawlessness. In this quote, Nixon refers to the fact that even in spaces such as New Hampshire, a predominantly white state with minimal concerns about crime at the time, the logic of law and order carries political power. He draws on white fears of Blacks to mobilize support for law-and-order policies. This is further exemplified in the diary of H. R. Haldeman, Nixon's chief of staff: "[President Nixon] emphasized that you have to face the fact that the whole problem is really the blacks. The key is to devise a system that recognizes this while not appearing to" (Parenti 12). The policies that develop to contain the *crime crisis*, including the war on crime and the criminal legal system buildup, are thus policies constructed in relation to Black bodies.

The criminalization of poor urban communities of color continues. Drawing from Hall et al. (1978), Macek (2006) argues that during the 1980s and 1990s a racialized paranoia about urban spaces—particularly in regard to young men of color—was ideologically produced. This production was a "confused response to a set of interlocking demographic, economic, and social changes that polarized our metropolitan regions along lines of race and class" (1). The changes Macek addresses are suburbanization, ghettoization, and economic restructuring. These social transformations led to constructing urban spaces as poor communities of color that faced significant social problems while simultaneously providing support for suburban communities that remained affluent and white. The divergent conditions of these racialized spaces were publicly explained by pathologizing poor communities of color. Macek cites William Bennett, former secretary of education:

> Current trends in out-of-wedlock births, crime, drug use, family decomposition, and education decline, as well as a host of other social pathologies, are incompatible with the continuation of American society as we know it. If these things continue, the republic as we know it will cease to be. (39)

It is within this neoconservative and white supremacist ideological context that the state engaged communities of color.

Criminalization must also be considered within the larger development of global neoliberalism. In the late 1960s and early 1970s, incarceration assumed important neoliberal labor functions. The creation of post–World War II policies—including the expansion of Roosevelt's New Deal policies—fueled social transformations that were mobilized by the various social movements of the 1950s and 1960s. In turn, this presented a threat to the interests of capitalists whose profits were affected by the state's intervention in the economy. The global economic recession of the early 1970s offered capitalists an opportunity to critique the role of the state in social redistribution (Marable 1999). The ideology of criminalized dependency that developed around Black motherhood provided US capitalists important ammunition to promote the neoliberal logic of minimal state intervention in the redistribution of wealth.

Central to neoliberalism is a flexible, and thus exploitable, labor force. Prisons serve a key purpose in that they are sites that address the massive economic redundancy created by neoliberal policies. Such policies include deindustrialization. Individuals who are greatly targeted for imprisonment have no place within the existing labor economy and are consequently constructed as redundant and unemployable, and prisons serve as spaces for their warehousing. As noted previously, gains made by Blacks during the 1950s and 1960s were in part the result of their ability to draw on their rights as citizens. These rights were successfully eliminated as global neoliberal economic restructuring constructed Blacks as undesirable workers as their rights afforded through US citizenship limited their flexibility, rendering them racial neoliberal excess. Prisons thus became a *fix* for the human excess created by neoliberal policies. Loïc Wacquant argues that the increase in incarceration directly correlates with the neoliberal retrenchment of the welfare state and urban deindustrialization.[35] At this historical juncture, undocumented (im)migrant labor assumes a pivotal role in neoliberal labor relations.

Furthermore, the act of incarcerating people and denoting them as criminal generates an entire population of flexible laborers. Nowhere is this made more apparent than in the fact that people in prison often perform some of the labor necessary to operate these facilities, such as cooking, cleaning, gardening, and office work. Also of significance, private corporations employ the labor of people in prison at an extremely low wage. However, compared to state and federal prisons, this is a rather small number often exaggerated by liberal and progressive activists in order to draw parallels between slavery and prison labor. Finally, incarceration creates a flexible labor force by decreasing the marketability of individuals with criminal records. In the case of (im)migrants, however, incarceration provides another type of "fix." During moments of perceived national crisis, including economic recessions, incarceration serves to legally transform (im)migrant bodies, whether documented or undocumented, into deportable "criminal aliens" and thus irrecuperable subjects.[36]

## Manufacturing of Racialized and Gendered (Im)migrant Criminality

The production of Black lawlessness and disorder merged with changes occurring to the welfare state. During the 1960s, the doors of the welfare system were forced open to allow access to previously excluded people (Fujiwara 2008, 33). This included people of color, particularly Blacks; individuals who were divorced, separated, or had been deserted; and increasingly, never-married women—all people defined as the *undeserving poor* (Katz 1989). These changes directed the public's anxiety toward single Black mothers, children born to single mothers, and generational dependency on social welfare (Abramowitz 1988; Collins 2000, 88–89; Fujiwara 2008, 33–35). Single poor Black mothers were mainly constructed as morally deficient; in contrast, "deserving" mothers were either dependent on their husbands or self-sufficient (Handler 2002). Historically, welfare policy has served to pass moral judgment by selecting who merits state protection.

In his examination, historian Michael B. Katz (1989) discusses the construction of the undeserving poor through the discourse of personal choice. Under the neoliberal logic of personal choice, poverty allegedly acts as a self-made outcome resulting from poor choices—in this way, the poor are constructed as undeserving. He writes, "They remained different and inferior because, whatever their origins, the actions and attitudes of poor people themselves assured their continued poverty and that of their children" (16). According to Katz, this notion of self-perpetuated poverty disallowed poor people from becoming morally *deserving*. By the 1980s, there was alarm about and hostility toward people in poverty.

> What bothered observers most was not their suffering; rather, it
> was their sexuality, expressed in teenage pregnancy; family pat-
> terns, represented by female-headed households; alleged reluctance
> to work for low wages; welfare dependence, incorrectly believed to
> be a major drain on national resources; and propensity for drug use
> and violent crime, which had eroded the safety of the streets and the
> subways. (185)

Through the rhetoric of personal responsibility, families with single Black mothers were held responsible for social problems, such as low levels of education, teen pregnancy, and poverty, all of which coalesced in the national imaginary as leading to increased crime.[37] Black feminist scholar Dorothy Roberts writes, "Society penalizes Black single mothers not only because they depart from the norm of marriage as prerequisite to pregnancy but also because they represent rebellious Black culture" (1995, 238). Considering Parenti's argument that Black rebelliousness was made criminal through the logic of law and order, Black women's reproduction was thus made responsible for "breeding" this imagined crisis. Not only were welfare recipients largely conceptualized as Black women, they were also rendered unfit to pass on national culture. Punitive practices against this group, including curtailing their reproduction, were legitimized (Collins 1999, 126).

The re-mapping of gendered criminality onto brown bodies occurs in large part through the notion of (im)migrant (il)legality. The criminalization of (im)migrants is secured through their assumed "illegal" entrance into the United States. Images of (im)migrants "flooding" the US-Mexico border saturate the media and contribute to a perceived crisis of invasion (Chavez 2001 and 2008; Ono and Sloop 2002; Santa Ana 2002). As in the case of the criminalization of Blacks, women's reproduction is also targeted. (Im)migrant women are imagined as crossing the border "illegally" to secure not only their children's citizenship, but also, eventually, their own. Socially, these children are marked as "anchor babies."[38] This group is also imagined as undeserving of resources such as health care and education (Chang 2000; Fujiwara 2008; Park 2001 and 2011). Whereas "working-class Black women are constructed as the enemy within, the group producing the population that threatens the American national interest of maintaining itself as a 'White' nation-state" (Collins 1999, 126), Latina (im)migrants are constructed as the enemy from without, crossing the border "illegally" to have children and making use of state resources (Chang 2000, 4; Park 2011). Following this logic, (im)migrant mothers are the ultimate thieves since, through their motherhood, they are able to "steal" that which is valued most by the US body politic—citizenship.[39]

The re-mapping of dependency and criminality developed in relationship to Black motherhood is evident in the concerns expressed during the 1990s by conservative voices over Latina (im)migrants' reproduction. Similar to the construction of Black families as pathological, conservatives concerned themselves with the potential consequences of the *Latinization* of the United States. Gutiérrez (2008) cites a commentator from the conservative journal *National Review*:

For those who cluck cheerfully about the "strong family ties" of Hispanic immigrants, the new figures are ominous: two-thirds of young Latina mothers have no husbands. . . . Because the Latino share of the population is expanding, any burgeoning Latino culture of poverty will make its impact widely felt. Thirty-three years ago Sen. Daniel Patrick Moynihan (D-NY) gave a prescient warning about the breakdown of the African American family, for which he had no easy remedy. Now, thanks to feckless immigration policies, the United States is sowing difficulties which could prove of at least comparable scope. (3)

This passage draws direct connections between the gendered racialization of Blacks, particularly Black families, as pathological, and the perceived deviancy of Latinas and their families.[40] While the construction of Latinas (especially Mexican) as problematically hyper-fertile is rooted in Spanish colonialism and has historically been constructed as a threat to the United States as a white nation (10), the criminalized discourse of *public charge*—the idea that some individuals are unable to care for themselves and will therefore become dependent on the state— takes a different form during the 1990s. The merging of criminality and state dependency during this time functions to regulate and control (im)migrants while disciplining them into ideal American-ness (read: whiteness). However, before examining the criminalized deployment of the notion of public charge during the 1990s, it is important to historically contextualize the development of this concept.

The use of the concept of public charge in (im)migration law has historically functioned to discipline women into domesticity (Gardner 2005; Luibhéid 2002; Mattingly 1997). Martha Gardner (2005) examines how, from the late nineteenth century to 1965, (im)migration law was used to regulate normative gender roles. Entrance into the United States largely depended on a person's likelihood to become a public charge (87). "Likely to become a public charge" (LPC), according to Gardner,

was uniquely gendered in ways that reflected a constrained diminished evaluation of women's role in the economy. During the early twentieth century, immorality was linked to indigence, and laws against poverty were layered onto those directed at patrolling women's morality and their roles within a family economy. Regardless of their work skills, women arriving during the early twentieth century who were alone, pregnant, or with children, or with a checkered moral past were routinely found to be LPC. LPC stigmatized women's work outside the home by dismissing the ability of single women, divorced women, or widows to support themselves and their families. Poverty, in essence, was a gendered disease. (87)

Through her discussion of public charge, Gardner demonstrates that (im)migration law evaluated women's level of domesticity to allow or deny entrance into the United States. If women entered as "proper" domestic subjects, such as wives or daughters of men, or to labor domestically, their likelihood of being allowed to enter increased. However, if they attempted to enter as single, widowed, divorced, or as non-domestic laborers, their entrance was often denied. Gardner's study ends in 1965, the year that the Immigration and Nationality Act (INA) was enacted. Similar to previous (im)migration regulation that policed women into domesticity, the (im)migration regime established in 1965 reinforced patriarchal relations. INA implemented three major reasons for (im)migrant legal entrance into the United States: family reunification, fulfillment of the nation's skilled and unskilled labor needs, and refugee status (Lowe 1996, 21; Massey, Durand, and Malone 2002, 40).

INA's gendered workings are evident in the 1986 implementation of the Immigration Reform and Control Act (IRCA) that allowed almost 3 million undocumented (im)migrants to legalize their status. Due to the privileging of agricultural labor and other mechanisms, the vast majority of (im)migrants able to access legalization were men. However, family reunification provisions allowed the families of those able to access legalization to (im)migrate. The wives and children of these individuals were the main groups allowed to (im)migrate. Feminist (im)migration scholar Grace Chang (2000) states that the fashioning of IRCA was informed by fears about the mass legalization of undocumented (im)migrants, as well as the considerable strain this would place on social service funds. Thus, "Congress included in IRCA a provision barring legalization applicants from most federal assistance programs, including AFDC, food stamps, and certain forms of Medicaid. The bar period extends for five years from the time someone applies for temporary residency" (61). Chang provides an important reading of IRCA and its retention of the "likely to become a public charge" test. When considering past history of public assistance, it is not a determinative factor "if they can show that they are currently employed or able to provide for themselves and their family" (61). This exception was integrated in part due to critiques that the "likely to become a public charge test" served to exclude women. However, exclusion through the construction of public charge is implicitly upheld since individuals requesting legalization still must demonstrate that they are financially independent.[41]

Recognizing that while many undocumented (im)migrants were working poor, they were "unlikely to become dependent on public benefits despite their low incomes," Congress implemented a special rule for people to overcome the public charge test (62). The individual must demonstrate a history of self-support without the use of public assistance. Chang notes that while Congress attempted to liberalize the public charge test through this special rule, "the INS did not utilize the 'special rule' properly and instead implemented its own interpretations of the law. . . . The result of this practice was that many undocumented women who had received public assistance for their children were wrongfully denied amnesty" (62). The example of IRCA's special rule again highlights how (im)migration policies intervened in women's private lives, hindering their ability to sustain their families. Furthermore, IRCA merged state dependency and criminality as it restricted (im)migrants' access to social services, participated in (im)migrants' criminalization by expanding the war on drugs, and contributed to the militarization of the border. I provide further discussion of this below.

The increased presence of Latina (im)migrants post-IRCA intensified the public attention they received, particularly within the realm of social policy. Park (2011) examines how (im)migration, health care, and welfare policies intertwined during the 1990s, officially re-igniting the concept of public charge. This served not only to target Latina and Asian (im)migrant women's reproduction, but also to discipline (im)migrants in general against using public resources.[42] In earlier work, Park (2001) provides an analysis of the notion of public charge in conjunction with the 1996 Welfare Reform Act. She argues that "the social contexts that helped garner support for such anti-(im)migrant legislative measures created an environment that essentially criminalized motherhood for low-income (im)migrant women—whether they are documented or undocumented" (1161). As Park notes, the notion of public charge carried over the connotation of criminality associated with state dependency.

California Proposition 187, the 1994 ballot initiative also known as "Save Our State," exemplifies the merging of criminality and state dependency during the 1990s.[43] Section 1 begins:

The people of California find and declare as follows:

That they have suffered and are suffering economic hardship caused by the presence of illegal aliens in the state.

That they have suffered and are suffering personal injury and damage caused by the criminal conduct of illegal aliens in this state.

That they have a right to the protection of their government from any person or persons entering this country unlawfully.

Proposition 187 intended to limit undocumented (im)migrants' access to education and health care, public resources primarily accessed by women and children and imagined as the appeal for (im)migrant women's (im)migration.[44] According to Gutiérrez (2008), this policy drew from the idea that "poor pregnant (im)migrant women, who, with their children, come to the United States to give birth in publicly financed county hospitals, allowing the newborns to become US citizens, and all their children to receive public assistance, medical care, and public school education" (4).

The above introduction to Proposition 187 discloses how the identity of (im)migrant became associated with state dependency and criminality. Employing similar discourse on Latina (im)migrants as that used to criminalize Black women serves to discipline them into "ideal" citizen behavior, with an intended purpose of barring access to state resources. During the 1990s, the unworthiness of (im)migrants was voiced within the language of dependency, and specifically public charge, a notion originally developed in the nineteenth century in relation to southern and eastern European women (Gardner 2005) and linked to Black motherhood through ideas of unchecked lawlessness.

The gendered and racialized anti-(im)migrant sentiment developed during the 1990s meaningfully affected social policy. Two of the most significant pieces of legislation, the Illegal Immigration Reform and Immigrant Responsibility Act (IIRIRA) and the Personal Responsibility and Work Opportunity Reconciliation Act (PRWORA, also known as the Welfare Reform Act), were both enacted in 1996.[45] IIRIRA was presumably passed to target "criminal aliens." In partnership with the Antiterrorism and Effective Death Penalty Act (AEDPA)[46] passed during the same year, IIRIRA increased the number of deportable (im)-migrants. Together, these two legislations amended and added new offenses to the definition of aggravated felony, making this new definition apply retroactively (Coutin 2013, 237; Dowling and Inda 2013, 15; Luibhéid 2002, 28; Stumpf 2006, 380–390). Thus, even if (im)mi-

**Table 1.1 (Im)migrants Removed: Fiscal Years 1991–2004**

| Year | No. People | Year | No. People |
|------|-----------|------|-----------|
| 1991 | 33,189 | 1998 | 173,146 |
| 1992 | 43,671 | 1999 | 181,072 |
| 1993 | 42,542 | 2000 | 186,222 |
| 1994 | 45,674 | 2001 | 178,026 |
| 1995 | 50,924 | 2002 | 150,542 |
| 1996 | 69,680 | 2003 | 189,368 |
| 1997 | 114,432 | 2004 | 202,842 |

*Source*: Office of Immigration Statistics. 2006. "2004 Yearbook of Immigration Statistics." Washington, DC: U.S. Department of Homeland Security.

grants engaged in these activities several decades before, they legally became deportable "criminal aliens."[47] The merging of (im)migration enforcement and the criminal legal system has been termed "crimmigration" (Stumpf 2006).[48]

The impact of the 1996 legislative changes is evident in the immediate upsurge of removals.[49] Table 1.1 shows the increase in the number of (im)migrant removals between 1991 and 1995. A meaningful jump of 18,756 additional removals between 1995 and 1996 shows that, even prior to the 1996 legislations, (im)migration enforcement efforts were already intensifying. The devastating impact of the 1996 legislations on (im)migrants is highlighted in the 44,752 additional removals that occurred between 1996 and 1997.

The policy changes implemented in 1996 created a "criminal alien identification system," intended to locate (im)migrants with prior convictions who were now made deportable (Library of Congress 1996). This facilitated the deportation of imprisoned (im)migrants, regardless of their legal status. The thousands of individuals affected by this legislation underscore the significance of these policies. In 1998, 62,108 people were removed for criminal status. By 2007, the number had increased to 99,924, a 38 percent increase within nine years (Office of Immigration Statistics 2008). The highest (im)migrant removal rate was reported in 2012: of 409,849 people, 55 percent, or 225,390, had previous criminal convictions (US Immigration and Customs Enforcement 2012).[50]

The racialization of (im)migration enforcement is made clear with a comparison between who constitutes the unauthorized (im)migrant population in the United States and who is removed. While individuals from Mexico, El Salvador, Guatemala, and Honduras make up the majority of undocumented (im)migrants in the United States (Baker and Rytina 2013), these countries, except for El Salvador, are over-represented in removals (Simanski 2014).

Table 1.2 and Table 1.3 demonstrate that while individuals from these four Latin American countries made up 72.6 percent of the US unauthorized (im)migrant population in 2012, they constituted more than 95 percent of removals in 2013, indicating that (im)migration, especially undocumented (im)migration, is largely racialized in relation to brown bodies. The over-representation in removals of people from Mexico, Guatemala, and Honduras demonstrates that these bodies have become the racialized targets of (im)migration surveillance, policing, and enforcement.

In addition to contributing to the racialized expansion of deportable (im)migrants, the legislative changes of 1996 also included severe restrictions for (im)migrants' access to state resources. IIRIRA, in particular, contains a section titled "Restrictions on Benefits for Aliens." The following is a summary of this section provided by the Immigration and Naturalization Services (INS) in 1997:

> Title V contains amendments to the welfare bill, the Social Security Act, and the INA, which are directed at limiting aliens' access to public benefits. Proof of citizenship is required to receive public benefits and verification of immigration status is required for Social Security and higher-educational assistance. A transition period (until April 1, 1997) is established for aliens who are currently receiving food stamps.

What is of special significance here is the punitive nature of these policies that criminalize and expand the number of (im)migrants who can be deported, which, according to the logic of IIRIRA, conflates (im)migration with state dependency and criminality.

Enacted the same year as IIRIRA, the Welfare Reform Act incorporated many of the restrictions that California's Proposition 187 sought to implement by targeting (im)migrants' use of public resources.[51] Proposition 187 proposed to restrict access to Medicaid, food stamps, cash assistance for poor families, and aid for the disabled and elderly (im)migrants. In addition to severely limiting (im)migrants' access to these benefits, the Welfare Reform Act targeted people convicted for felony drug offenses by banning them for life from certain resources, including the Food Stamp Program.

**Table 1.2 Country of Birth of Unauthorized Immigrant Population: January 2000, January 2010, January 2012**

| | Year | | |
|---|---|---|---|
| | *2000* | *2010* | *2012* |
| *Country* | *No. people per country (Percent of total migration)* | | |
| Mexico | 4,680,000 (55.3) | 6,640,000 (61.8) | 6,720,000 (58.8) |
| El Salvador | 430,000 (5.0) | 620,000 (5.8) | 690,000 (6.0) |
| Guatemala | 290,000 (3.4) | 520,000 (4.8) | 560,000 (4.7) |
| Honduras | 160,000 (1.9) | 330,000 (3.1) | 360,000 (3.1) |

*Source*: Bryan Baker and Nancy Rytina. "Estimates of the Unauthorized Immigrant Population Residing in the United States; January 2012." Washington, DC: Office of Immigration Statistics, 2013.

**Table 1.3 Countries of Removal by Citizenship**

| *Country* | *FY 2013* No. people (percent total removal) |
|---|---|
| Mexico | 314,904 (71.8) |
| El Salvador | 20,862 (4.76) |
| Guatemala | 46,866 (10.7) |
| Honduras | 36,526 (8.3) |

*Source*: John F. Simanski. "Immigration Enforcement Actions: 2013." Washington, DC: DHS Office of Immigration Statistics, 2014.

Again, similar to that of IIRIRA, the logic of the Welfare Reform Act merged (im)migration, crime, and state dependency. In discussing these anti-(im)migrant policies, scholar-activist Syd Lindsley (2002) argues that the criminalization and attacks that (im)migrants undergo, particularly Mexican (im)migrant women, at the most basic level, have little to do with the costs that this group has on the state and the nation. Rather, these policies "reflect assumptions about the value of (im)migrant mothers in US society" and their passing is "an attempt to regulate and control (im)migrant women's mothering" (185).[52] The context that I present here illustrates how (im)migrant women and their communities are made violable by the state. Militarizing the border, criminalizing (im)migrants, limiting access to public resources, and expanding mechanisms for the deportation of both documented and undocumented people results in increased levels of both poverty and violence. This contributes to the substantial family separation that is occurring as (im)migrants are held by the state in detention centers, jails, or prisons and then deported.

## Border Warfare and Consequences for (Im)migrants

The 1990s also brought about the end of the Cold War, which had ramifications for (im)migrants, especially in how criminalization is lived. Kent A. Ono and John M. Sloop (2002) maintain that the Cold War enabled the construction of the United States as a land of freedom and opportunity, in contrast with communism, which was ideologically constructed as unfree and undemocratic. According to the authors, a need for new enemies characterized the post–Cold War era, and, as a result, "the projection of fears onto 'alien invaders' was a natural after-effect of the Cold War and the concomitant dissolution of a clear and coherent enemy, the Soviet Union" (35). This serves as yet another moment when the United States turned attention from the "enemy outside" to the "enemy among us." Even during the post–Cold War, the United States maintained an *us* versus *them* worldview. However, in the postmodern United States, those who constitute "the other," "the enemy among us," have changed and are now manifest in a multiplicity of representations, depending on the geopolitical moment. According to Ono and Sloop, the "news media represent many different versions of enemies who threaten the moral, cultural, and political fabric of the nation-state and therefore must be evicted, eliminated, or otherwise controlled" (35).[53]

In the case of (im)migrants, the notion of war significantly informs their (im)migration experiences. According to border historian Jose Palafox (2000), the shift into the post–Cold War United States was accompanied by a conflation of law enforcement and military, increasing not only the cooperation between these institutions, but also creating a joint infrastructure. Similar to arguments made by border scholar Timothy Dunn, Palafox contends that the military presence at the border operates as a form of low-intensity warfare against (im)migrants. Peter Andreas and Richard Price (2001) discuss this transformation as a change from "war fighting to crime fighting." Like Palafox, Andreas and Price argue that there was a blurring of boundaries between the police and the military, where the military has undergone domestication while policing has been militarized. Thus, the criminalization of (im)migrants acts as an inherent part of the wars waged at the border.

The war on drugs that developed in part to contain Black rebelliousness was essential to wedding criminality to the border. While the border was already a legally contested space, given the production of undocumented (im)migration, the war on drugs served to fuse criminality to the US-Mexico border (Payán 2006, 11–12). According to political scientist Tony Payán, the declaration of the war on drugs by President Nixon transformed that border into "the frontline of a never-ending war between the US government and the drug smuggling cartels" (2006, 23). The perception of drugs being trafficked through the border to be sold and consumed in US Black urban cities designated the border as a crucial site where criminality, as linked to drugs, made its way into the nation. In addition to "illegal" (im)migration, drug trafficking became conceptualized as a threat to the nation and served as another reason to control the border and contain (im)migrant bodies. In other words, the war on drugs served to fix the border as a space of criminality and its inhabitants as inherently criminal. The border became both another productive space where the logic of law and order contributed to the war on drugs and an additional space where the expansion of the US criminal legal system takes place.

Prior to President Nixon declaring the war on drugs, one of the first mobilizations against drugs, Operation Intercept, was deployed in September 1969 at the US-Mexico border. This measure was intended to compel Mexico to participate in the battle against drugs. The concern over drugs entering the United States was largely centered on their destinations and the bodies that inhabited these spaces: primarily urban cities and Black bodies imagined to be engaging in criminalized activities to continue their drug addiction.

Through an analysis of Operation Intercept, senior analyst Kate Doyle (2003) provides insight into the US-Mexico relationship as affected by the war on drugs.[54] She notes that two months after Nixon took office, he established the Special Presidential Task Force. This task force regarded Mexican "free-lance smugglers and organized traffickers" as "responsible for the marihuana and drug abuse problem." Their recommendation was to launch Operation Intercept, which, according to Doyle, was not necessarily intended to stop drug trafficking, but rather, was an attempt to compel the Mexican government to address the drug problem within its borders. Launched on September 21, 1969, and with little notification to the Mexican government, the operation consisted of the meticulous inspection of everything crossing the border, a process that severely slowed all border crossings. Doyle cites the autobiography of G. Gordon Liddy, senior advisor in the Department of Treasury at the time, which notes that rather than deterring illegal drug trafficking, the implementation of Operation Intercept was about forcing Mexico to comply with the wishes of the United States. Liddy wrote:

> For diplomatic reasons the true purpose of the exercise was never revealed. Operation Intercept, with its massive economic and social disruption, could be sustained far longer by the United States than by Mexico. It was an exercise in international extortion, pure, simple, and effective, designed to bend Mexico to our will. (185–186)

Liddy's comments signify how the war on drugs served as a political mechanism deployed to meet the desires of the existing administration. The US-Mexico border was thus central to the expansion of the war on drugs (Doyle 2003; Andreas 2000, 41).

While Operation Intercept was largely waged by the United States to compel Mexico to increase the policing of drug trafficking, the war on drugs has been waged by both nations. An example of Mexico's participation is Operation Condor, launched in 1975. The operation used aerial herbicides, military troops, and "law enforcement collaboration between the United States and Mexico, including intelligence sharing, surveillance, and training" (Andreas 2000, 41). While law enforcement strategies such as this one were largely perceived as successful, political scientist Peter Andreas demonstrates that the increased enforcement largely resulted in a restructuring of the drug trade that made it more dangerous and more profitable.[55]

During the Reagan administration, the war on drugs continued to escalate (Payán 2006, 12). When the number and settlement of Mexican (im)migrants re-emerged as an issue of national concern, Congress passed the Immigration Reform and Control and Act in 1986 and, as a result, the war on drugs at the border was extended. According to leading border studies scholar Timothy Dunn:

> Following the passage of IRCA in 1986, the issue of illegal drug trafficking gained ascendency, eclipsing undocumented (im)migration as the most urgent border-control matter. The issue was formally designated as a threat to national security by President Reagan in 1986, and the ensuing war on drugs was a prominent element of both US domestic and foreign policy. (1996, 2)[56]

Similar to its deployment in urban cities, the war on drugs deployed at the border serves to create the appearance that the government is cracking down on crime while at the same time contributing to the criminalization of (im)migrants and border militarization by increasing the violence in this space.[57] The war on drugs served to characterize the US-Mexican border as a space of criminality and violence. Bodies that inhabit and travel through this space are subjected to its racialized criminalization and to the policies intended to bring the border under state control, a bilateral effort between the United States and Mexico. Since the 1960s, Mexico has offered an increasingly militarized response to drug production and trafficking, with great focus on the border. Similar to the United States government, the Mexican government criminalized the border, resulting not only in criminalizing people engaged in illicit actions such as drug trafficking, but also in mapping criminality onto (im)migrants and people residing in the borderlands. Similar to the US militarization of the border, Mexico also engages in militarizing efforts. For example, between 1994 and 2000, President Ernesto Zedillo assigned the Mexican army, in addition to the federal judicial police, to combat drug trafficking (Chabat 2002, 139).[58]

IRCA's relation to the war on drugs cannot be divorced from its overall effect. In general, IRCA added three important provisions: employer sanctions, amnesty for a large number of people residing and working in the United States for a fixed number of years, and border militarization. The law was intended to provide enough laborers—hence the amnesty provision—while at the same time attempting to curtail future (im)migration in order to alleviate public discontent over a perceived crisis of undocumented (im)migration. However, rather than curtailing (im)migration, the law actually increased it since, as noted above, it included a provision for family reunification that included the (im)-migrants' spouse, children, parents, and siblings (Luibheid 2002, xxiv, 24).[59] While female (im)migration was already increasing prior to the passing of IRCA, the family reunification provision fueled the female (im)migration trend since those who could receive amnesty and prove they could sustain a family were mainly men who had been working in the United States and could then petition for their wives and family (Lindsley 2002, 177; Hondagneu-Sotelo 1994, 24). The increased (im)migration of Mexican women and their families focused attention on this group and intensified nativist sentiment. Thus, while the criminalization of the border was well underway, the centrality of women's bodies in (im)migration control gained significance.

A consequence of the intensified racialized and gendered focus on (im)migrants' settlement and social lives is the expansion of (im)migration enforcement into the interior of the United States. Central to this process is the strategy of "attrition through enforcement." Its logic is to make life so difficult for unauthorized (im)migrants that they will leave of their own volition.[60] Attrition through enforcement policies take place at the federal, state, and local levels.

An example of this strategy at the federal level is the US Immigration and Customs Enforcement's (ICE) Secure Communities Program. This program created partnerships among local, state, and federal law enforcement agencies to capture and transfer (im)migrants considered by ICE to be "criminal aliens" for removal (US Immigration and Customs Enforcement, "Delegation"). On the ground, however, Secure Communities was used very broadly and affected (im)migrants in general, resulting in massive detentions and removals. (Im)migrants do not just fear federal (im)migration agencies; indeed, fear has been distributed across space. President Barack Obama's executive action on (im)migration replaced Secure Communities with the Priority Enforcement Program (PEP), which is intended to target "enforcement priorities," particularly "criminal aliens" (Johnson 2014b; Office of the Press Secretary 2014a).[61] Thus, people marked as "criminals" are targeted and the binary between deserving and undeserving (im)migrants is reinforced.

The spatial expansion of the fear of deportation continues with the federal E-verify Program. Employers are required to determine the legal ability of potential or current employees to work in the United States. E-verify is a federal database that allows employers to submit documentation to make such determinations. This functions to limit unauthorized (im)migrants' ability to work and sustain themselves.

An example of state attrition through enforcement is Arizona's S.B. 1070, the Support Our Law Enforcement and Safe Neighborhoods Act (O'Leary and Sanchez 2011), which received significant public attention. Among many of its provisions, S.B. 1070, passed in 2010, requires law enforcement officers who have "reasonable suspicion" that an individual is undocumented to detain that person for further investigation and possible transfer to federal immigration authorities. On the ground, S.B. 1070 racially works to target Latinas/os in general (Williams 2011). In 2012, the US Supreme court ruled on the constitutionality of this legislation and overall maintained that federal law preempts most of its provisions. This included making it a state misdemeanor crime to be undocumented and working without legal permission. However, the requirement that law enforcement officers detain suspected unauthorized (im)migrants was upheld (Wessler 2012).

Local city governments are also participants in the attrition through enforcement strategy. A common way for city governments to engage this practice is to pass ordinances against renting to unauthorized (im)-migrants (McKanders 2007). For example, in early 2014, Fremont, Nebraska voted (by 60 percent) to uphold a ban on unauthorized (im)-migrants' ability to rent housing (Fitzsimmons 2014). In other words, private citizens are active participants in (im)migration control and enforcement (Walsh 2014) in attempts to make life unlivable for unauthorized (im)migrants so that they will leave "voluntarily."

The attrition through enforcement strategy exemplifies how (im)migration enforcement is disarticulated across space and penetrates the most intimate spaces of (im)migrants' lives. These efforts reveal the ways in which the state attempts to spatially organize society and manage and discipline (im)migrants.

## Conclusion

This chapter roots the criminalization of Latina (im)migrants within the longer history of captivity lived by Blacks in the United States, which has serious social implications. This conceptualization displaces the competition paradigm that dominates our understanding of the relationship between Blacks and Latina/o (im)migrants and instead highlights the centrality of criminalization in racially organizing society. The reliance on incarceration that developed during the late 1960s and 1970s occurred simultaneously with the increased production of an undocumented (im)migrant labor force and exclusion of Black citizens. The relational analysis of the criminalization of Black and Latina motherhoods exposes how targeting women's reproduction serves to control racialized neoliberal labor relations, and the centrality that incarceration assumes in this process. In the post–civil rights era, Blacks became less attractive as laborers because their claims to US citizenship theoretically afforded them some legal protections. Their undesirability should also be attributed to the lasting afterlife of Black insurgency and civil disobedience. Their construction as inherently deviant contributed to their disposability in the labor market as racialized neoliberal *excess*. Furthermore, notions developed in relation to Black motherhood—including laziness, dependency, and criminality—provided ideological grounds for the expansion of the US prison regime as a *fix*. A central development of this dynamic is the creation of exploitable, "criminal," and predominantly Black bodies that can labor while they are held captive and, if released, extends their vulnerability within the labor market through their records of criminality.

As noted, the increased imprisonment of Blacks is accompanied by an increased reliance on undocumented labor. The presence of (im)migrant women and their families is partially a result of the neoliberal shift that polarizes the labor market into two main forms of labor—one that is feminized, "unskilled," and exploitable, and the other that is masculinized, "skilled," and protected. The criminalization of (im)migrant motherhood functions through tropes developed in relation to Black women's reproductive bodies and provides rationalization for the policing, incarceration, detention, and deportation that (im)migrants in general confront. (Im)migrants are tolerated as laborers and punitive practices of capturing, warehousing, and disposing of their bodies participate in regulating the neoliberal labor market by reinforcing their exploitability as workers and separating their productive from reproductive capacities, which occurs in part by breaking up (im)migrant families. Contextualizing the anti-(im)migrant moment within the history of incarceration of Blacks and focusing on women's reproduction dislodges exceptionalist frameworks and allows us to see the ways in which criminality is central to racialized global neoliberal governance. Rather than label this as unique, the contemporary anti-(im)migrant moment is a natural extension of the racialized and gendered methodologies used in the constant remaking of the United States.

While the framework afforded throughout this chapter indicates the relational dimensions of the gendered racialization of Black women and Latina (im)migrants, the following chapter demonstrates how this framework guides responses to the violence that the gendered criminalization of (im)migrants creates. The analysis of dominant (im)migrant rights discourse developed in response to the criminalization of (im)migrants illustrates an attempt to distance (im)migrants from criminality, with little interrogation of criminalization, and an attempt to distance them from feminized domesticity, with limited questioning of the retrenchment of the welfare state.

CHAPTER 2

# Reinforcing Gendered Racial Boundaries: Unintended Consequences of (Im)migrant Rights Discourse

The intensified criminalization of Latina/o (im)migrants during the past two decades has brought about many responses, including the (im)migrant rights movement's claims that "(im)migrants are not criminals, (im)migrants are hard workers." This dominant message, espoused by pro-(im)migrant voices, intensified during the mass marches that began in 2006. Similarly, the declaration "Nadie es Ilegal/No One is Illegal" became an axiom for (im)migrant rights. These messages have been used to distance (im)migrants from criminality in an effort to secure the innocence and safety of (im)migrant communities that find themselves under intense policing and violence.

However, these decriminalizing motions turn into violent acts themselves when the innocence of some (im)migrants is secured at the expense of others. These discursive utterances present the identity of (im)migrant and criminal as mutually exclusive, thus constructing (im)migrants as innocent while criminalizing an unspoken *other*. When (im)migrants' innocence is explicitly articulated, society is left to ask, "What about (im)migrants that do engage in crime? Also, if (im)migrants are innocent, then who is guilty?" In *Social Death: Racialized Rightlessness and the Criminalization of the Unprotected*, Lisa Marie Cacho addresses processes of valuing. She maintains that human valuing is inherently a process of devaluing (an)other and "made intelligible through racialized, sexualized, spatialized, and state-sanctioned violences" (2012, 4). Attempts to value (im)migrants by distancing them from criminality has two consequences.

First, an effort is made to distance (im)migrants from the identity of criminal by implicitly (and at times explicitly) asking for the punishment of "criminal" (im)migrants while simultaneously demanding the protection of "American-behaving" (im)migrants. DREAMers, children brought to the United States without proper documentation by their families and marked as "American-behaving," are the most recent example of this development.[1] The DREAMers' framework maintains the youths' innocence since they seemingly had no role in deciding to enter the United States undocumented. At the same time, it categorizes their parents as conscious violators of the nation's laws.[2] Diaz-Strong et al. (2009) argue that (im)migrant rights organizing strategies largely depend on tropes of "innocence" and "merit." Employing such tropes tends to "reinforce the idea that there are 'real' criminals and undeserving or guilty immigrants who should legitimately be denied access to pathways for legalization" (74).[3]

The second consequence of attempts to distance (im)migrants from criminality is the reinforcement of boundaries between Blacks and Latina/o (im)migrants. As exemplified in the previous chapter, criminality in the United States has been historically constructed in relation to Blackness and Black bodies. Thus, when the claim "(im)migrants are not criminals" is made, the fundamental message, whether intentional or not, is that (im)migrants are not going to be another "Black problem."[4] Tracing the construction of criminality in relationship to Blackness and how it is re-mapped onto brown bodies through the notion of (il)legality demonstrates the ways in which criminality allows a reconfiguration of racial boundaries along notions of Blackness and whiteness that serves to discipline Latina/o (im)migrants and other bodies racialized as non-white.[5]

Moreover, it is crucial to examine how gender informs the remapping of criminality onto brown bodies. In chapter 1, I noted how in the United States criminality historically has been conceptualized as birthed by Black women. Constructs such as the "welfare queen" and the "crack mother" that aided in configuring this group as public charges were particularly useful (Jordan-Zachery 2009; Roberts 1997; Neubeck and Cazenave 2001; Flavin 2007). How does this history inform the criminalization of (im)migrants? The merging of criminality and state dependency takes place largely through the notion of dependency. This results not only in attempts to distance (im)migrants from Blackness, but also fosters the criminalization of (im)migrant women by distancing them from womanhood. Consequently, (im)migrant rights discourse, in addition to affirming that (im)migrants are not criminals, tightly adheres to masculinized claims of (im)migrants as hard workers.[6]

The centrality of the figure of the "worker" for Mexican and Mexican American social and cultural politics is depicted in *Migrant Imaginaries: Latino Cultural Politics in the US-Mexico Borderlands* (2008) by transnational migration scholar Alicia Schmidt Camacho. She demonstrates that Mexican (im)migrants and Mexican Americans, due to their perpetual status as foreigners in the United States, have engaged in imaginings of social belonging that "resist subordination to the nation-state" (9). Schmidt Camacho writes:

> Mexican and Mexican American cultural politics have emerged from imaginaries shaped by the experience of laboring for the nation without the promise of inclusion into its community as the bearers of rights. *Migrant Imaginaries* argues that the particular formation of Mexicans as a *transborder laboring class* (emphasis added) forced immigrants to articulate expansive definitions of civic life and community that defied conventions of national citizenship in both Mexico and the United States. (9)

Schmidt Camacho's analysis signals the significance that labor assumes for ethnic Mexicans' understanding of their position in the United States. While she reinforces the significance of ethnic Mexicans' cultural politics in producing imaginaries of social belonging outside of citizenship, these imaginaries are mainly produced around the figure of the Mexican (im)migrant as worker. Thus, it is through the identity of worker that claims to rights and belonging are widely made, whether these claims are made on the nation-state or some other transnational entity.

The dominant narrative of Mexican (im)migrant workers centers on a male experience and largely ignores the ways in which women experience belonging (or non-belonging). Great pains are taken to demonstrate how much work (im)migrants contribute to the United States and how the labor of (im)migrants contributes to the economy.[7] Attempts to claim belonging based on the masculinized identity of workers contrast with the historical racialization of Blacks as dependent and serve to reinforce boundaries between these communities. Thus, while I acknowledge that for many (im)migrants and (im)migrant advocates dignity may be derived from the identity of hard worker, my contention is that in the United States this identity is constructed against Blacks, who were ideologically represented as the main beneficiaries of social welfare. Given the historical development of the concept of dependency and the fact that Blacks have the highest level of unemployment in the

United States in terms of race and ethnicity (US Bureau of Labor Statistics 2014), is it possible for Latina/o (im)migrants to present their value as hard workers without devaluing Blacks? I argue that, even if unintentional, seizing the identity of hard workers to claim rights and belonging reinforces boundaries between Latina/o (im)migrants and Blacks.

The importance that multicultural neoliberalism assumed after the 1960s social movements affects efforts by (im)migrants and their supporters, including some media outlets, to advocate for (im)migrant rights. Critical race scholar Jodi Melamed (2006) discusses this shift and maintains that central to neoliberal restructuring is the deployment of multiculturalism, the idea that different cultures can coexist and equally contribute to society. Melamed maintains that neoliberal policy

> engenders new racial subjects, as it creates and distinguishes between newly privileged and stigmatized collectivities, yet multiculturalism codes the wealth, mobility, and political power of neoliberalism's beneficiaries to be the just desserts of "multicultural world citizens," while representing those neoliberalism dispossesses to be handicapped by their own "monoculturalism" or other historico-cultural deficiencies. (1)

Neoliberal capitalist hegemony is thus in part secured through multicultural discourse and the representation of the resulting inequality, which is inherently racialized, as self-made. In this sense, (im)migrant rights discourse that attempts to denaturalize (im)migrant criminality and fasten the identity of (im)migrant to hard worker is in great part structured by neoliberal multiculturalism. Claims of belonging based on (im)migrants' merit presuppose an open society where membership is ascribed based on individuals' social contributions. The contributions of Latina/o (im)migrants have been historically relegated to that of exploitable labor. (Im)migrant rights advocates discursively draw from this notion to advance their efforts. For Blacks, however, the neoliberal shift contributed to further constructing them as dependent and prone to crime, attributes from which (im)migrants incessantly attempt to distance themselves. (Im)migrant rights advocates inadvertently participate in bolstering neoliberal capitalist hegemony that relies on the racialized subordination of both communities.

Part of the dilemma for most Latina/o (im)migrants is that they are trapped in a perverse relationship within neoliberal capitalism where many depend on this very exploitative system to sustain themselves and attempt to make their way out of poverty. Thus, the neoliberal capitalist economy depends on their exploitability while Latina/o (im)migrants depend on the jobs made available specifically for *them* (exploitable workers) by this system. However, as the (im)migrant rights movement demonstrates, Latinas/os are engaged in resisting this relationship, in part by making demands for a path to legalization, which would reduce their condition of exploitability. The demands for (im)migration reform were addressed by President Barack Obama's 2014 executive action on (im)migration. This action provides both temporary relief from deportation for qualifying undocumented (im)migrants (approximately 5 million) and temporary work permits for three-year periods. However, it is not a path to legalization or citizenship. Thus, it maintains (im)migrants' vulnerability.

In this chapter, I examine some of the limitations presented by dominant (im)migrant rights discourse that centers around the logic "(im)migrants are not criminals, (im)migrants are hard workers." The critique is in part informed by Gonzales (2014), who also addresses the limitations of the dominant (im)migrant rights framework. He makes use of Gramsci's theory of hegemony to explain how, despite the ability to mobilize massive numbers of people, the (im)migrant rights movement has been unable to secure justice for (im)migrants. He attributes this to the ideological and material work carried out by what he terms the "anti-migrant bloc." The anti-migrant bloc is composed of academics, public personalities, elected officials, and state representatives who seek to expand what Gonzales and others term the "Homeland Security State" (7). The anti-migrant bloc has been successful in securing the debate over (im)migration within the good/bad (im)migrant binary and erasing the structural issues that lead to massive displacement of people. The (im)migrant rights movement's inability to subvert this framework has prevented it from bringing about justice for (im)migrants. Gonzales's argument significantly informs this chapter, and I expand upon it by providing a comparative and relational analysis between Latina/o (im)migrants and Blacks and also by deploying a feminist critique of the limitations of the (im)migrant rights movement.

To provide a comparative and relational analysis of Blacks and Latina/o (im)migrants, I make use of critical anthropologist Nicholas De Genova's (2005) *Working the Boundaries: Race, Space, and "Illegality" in Mexican Chicago*. De Genova examines how "Mexican (im)migrants in Chicago negotiated their own racialization as Mexican, always in relation to both a dominant whiteness and its polar opposite, a subjugated and denigrated Blackness" (8). He illustrates how the anti-migrant politics of the 1990s were inherently tied to the criminalization and dismantling of social welfare for impoverished US citizens, largely imagined as Black. What results is what he calls "double discipline" (206). On the one hand, (im)migrants are made responsible for "taking American jobs." On the other, their vulnerability as (im)migrant workers encourages them to generate distance between themselves and impoverished US citizens constructed as lazy and racialized as Black.[8] Claiming the identity of hard workers led to disparaging the supposed laziness of impoverished citizens who had advantages over (im)migrants such as citizenship and knowledge of the English language (206). According to De Genova:

> Because immigrant workers were always at pains to demonstrate to their overseers that they were "hardworking" and not "lazy," the momentum of their efforts at self-defense served to subvert the possibilities for resistance, and they effectively participated in their own intensified exploitation. (206)

De Genova's examination draws attention to the way that the white supremacist social order of the United States has fixed (im)migrants, particularly Latinas/os, spatially between whites and Blacks. However, the racial "foreignness" of (im)migrants, which is marked through (il)legality, has permanently dislodged them from assuming an American identity. (Im)migrants' attempts to claim any form of American belonging are perpetually obstructed by their racialized (il)legality. Their continued attempts at inclusion contribute to maintaining racial boundaries. In this chapter, I reinforce De Genova's position that (im)migrants' negotiation between the polarized racial boundaries of the United States often results in bolstering white supremacy. However, I also define this boundary work as a particularly violent patriarchal negotiation that reinforces the irrecuperability of imprisoned (im)migrant women.

Boundary work, or social valuing (Cacho 2012), does not strictly work along racial lines. Instead, other markers of identity also participate in constructing these divisions. For example, in *The Boundaries of Blackness: AIDS and the Breakdown of Black Politics* (1999), Cathy J. Cohen considers the responses of Black communities to the issue of AIDS. She demonstrates how even though these communities are predominantly represented as a unified entity driven by a common political agenda, the levels of stratification result in what she terms "secondary marginalization." The inability of Blacks to exercise control over resources that shape their lives serves to marginalize this community (25). However, particular members within Black communities face further marginalization, which is the case of individuals identified as HIV positive.[9]

Cohen's work enables an understanding of how boundary work functions not only to create and reinforce divisions between racial groups, but also within these groups. It also demonstrates how the actions and attitudes of marginalized communities are shaped not only on a national level by dominant institutions and systems, but also on a regional level by community leaders and organizations. This chapter highlights the boundary work carried out between Latina/o (im)migrants and Black communities as well as within (im)migrant communities.

## Road Map

In this chapter, I consider two different sites where dominant (im)migrant rights discourse emerges and demonstrate its limitations, particularly as it serves to reinforce the racialized good/bad (im)migrant binary. In the first part of the chapter, I focus on families facing separation as a result of parents' deportation as evident in the *Los Angeles Times*.[10] I focus on news articles dated January 1, 1994, to December 31, 2008.[11] The year 1994 proved a significant moment in the nation's understanding of (im)migration. It was the year that California passed Proposition 187, which focused on the alleged criminality of (im)migrants and their undeserved use of public resources. I selected twenty-four articles that profiled families facing deportation and analyzed how the authors, who participate in constructing civil society's common sense, presented the families in relation to the dominant framework used to discuss (im)migration. The analysis of these texts reveals their engagement in a struggle over the production of an ideological common sense that attempts to decriminalize (im)migrants while simultaneously drawing from and reinforcing hegemonic ideologies, including the sanctity of the heteronormative nuclear family and American exceptionalism.

In the second part of the chapter, I draw from my ethnographic research and analyze the story of Esther and her fifteen-year-old daughter, Elisa. Esther was deported in June 2008, after serving a five-year prison sentence.[12] After her deportation, she and Elisa, who traveled from the United States to be with her mother, immediately became involved in the (im)migrant rights movement in Tijuana. Their story received a great deal of attention from activist groups, media, and government authorities. However, the story Esther and Elisa were compelled to tell presented Esther as a hardworking mother and Elisa as the victim of punitive US (im)migration policies. This strategy completely erased their experiences as shaped by Esther's imprisonment. Their adapted narrative could not account for their five-year separation. Their story highlights how the (im)migrant rights movement attempted to transform the commonsense understanding of undocumented (im)migrants as criminals and public drains. Instead, they were presented as hard working, and, in the case of Esther, as a "good" mother. The analysis underscores the constraints imposed by hegemonic ideologies. The challenges generated by incarceration were strategically erased from their story in order to represent this family as deserving.

Information on Esther's experiences as an (im)migrant rights activist comes from our weekly visits and conversations that ranged from one to three hours.[13] I interviewed Elisa on the day she returned to the United States to resume school. Her experience as a representative for children of deported parents was one of the topics we discussed. Through my analysis, I argue that dominant (im)migrant rights discourse negotiates the inclusion of "American-behaving" (im)migrants while unintentionally re-criminalizing those outside the "good" (im)migrant identity. This reinforces racialized boundaries of worthiness that assemble some (im)migrants as deserving of belonging while reinforcing the expendability of others.

## From Public Charges to Ideal Potential Citizens: *Los Angeles Times* and (Im)migrants' Representation

In chapter 1, I discussed the racialized and gendered ideological construction of (im)migrants as public charges. This construction represents (im)migrants as undeserving of belonging because, rather than contribute to society, they are assumed to drain public resources. The identity of public charge was merged with criminality, particularly in relation to Black motherhood. The representation of women of color as dependent on the state served to designate them as poor mothers who passed on to their children deficient moral values that include laziness, dependence, and undeserved entitlement—ideas that are linked to criminality. The re-mapping of dependency and criminality onto (im)-

migrant women—which in large part occurs through media representation, political debate, and social policy—constructs this group as criminal threats to the nation and generates an environment that condones violence against them and their communities. This includes interpersonal forms of violence (e.g., intimate partner and sexual violence),[14] as well as deaths at the border, ICE raids, massive detentions, deportations, and family separations. These outcomes are conceptualized as logical consequences to (im)migrants' assumed "illegal" border crossings.[15] De-criminalizing efforts are responses to the violence encountered by these communities.

Attempts to afford some level of protection for (im)migrants come from many venues, including the media; however, the current framework available to discuss (im)migration limits these efforts. In this section, I analyze strategies employed by *Los Angeles Times* writers to sympathize with (im)migrant families facing separation due to deportation. Within the current neoliberal moment, capitalist hegemony is in part secured through the logic of multiculturalism (Melamed 2006). The social inclusion of communities of color serves to obscure the work of racism and white supremacy in structuring society. However, this inclusion is conditional and grounded in the abilities of the people of these communities to fulfill their roles within neoliberalism. This dynamic greatly informs the framework available to advocate for (im)migrants.

What is witnessed in the analysis of the representation by the *Los Angeles Times* of undocumented (im)migrant families is that the authors contest, while at the same time reproduce, dominant ideologies. In order to advocate for (im)migrant families, they challenge the criminalization of (im)migrants while simultaneously drawing on powerful ideals, including the sanctity of the nuclear family and American exceptionalism. All twenty-four articles sympathize with (im)migrant families affected by deportations. This complicates our understanding of power relations, given that all these cases attempt to generate support for the (im)migrant families discussed. However, not all (im)migrants are considered worthy of support. The examination reveals how the binary constructions of redeemable "good" (im)migrants—those who "work hard" and do not engage in criminalized acts—and disposable "bad" (im)migrants—those who are "lazy" and engage in criminalized acts—work to discipline (im)migrants into behaving like "ideal" citizens while normalizing the violence that occurs to those who deviate from this norm. Furthermore, it highlights how, in the public imagination, the (im)migrant identity is feminized through the notion of public charge. Claims made to disassociate (im)migrants from state dependency are thus attempts to re-masculinize the (im)migrant identity as (exploitable) workers.

The media, in this case the *Los Angeles Times*, participate in the production of common sense regarding issues of (im)migration that instantaneously draws from existing hegemonic ideals that dictate what it means to be a US citizen. In doing so, the media influence the ideological framework of the mainstream (im)migrant rights movement. As noted earlier, the nature that the (im)migrant rights movement assumes, including its actions and attitudes, is formed by dominant institutions and systems, including the media, as well as by (im)migrant community leaders, organizations, and institutions. Serious tensions exist within the (im)migrant rights movement and (im)migrant communities over the frameworks and tactics employed to bring about change.[16] The extent to which the (im)migrant rights movement genuinely accepts this commonsense narrative, in part produced by media outlets such as the *Los Angeles Times*, is difficult to assess. Segments of the (im)migrant rights movement and (im)migrant communities do not only espouse, but, in fact, believe and agree with these narratives that attempt to present them positively. However, as I demonstrate in the second part of this chapter, the espousal of such ideas can also be strategic.

The stories considered in the analysis follow similar patterns, including families paying taxes, owning homes, having children who excel academically—that is, essentially fitting into the dominant family ethic. These stories kept making news in large part because they problematize the American myth of the United States as a land of (im)migrants and opportunity and, in doing so, disrupt the logic of multicultural neoliberalism. In these cases, according to the authors, these families "did everything right" and yet were denied the American Dream. More than apprehension for these families, these stories highlight concerns for the nation and how, in these cases, it fails to meet its expectations.

I begin my analysis with a brief discussion of how the racialization of Asians in the United States as model minorities ideologically works to construct the "good" (im)migrant identity. These articles especially profile South Asians. Significantly, of the twenty-four articles considered, five focused on the stories of Asian (im)migrants. The construction of the Asian American model minority serves to discipline Asians by defining their worth in accordance to how closely they follow the model minority myth (Park 2005). This myth maintains that Asian Americans can integrate themselves into US society because their cultural values are similar to those of Americans. These values include hard work, diligence, and self-motivation. Society deems Asians who do not adhere to this construction less deserving because they do not have the characteristics that are idealized to form part of the American society (23–24). This construction not only informs the experiences of Asians, but also serves to discipline other racialized groups, including Blacks and Latinas/os. At the root of the model minority myth is the question: "If they made it, why can't you?"[17] In addition to functioning as a mechanism to discipline Blacks and Latinas/os, this myth also ignores the histories of Asian Americans and their continued struggles for social inclusion. The fact that several of the articles profiled Asian American families attests to the continued significance of the model minority myth and its use to differentiate between deserving and undeserving (im)migrants.

The ideological workings of the model minority myth are evident in two articles written by journalist Ann M. Simmons (2004 and 2005), which covered the story of Jayantibhai and Indiraben Desai. The couple, Jayantibhai, an Indian national, and Indiraben, a British national, overstayed their visas in the early 1980s, but they continued to live in the United States. Central to this discussion is Simmons's attempt to portray the Desais in a positive light by contrasting them with the dominant image of (im)migrants as public charges. In three different places, within two articles, Simmons makes the point that the Desais pay taxes. Their representation directly contrasts them with general notions that (im)migrants do not contribute to the economy and instead deplete resources. Simmons writes, "For more than 20 years, the Norwalk couple worked hard. They bought a house, paid taxes and sent their two sons off to college. They were a success story in the making, but for one thing: Their status as illegal immigrants" (2004). She includes these details more than once, attempting to further separate the couple from the image of public charge.

Implicit in Simmons's 2005 article is an attempt to distance the Desais from the identity of criminals. The author struggles to answer questions of when and why (im)migrants are deported. She devotes a significant amount of text to a discussion about deportation based on issues of criminality and argues that (im)migration policies are less forgiving than in prior years. In doing so, she implies that these policies are having negative effects on deserving families. Throughout her two articles, she includes the fact that the Desais have two sons, both of whom are in college, which further constructs them as deserving (im)migrants.

The framework she employs is a contrast between "good" and "bad" (im)migrants. The Desais are different from other (im)migrants; they are not criminals or public charges, implying that they have earned the right to remain in the nation. Their representation works in contrast to criminals, who are implicitly undeserving and who should be targeted by these policies. Simmons cites Carl Shusterman, the couple's attorney, who states that (im)migration judges were formerly more lenient with people who had put down roots in the United States, paid their taxes, and proved themselves to be model members of society (2005). Again, the "good" (im)migrant is one who pays taxes, owns a home, sends children to college, and does not engage in criminalized activities. These are the deserving (im)migrants who should be given special considerations versus (im)migrants who become public charges and engage in criminalized activities.

Patrick J. McDonnell (1997) begins his article, "Criminal Past Comes Back to Haunt Some Immigrants," with the story of Saeid Aframian. The article was published one year after the enactment of 1996 federal legislation that expanded the definition of "deportable criminal alien" and applied it retroactively. McDonnell begins the article:

> To visit with Saeid Aframian is to spend time with a condemned man, someone far removed from his previous life as a prosperous jewelry salesman and family man with a home in Bel-Air.
>
> His bearded face is skeletal, his deep-set eyes bloodshot and he shuffles about in plastic slippers and a government-issued red jumpsuit like a haunted soul.
>
> "It's like a shadow has been following me and has finally taken over my life," a sobbing, gaunt Aframian said recently during an interview at the US Immigration and Naturalization Service lockup on Terminal Island in San Pedro. "I really need one more chance. It's a matter of life or death."
>
> Aframian, one of thousands of Persian Jews who fled to Southern California after the Islamic revolution in Iran, faces deportation to a homeland where human rights advocates say religious minorities continue to be persecuted.

Although McDonnell covers various stories of (im)migrants awaiting deportation, it is important to note that he frames his article through the story of Aframian, an (im)migrant whom McDonnell attempts to socially recuperate. The author regards Aframian's story as significant in several ways. Most notably, he characterizes the (im)migrant as a "prosperous jewelry salesman," a "family man," and a homeowner in Bel-Air. In this depiction, Aframian embodies what are considered to be ideal American characteristics: a hardworking, family-oriented man, who is also affluent, as signaled through his home's location in Bel-Air. McDonnell draws on the myth of American exceptionalism and makes a case for Aframian's stay. He symbolizes Iran as a site of violence and persecution, while he implicitly represents the United States as a haven for (im)migrants. Hengameh, Aframian's wife, further highlights this point: "I don't understand it. . . . This is supposed to be the land of freedom."

While McDonnell demonstrates concern over Aframian's deportation, the article in large part centers on the contradictions that these deportations represent for American exceptionality and liberal democracy. McDonnell critiques the federal policies enacted the previous year, noting that "it makes no difference if the offenses triggering deportation for those defined as aggravated felons occurred last week or decades ago, or whether the person targeted has led an exemplary life since completing his or her sentence." The irrecuperability of (im)migrants enforced by the new laws contradicts notions of America as the land of freedom and opportunity. Thus, more than deportation, what is at stake is the failure of the United States to live up to its claims of exceptionality.

Within the same article, McDonnell presents Refugio Rubio's story. Rubio was arrested and convicted in 1972 for drug possession and served his sentence. Because of anti-(im)migrant backlash, Rubio attempted to obtain citizenship in 1997. Through fingerprinting, his 1972 conviction was exposed, setting the stage for his deportation. McDonnell describes Rubio: "A longtime field hand and laborer who has lived legally in the United States for almost 34 years, Rubio built his own home in the Bay Area community of Vallejo, and is the patriarch of a family that includes seven sons, all US citizens, and seven citizen grandchildren." In this example, the reader witnesses the implicit contrast between "good" and "bad" (im)migrants. McDonnell describes Rubio as a hardworking, self-sufficient man with social ties to citizens. According to McDonnell, he is rehabilitated and is represented as significant because his story highlights how the legal status of individuals can change: in this case, Rubio is transformed from a legal resident to an "illegal alien." McDonnell cites Rubio, "If I was a person who continued doing bad things, I could understand this. . . . But I never had trouble with the law again. I've always worked hard and paid my taxes, and my family has never depended on the government." In part, these stories illustrate the impact that the language of public charge has on the (im)migration debate where their defense largely centers on demonstrating their financial independence. The following stories further mark this point.

Journalist Teresa Watanabe published two articles (2003a and 2003b) in the *Los Angeles Times* that cover the story of the Cabrera family. Benjamin and Londy Cabrera resided in the Bell Gardens area of Los Angeles with their two daughters, Diana, eleven years old, and Jocelyn, nine years old. Benjamin (im)migrated from Mexico, and Londy from Guatemala, and they established their lives in the United States despite their undocumented status. The couple faced deportation and fought to remain in the United States, largely justified by Diana's academic achievement and gifted status. The couple and their supporters maintained that Diana would be denied opportunities if her parents were deported. Watanabe writes:

> Eleven-year-old Diana Cabrera is a straight-A honors student, hits top scores on statewide achievement tests and has never missed a day of class. The Los Angeles native studies as much as six hours a day. "She's the smartest student I've had in 30 years of teaching," said JoAnn Burdi, who teaches Diana and other gifted sixth-grade students at Bell Gardens Intermediate School, which serves low-income, mostly Latino families east of Los Angeles. (2003a)

Watanabe also notes Diana's other accomplishments, including her two-year selection for a prestigious summer honors program at Johns Hopkins University. In 2002, Judge Bruce J. Einhorn allowed the couple to remain in the United States, citing the "exceptional and extremely unusual hardship" this would place on Diana and her academic achievement and noting that the family, "had paid taxes, committed no crimes and did not receive welfare." The federal Board of Immigration Appeals reversed the opinion based on the fact that it would open the door for undocumented (im)migrants with bright children like Diana to remain in the United States. Burdi is quoted again, "This is a family that does not rely on welfare. They speak to us in English. They've done it all on their own. This is something our society should be proud of and open our arms to and say: 'This is what should be a model of what's possible in America.'" Watanabe also notes the couple's acquisition of a $150,000 home and a brand new Nissan Frontier pickup.

In a second article (2003b), Watanabe continues the Cabreras' story and discusses the introduction by US Senator Dianne Feinstein (D-CA) and Representative Lucille Allard-Roybal (D-East Los Angeles) of legislation to grant permanent legal residency to the Cabreras. According to Feinstein, "Some cases deserve special consideration and this is one of them." In this second article, Watanabe once again cites Diana's brightness and Einhorn's statement that the family, "paid their taxes, committed no crimes and had not received welfare." In both articles, Diana's academic achievements are offered as evidence of the Cabrera couple's civic performance as productive and contributing members of society. According to this logic, they are imparting the right morals and values onto their children, despite their undocumented status. Through the construction of the Cabreras' story, Watanabe reinforces notions of deserving and undeserving individuals and consequently contributes to the normalization of violence against people who deviate from the norm. Individuals who fall under the categories of public charge and criminal are thus made expendable.[18]

In another *Los Angeles Times* article, staff writer Anna Gorman (2007) describes as painful the separation of the Muñoz family by US (im)migration authorities. Zulma Miranda and her husband, Abel Muñoz, were undocumented and settled in San Diego. The article centers on the impact of their deportation on the lives of Zulma and Abel's three children: Leslie, sixteen; Marcos, thirteen; and Adilene, eight. The parents reside in Tijuana while the children live in their San Diego home. Leslie assumed the role of caregiver for her younger siblings, including the economic burden of paying bills and the home mortgage. Gorman describes the violence the children witnessed when (im)migration enforcement agents came to their home and detained their parents, and the many challenges the family faced due to the parents' deportation. She quotes Oswaldo Cabrera, director of the Latinoamerica International Coalition and initiator of the Adopt an Immigrant campaign, designed to symbolically show support for (im)migrants: "With these raids, they aren't just getting criminals. They are breaking up innocent families. This is a great injustice."

The innocence of the Miranda-Muñoz family is secured by differentiating criminals from innocent families, naturalizing the punishment of criminals while attempting to secure protection of "good" (im)migrants. Gorman describes the family:

> Muñoz supported the family by working as a landscaper and butcher and then as an electrician, eventually earning up to $1,000 a week, he said. Miranda stayed home with the children, and both parents volunteered in their schools. The family bought a home and remodeled it. They paid taxes. They took trips to Universal Studios and Las Vegas. They became involved in their church.

She also cites the parents' court testimony as they described their children as strong students who earned numerous awards. She constructs the Miranda-Muñoz family as the ideal American family. Abel works and earns enough money to sustain his family, while Zulma stays at home and cares for the children. They are both actively involved in their children's lives and in their church, they own their home, they pay taxes, and their children are excellent students. Gorman presents the family as deserving (im)migrants who, because of unfair (im)migration policies, face the painful separation of their family. According to her narrative, (im)migration authorities caught the wrong (im)migrants. Gorman centers on the idea that, in America, the sanctity of the family and the protection of the children are imperative.

There is an explicit attempt in these stories to represent (im)migrants as deserving, evidenced by owning their own homes, being independent from the state, working hard, and having their "academically gifted" children in or on the road to college. These narrow definitions of criminality and dependency limit the framework available to advocate for (im)migrants. The articles suggest that many of the families affected by (im)migration authorities' practices are deserving members of society. However, they also work to simultaneously and unintentionally rationalize the violence that occurs to those who do not fit this category. The idea of deserving members of society is constructed so narrowly, so bounded, that it becomes extremely difficult to meet the requirements. The compliance with this definition depends on the conformity to racialized, gendered, sexualized, and class-based expectations that uphold existing hierarchical relationships of power.

The ideological work of multicultural neoliberalism is evident in these cases. The authors lament the fact that even though these families fulfill their neoliberal role, in the sense of being self-reliant, and appear to contribute socially by imparting the proper morals and values onto their families, they are denied social membership. The authors' claims for inclusion of these families are grounded largely on representing them as ideal potential neoliberal citizens. What the authors miss, however, is the work of racism and white supremacy and the fact that (im)migrants racialized as non-white are not desired as citizens. This is the case irrespective of how multicultural society appears to be. The value of these (im)migrants continues to be relegated to exploitable labor. Their non-white racialization and legal status, regardless of how socially American they may appear, make them vulnerable to exclusion.

For those constructed as "criminal aliens," deservingness is permanently foreclosed. Their ideological undeservingness rationalizes any consequences they may face during their lives, including various forms of violence. The notion of public charge, used in reference to Black women and then re-mapped onto Latina (im)migrants, informs the criminalization of (im)migrants and limits the framework of the debate around (im)migration. The fusing of criminality and state dependency that occurred with the production of images such as the "welfare queen" and the "crack mother" serves to discipline (im)migrants into "good" potential Americans. The dichotomous relationship addressed is not necessarily intrinsic to the (im)migrant rights movement, but rather, reflects the inherent, unequal relationship created through legal citizenship. The citizen is defined in direct relationship to non-citizens. Citizenship is given social meaning through the rights, protections, and privileges that can be denied to the non-citizen. This establishes the framework available for (im)migrant rights advocacy that centers on legalization and citizenship.

Together, these media stories demonstrate how difficult it is to engage in counter-hegemonic struggle. Again, while the authors demonstrate sympathy toward (im)migrant families affected by deportations, dominant ideals related to criminality and state dependency inform the narratives and in turn reinforce boundaries between (im)migrants.

## Negotiating Belonging and Its Consequences: The Story of Esther and Elisa

The attempts to recuperate (im)migrants as worthy of belonging, as noted in the previous section, are informed by the increased criminalization of (im)migrants and its consequences. Since the mid-1990s, the number of (im)migrants—particularly Mexican (im)migrants—in US prisons has expanded considerably. For example, in 1995, a year before the enactment of several federal laws targeted at (im)migration, the percentage of Latinas/os in US federal prisons was 27.2 percent (Federal Bureau of Prisons 1995, 3); in 2010, that percentage had increased to 32.6 percent (Federal Bureau of Prisons 2010, 3).[19] Rather than indicating (im)migrants' increased engagement in criminalized acts, this growth reflects changes in legislation that re-defined the meaning of crime and punitively penalized (im)migrants. The 1996 Illegal Immigration Reform and Immigrant Responsibility Act (IIRIRA) ordered (im)migration enforcement authorities to deport non-citizens convicted of an aggravated felony. The law also expanded the definition of "aggravated felony": crimes that carry a one-year sentence, including misdemeanors such as shoplifting, are considered aggravated felonies and are applied retroactively. This highlights the fact that, rather than (im)migrant criminality increasing, what changed was the definition of crime, expanding the boundary for deportable non-citizens.

However, the current debate over (im)migration obscures this practice of criminalization and institutional targeting of (im)migrants and instead centers on the binary between "good" and "bad" (im)migrants. This places the responsibility on (im)migrants themselves to behave "like" Americans or face the consequences. These confines delimit the boundaries of the American identity, not only informing (im)migrant experiences but also American belonging in general. Thus, it not only serves to discipline (im)migrants, but also citizens. This dominant framework limits the possibilities for resistance. Instead, it enlists some of the voices of resistance, including (im)migrant rights advocates, to perform the work of policing the racialized and gendered boundaries between deserving and undeserving bodies.

In this section, I analyze the story of Esther, an (im)migrant woman deported in June 2008, after being imprisoned for five years, and Elisa, Esther's fifteen-year-old daughter. Both mother and daughter became involved in the struggle for (im)migrant rights when they confronted Esther's deportation and the uncertainty of their relationship created by their forced re-separation. When Elisa joined Esther in Tijuana, she became the voice for children of undocumented parents. Elisa was interviewed by the media and scheduled to speak at the 2008 Democratic National Convention in Denver, Colorado. However, the story that they were asked to tell was very different from their actual experiences. Rather than recounting Esther's imprisonment and describing the impact of the US prison system expansion on (im)migrants, their narrative was limited to representing Esther as a dedicated, working, undocumented mother who was recently detained by police and then transferred to ICE for deportation.

Their story highlights the limitations of the current (im)migrant rights discourse and shows how it is used to discipline individuals to act "American" and reinforce the violability of those who transgress these boundaries. The analysis illustrates how this dominant discourse operates to secure the boundaries of the American identity and reinforces the irrecuperability of particular bodies. Rather than interrogating the idea of crime and criminalization, many of these voices struggle to demonstrate (im)migrants' "American-ness" and seek (im)migrants' inclusion into the nation. The exercise of seeking inclusion, without questioning how the American identity is inherently policed by racialized and gendered boundaries, fails to acknowledge how this limited identity is constituted precisely through difference. It erases how marking differences between "good" and "bad," deserving and undeserving, recuperable and irrecuperable bodies serves to maintain relationships of power based on race, gender, sexuality, class, national origin, and body ability, among other factors, and these relationships are used to regulate the makeup of the United States.

Esther's presentation as a working mother reinforces the disciplining ideas of both "good" (im)migrants and "good" mothers, defined by the individual's proximity to American-ness. It reinforces white supremacist ideas about who deserves protection and punishment, as well as who can be recuperated or disposed of. For one, rather than questioning the criminalization of (im)migrants, Esther and Elisa's media story reinforces the masculinized construction of the (im)migrant identity as hard workers. Two, Esther's work ethic is presented to include her in the identity of "good" mother. This identity is mainly limited to women who are both biological and social mothers and self-reliant, preferably through marriage (Collins 1999). However, there are efforts to expand this definition to include (im)migrant mothers and their pains to provide emotional and economic support for their children.[20] Their assumed state dependency serves to place (im)migrant mothers outside of deservingness. For Esther, her imprisonment foreclosed any opportunity of assuming the position of "good" mother since she was not able to provide economically or be physically and socially present for Elisa. However, Elisa was the ideal representative for children with deported parents. At the time, despite being fifteen years old, she looked extremely young; she was bilingual, and she traveled a long way to be with her mother. (Im)migrant rights advocates asked Esther and Elisa to tell "their" story. However, in an effort to meet the requirements that the dominant good/bad (im)migrant binary presents, they were asked to leave out Esther's imprisonment. Esther's image was adapted to fit the identities of a "good" (im)migrant and mother because of her hard work. Elisa was represented as a child victim of punitive US (im)migration policies. The analysis of their story highlights how the (im)migrant rights discourse negotiates the inclusion of some while re-criminalizing and reinforcing the irrecuperability, and thus violability, of others.

The day I met Esther, she was searching for a job, which she found working at a restaurant in downtown Tijuana. We struck up a conversation about my research, and she shared that she was recently deported after being imprisoned for five years. She began to talk about her experiences, and we decided to continue our conversation in downtown Tijuana where we could get some lunch since she had not eaten that day. Esther relayed that she had arrived at Instituto Madre Assunta (Instituto), an (im)migrant women's shelter, in June 2008.

As we walked to the bus stop, Esther told me about how she did not initially disclose to Sister Orilla, Instituto's director, the fact that she had been incarcerated because she was afraid of being alienated. Esther's worries were confirmed. Sister Orilla initially offered her a job at the shelter, doing domestic chores. However, when Esther eventually acknowledged her past imprisonment, Sister Orilla stated that, under the shelter's regulations, she could not hire her and withdrew the job offer. Despite her disappointment, Esther decided that she would attempt to continue to have a good relationship with the shelter and its staff. It was important for her to be a link between women in prison who faced deportation and the shelter. She set out to connect imprisoned women she knew with places that could provide assistance after deportation. While in prison, she developed an intimate relationship with Sonia, an (im)migrant woman serving a life sentence. Esther wanted to work with Sonia to relay information to (im)migrant women in prison.[21] We spoke for two hours about her experiences in prison, her separation from her daughter Elisa, the particular challenges of being an (im)migrant woman in prison, her deportation, and her plans for the future.[22] She hoped to reunite with Elisa, her daughter, and settle in Tijuana. We remained in contact thereafter.

We met almost every week. At Instituto, (im)migrant women are usually limited to a two-week stay. After her time concluded in early

July 2008, Esther moved to Casa Refugio Elvira, another (im)migrant women's shelter in Tijuana.[23] While at Casa Refugio Elvira, Esther immersed herself in the (im)migrant rights movement. She cooked for fundraising events, distributed leaflets at the border informing deported (im)migrant women of the shelter, attended events and meetings, and volunteered to run the thrift store located on the first floor of the shelter. Esther enjoyed the work and felt useful. She was allowed to stay at the shelter as a volunteer and remained there through August.

Esther continued to work at the restaurant during the day and run the thrift store during part of the afternoon and into the evening. During her stay at the shelter, her fifteen-year-old daughter Elisa visited and stayed with her for a while. Elisa traveled via bus from Union City, California, to Los Angeles and stayed with family friends who then drove her to Tijuana to be with Esther. While there, Elisa offered to set up a website to help promote the struggle of women in prison. She created a myspace site for Esther—"Mujeres en Prisión: A Alguien le Importas . . . a Mi!" ("Women in Prison: You Matter to Someone . . . to Me!")—to try to secure support for Latina (im)migrants in prison.[24]

While in prison, Esther made rings, bracelets, and necklaces out of beads to support herself. Once Elisa joined her in Tijuana, they both began making similar jewelry to raise funds for women in prison. They gathered seventy dollars and sent it to Esther's partner Sonia to help other women in need. Esther also mailed Sonia flyers about Casa Refugio Elvira to be distributed among women who faced deportation.

Throughout this period, Casa Refugio Elvira received a lot of media and general public attention. The attention also focused on Elisa as the daughter of a deported mother. She was interviewed by Tijuana- and San Diego-based newspapers and radio and television shows, and she spoke with government authorities on the experiences of children of deported parents. For example, Alicia Llanos de Ramos, president of Tijuana's Desarrollo Integral de la Familia (DIF)[25] and wife of the city's mayor, Jorge Ramos, visited the shelter and made donations. (She met Esther and Elisa at the shelter, but she did not visit there specifically to meet with them.) Elisa talked at length with Llanos de Ramos, and the DIF president committed to continue her efforts to address the needs of deported (im)migrants. Llanos de Ramos states, "We want the migrant population to receive dignified treatment and appropriate attention by government bodies in charge of this complex subject, that their rights be secured" (XIX Ayuntamiento en Tijuana 2008, author's translation).

Elisa and Esther were also asked to participate at (im)migrant rights events. They were invited to speak at an ecumenical gathering at the San Diego-Tijuana Friendship Park on August 3, 2008.[26] Esther spoke about the difficulties faced by deported parents and introduced Elisa, saying, "It is very difficult, very difficult. More than anything, the separation of the family. Material stuff is just material stuff, but our loved ones, especially our children suffer a lot. And here is my daughter to tell you something" (Ramirez 2008). Elisa took the microphone and, with tears in her eyes, said "Hello, good afternoon. I am Elisa, and I am actually a citizen of the United States. And I am not only here to help and support my mom, she's from Mexico, but everybody here on the other side of the border. . . . I really don't like what is happening right now." Elisa then returned the microphone, unable to continue because of her emotions, and she and her mother hugged for a moment.

Elisa and Esther's participation in these events speaks to their significance in the Tijuana movement for (im)migrant rights. However, the story they told differed greatly from their actual experiences. Esther and Elisa's repeated narrative represented Esther as a working mother and Elisa as a distressed daughter left behind in the care of relatives, both victims of ICE raids. The following examples from various media sources illustrate the continued adaptation of their narrative. In part, the various adaptations were in response to requests made by (im)migrant rights activists who attempted to respond, through this mother and daughter narrative, to the urgency of the moment by making use of available tropes of deservingness. In other words, while these adaptations were deliberate on the part of (im)migrant rights activists, the tropes employed appeared to be the only viable ideas to provide protection for (im)migrants in general. For Esther and Elisa, their own sense of urgency also informed their decisions to participate in these narrations. Esther personally experienced detention and deportation and was aware of the immediate dangers presented to deportees, as well as the long-term effects, including limited life opportunities and family separation. For Elisa, being separated once again from Esther and witnessing the experiences of other (im)migrants compelled her to participate. Thus, they understood their participation as contributing to the larger goal of bringing about justice for (im)migrants.

Esther and Elisa's involvement included media interviews. On Thursday, July 31, 2008, they participated in a radio interview with Samuel Orozco, a Radio Bilingüe producer (Orozco 2008). The show, *Linea Abierta: Los Repatriados* (*Open Line: The Repatriated*), focused on the mental and physical health of children of deported parents. The interview begins with a nine-minute session with Esther followed by a two-minute interview with Elisa. In this case, Esther was represented as a single mother deported by immigration authorities in May after being stopped at a police checkpoint. She relates the process of being detained until (im)migration enforcement agents picked her up and talks about remaining in Tijuana instead of returning to Oaxaca, her home state, in order to be closer to Elisa. Then Esther describes her stay at the shelter. Orozco asks her what was the most difficult part of her deportation, and Esther says, "The family separation. The instability of my daughter because of her school." Next, she talks about how Elisa depends on Esther's family to sustain herself. "[P]recisely last night she was telling me that she missed many opportunities at school because she did not have money to pay . . . for school stuff. And I tell her that, well, that she should not feel bad, that she is very young and that she is going to get better opportunities. This is going to pass, and everything is going to be fine." Then Orozco interviews Elisa and asks why she decided not to follow her mother in her return to Mexico; Elisa responds that she needs to finish school first. Orozco asks, "What is the most difficult part of living this way? I know that it has not been that much time yet but in these few weeks that you have been separated, what is the most difficult?" Elisa responds, "Well that I see my friends . . . that they are with their mom and everything, and I feel bad because I have not been with my mom for two months. So, I missed her a lot. Then, well, I was feeling very bad." The interview ends with Esther sending a message to listeners: "Well, . . . what happened already happened and we have to move forward . . . and support those that supported you."

There are several important points in this interview. First, the construction of this narrative erases the fact that it was a five-year separation caused by Esther's imprisonment, an adaptation that seems necessary to fit their story into the current moment. Thus, the opportunities Esther notes that Elisa missed extend beyond a two-month period and instead span across five years of missed opportunities because of Esther's absence. Second, when Elisa responds to the question of what was the most difficult part, she could not include how she was harassed by her peers, who insisted she talk about why her mother was in prison, and the pain this caused her. Furthermore, she also could not discuss an important challenge: the absence of her mother during her teen years. This included witnessing her friends' relationships with their mothers—a constant reminder of what she was missing. Finally, to fit their story into the current (im)migration debate required an erasure of the violence generated by imprisonment. As Esther and Elisa's story demonstrates, violence against bodies constructed as criminal is justified by the suggestion that they brought it upon themselves for acting "un-American." In other words, the identity of "criminal" is in direct contrast with the "American" identity, and, as a result, social protection is rendered unavailable. In order to argue against (im)migrant family separation, Esther and Elisa are compelled to disavow Esther's criminalized identity.

Omar Millán González, contributor to *Enlace*, the San Diego *Union-Tribune* Spanish-language newspaper, wrote several stories about Casa Refugio Elvira. Part of his coverage included an *Enlace* article, titled "Quiero que Me 'Escuchen': Hija de Madre Deportada Hablará Durante la Convención" (August 22, 2008), and a shortened and translated version of this article in the *Union-Tribune*, titled "US Teen Whose Mom Was Deported to Tell Story at Convention" (August 25, 2008). I first discuss the shortened version in English and then consider the lengthier Spanish edition.

The account that Esther and Elisa provided González is a modified version of the actual story. According to this narrative, Esther was "a cook at a seafood restaurant and managed apartments," and Elisa was "a typical American teenager," until one day in May, "while at her best friend's house, Elisa received a call from her mother, who told the teen that she had just been deported." Elisa's world was suddenly shattered. González writes that Esther "was arrested by immigration authorities near her home in the San Francisco Bay area. The next day, at 4 a.m., she was dropped off in Tijuana, along with 50 others." Instantly, according to this narrative, Elisa "became one of the thousands of children caught up in the nationwide crackdown on illegal (im)migrants." González goes on to discuss Elisa's invitation to speak at the Democratic National Convention in Denver about her experiences as representative of all children suffering because of their parents' deportation. The article was published prior to the convention, and Elisa did not attend because of difficulties securing her passport. The director of Casa Refugio Elvira is cited as stating that Elisa was selected by Hermandad Mexicana, an advocacy organization for the human rights of (im)migrants, because "of the strength she displayed after her mother was arrested," referring to Esther's supposed ICE arrest. Elisa, according to the director, "represents the typical example of this humanitarian crisis that's happening when families are separated by immigration raids." The article ends by quoting Elisa: "I want to say that (the US authorities) are driving families apart, little by little. I want people to hear me, to hear us." This narrative presents Esther, a hardworking mother, and Elisa, a "typical American teenager," as victims of ICE practices of separating families.

An analysis of the *Enlace* article reveals additional erasures of their actual experiences. Elisa *is* "one of the thousands of children caught up in the nationwide crackdown" on (im)migrants. However, this account obscures how criminalization and prisons specifically are a fundamental part of this nationwide crackdown. As stated earlier, the numbers of imprisoned (im)migrants have dramatically increased in the last decades, resulting in family severances through state parental rights terminations. This is the case because imprisoned parents are often unable to meet the requirements to keep their children.[27] Additionally, the required deportation of non-citizens convicted of an aggravated felony creates an additional barrier that prevents deported parents from keeping their children. Thus, deportations and family separations are not new; instead, they have an extended history linked to imprisonment. In this respect, prisons have served as laboratories for the current state of (im)migrant families. However, the dominant (im)migrant rights discourse's efforts to distance (im)migrants from criminality limits the ability to include the experiences of people in prison and their families. As a result, imprisoned (im)migrants and their families become not only expendable, but also violable in the struggle for (im)migrant rights.

The construction of this narrative, in combination with Esther and Elisa's lived experiences, merged with the demands of the current moment to engage the (im)migration debate in the context of the good/bad (im)migrant binary. During an interview I conducted with Elisa, she described the event five years earlier when Esther was imprisoned. Similar to the story narrated to González, Elisa, then ten years old, was at a friend's house when she was suddenly separated from her mother. At the time, she was spending the night at her friend's house when a family friend arrived looking for her and asking to speak with her friend's mother. Elisa relates, "They went into the kitchen, and I got this really bad vibe . . . those vibes like, something bad is going to happen, or something happened." After they had talked, they told her that she would be picked up the next day. When she and the family friend arrived at the apartment in the morning, Elisa kept asking about her mother and was told she was working. That evening Elisa received a phone call from Esther. Rather than telling Elisa about her arrest and the events that led to it, Esther told her daughter that she had been deported and that she would be with her soon. Elisa kept asking Esther, "Why'd they take you? Why'd they take you?" The next day, her *nina* (godmother), fearing that Elisa would be placed in foster care, picked the girl up and took her to Union City. Elisa's world had been altered long before her mother's deportation was reported in the *Union-Tribune* story. Esther's imprisonment turned their lives upside down, separating them for five years, not the two or three months reported in the media, and leaving them unable to see each other. During Esther's imprisonment, Elisa remained with her *nina*.

The critical difference between Elisa and Esther's reality and the story told in the media represents the limitations of the dominant (im)migrant rights discourse. Mother and daughter are asked to tell a distorted version of their story to fit the category of deserving (im)migrants. The effort to distance Esther—and, by extension, (im)migrant mothers in general—from criminality reinforces boundaries between deservingness and undeservingness. Although there is a willingness to advocate for individuals like Elisa and Esther, that advocacy must occur within a paradigm that conforms to disciplining narratives of citizenship, particularly that of a hard worker with no criminal record. However, once lines are crossed, as in the case of Esther, who engaged in criminalized activities and was deported as a "criminal alien," the willingness not only dissolves but also, in some cases, turns into demands to punish individuals who transgress these lines in order to protect "American-behaving" (im)migrants.

For example, consider the protest/press conference held in front of the San Diego federal building on August 22, 2008. During the event, co-sponsored by several (im)migrant rights groups, Enrique Morones, president of Border Angels, spoke on behalf of (im)migrants and maintained that they are not "criminals."[28] Morones noted that if people crossing the border are found to be "criminals," they should be jailed, but otherwise, undocumented (im)migrants deserve protection. This points to the way in which dominant (im)migrant rights discourse fails to take into account how the line between criminal and non-criminal shifts, depending on the current socio-political climate. At one moment, individuals or actions can be classified as non-criminal; at another, changes in legislation can reclassify those same individuals or acts as criminal. Thus, the boundaries used to regulate deserving and undeserving, recuperable and irrecuperable subjects constantly change depending on the organizing logic of the moment. Simply demanding protection for "innocent" (im)migrants does not address the origins of criminality, which are located in the state's ability to classify and reclassify its meaning.

Currently, the logic of criminality organizes society in order to regulate racialized and gendered boundaries of belonging. In other words, the idea of crime is useful because its definition fluctuates by targeting specific bodies and behaviors while simultaneously erasing how this process is racialized and gendered. Thus, no matter how much of an effort is made to decriminalize (im)migrants, this boundary can be and is constantly shifting. However, efforts to expand American citizenship to (im)migrants are still productive in the sense that they strengthen divisions of belonging.

In González's *Enlace* article, the same story is told as in the *Union-Tribune* piece. It is a much lengthier piece, and it is important to note some of the differences. In the *Enlace* piece, González devotes a separate section to Esther. Here, Esther's "life" before and after deportation is presented. For example, González describes how thirty minutes after being deported, she was arrested by the local Tijuana police for "looking suspicious." She spent almost four hours in jail because she did not have any form of identification. She describes trying to contact a coyote—a person who guides undocumented (im)migrants into the United States—as she prepared to cross again, possibly during Christmastime. Finally, Esther states, "We are not displacing anyone in the United States. Immigrants, we are simply doing the job that many people in the US do not want to do. It is convenient for the government to have us work there because we stimulate the economy. We are not terrorists; we are people who want to work." Esther herself employs the rhetoric of hardworking (im)migrants, although, under the current logic of (im)-migration, she is considered a public charge because it costs the state thousands of dollars each year to house a person in prison.

This narrative, again, is the melding of Esther's actual experiences, such as being jailed after her deportation and looking to cross the border, and the dominant discourse on (im)migrant rights, which asserts that (im)migrants should not be targeted because they are economic assets to the United States. Esther's own effort to fit the identity of "good" (im)migrant reinforces her irrecuperability. Under this logic, "American-behaving" (im)migrants are socially salvageable while (im)-migrants such as Esther are made irrecuperable. In this case, even Esther reinforces these boundaries. It is significant that this discourse was not necessarily imposed on Esther. From our conversations, she showed firm beliefs about (im)migrants contributing to US society through their labor. Thus, while Esther, through her criminalized identity, cannot fit the ideal of a hardworking (im)migrant, she adheres to and espouses this logic.

During our interview, I asked Elisa about her participation in the movement for (im)migrant rights. She noted how the trip to Tijuana to reunite with her mother, whom she had not seen in five years, changed her already difficult life once again. On the day that Elisa arrived in Tijuana, she was dropped off on the US side by family friends and walked across by herself. Esther was holding a sign with Elisa's name on it, not because she did not know what she looked like, but rather, as a welcoming gesture. Elisa recounts her story:

> I walked over to her, and we were just staring at each other . . . and, okay, awkward silence moment. We were just staring at each other and . . . "what do we do now? . . . do we hug? do we cry? what do we do?" She took me to the bus and then we went to the house and then that same day we started working selling waters and sodas on the street . . . I was helping with that. It was fun. It was pretty awkward in the beginning because I hadn't seen her for five years. How do I . . . how am I supposed to react?

Elisa immediately immersed herself in the struggle for (im)migrant rights by working to raise funds for the shelter, speaking at (im)migrant rights events and with state representatives and media outlets about "their" experiences. During our interview, Elisa said, "It happened so fast, too. It was the first week, and I was already the voice for all the children of deported immigrants. And I was like, 'what the heck? How did this happen? Nobody told me.'"

In addition to reuniting and building her relationship with Esther, as well as establishing future plans, Elisa was trying to create positive changes for (im)migrants. Her desire to contribute to this struggle came from her personal experiences, but she was also motivated by the people she met at the shelter. Many (im)migrant women arrived at the shelter and shared their stories, and, as Elisa listened to them, she sympathized with their hardships. When asked about her organizing at the shelter, Elisa said:

> I had a lot of experiences there too, especially since like the whole border thing. They were going to put more walls up or something so people can't pass to America. . . . When I went there to the *muro* [Friend-

ship Park] where people could talk, I was like, "this is really intense." People would sit down and share food and eat. I was like, "wow." People joke about the *migra* and stuff "*la migra, la migra*," and I actually saw it. [T]he minutemen saying all these bad words to . . . Mexicans. . . . I never knew there were so many mean people against us, you know? It was so intense.

Although Elisa grew up with her mother and then her *nina*, who were both undocumented, she maintains that she did not comprehend the seriousness of the situation until Esther was deported. She notes that this had a significant impact on her and her understanding of what it means to be an (im)migrant. Similarly, Elisa acknowledges how her experiences at the shelter changed her as a person:

I knew about the *migra* . . . that they catch you and throw you back to Mexico, but I didn't think it was this bad. I see the news a lot now, since . . . all this happened, so I watch the news a lot and they talk a lot about migration and the deportations, and I was like, "wow." I wasn't really paying a lot of attention to my surroundings back then. I was just, oh, into my friends and having fun, you know? Now that I am older I see all of this and . . . I missed a lot.

Esther and Elisa's adapted story erases their experiences as shaped by Esther's imprisonment. During their five-year separation, they remained connected through a few phone calls, but mainly through letters. Elisa saw Esther once during this time when Esther was first held in a Los Angeles county jail. She sent Elisa an application to visit her in prison. However, she was unable to visit. Elisa recounts receiving Esther's letter:

At my *nina's* we are not supposed to open the mail. She opens it and gives it to us. But I opened it, and I got in trouble because I wasn't supposed to do that. And there was a form to allow us to go to Chowchilla, the prison where my mom was at. I got it, and I got in trouble because I wasn't supposed to do that. I had already filled it out and stuff and I told my *nina* and she said, "No, we can't go," and I asked, "Why can't we go?" And she said "First of all, because I am an immigrant." My *nina* is an immigrant and if they find out or something . . . she could go to jail herself. We didn't go.

Elisa's account speaks to the added dimension of (im)migrant families with relatives in prison as her *nina*'s undocumented status prevented them from visiting Esther. This is a challenge that many (im) migrant families confront, but it is rarely discussed within the (im)migrant rights movement. Elisa's alleged two- or three-month separation deserves attention *only* when the family fits the ideal (im)migrant profile. However, her actual five-year severance from her mother does not merit the same consideration once individuals cross the line between "criminal" and "innocent." Esther's undeservingness carries over to Elisa. Many in society view the children of deported parents as victims of punitive (im)migration enforcement policies, yet for children of imprisoned parents, the criminalization of their parents serves to diminish their worth. The prominence of the children of detained and deported (im)migrant parents within the (im)migrant rights movement and the silence on the situation of children with imprisoned (im)migrant parents speaks to the differentiating value afforded to these children.

Elisa was unable to speak at the Democratic National Convention in Denver, Colorado. When Esther was deported, Elisa's *nina* applied for a passport for Elisa so that she could visit Esther in Mexico. However, Elisa had waited so long to see her mother that she could not postpone it any longer. Consequently, she left with only her school identification, an expired California identification, and her Social Security card. Elisa's *nina* was unable to claim Elisa's passport because she was not the mother and needed proof of legal guardianship. The decision was made to not take Elisa to the convention and instead wait to see if her aunt could obtain her passport. She could not get the passport and the time came for Elisa to return to school. Esther, Elisa, and I decided that she would cross with me. The hope was that, in the worst-case scenario, Elisa would be held by the Border Patrol and questioned. Her desire to see her mother motivated her to leave without proper documentation. In doing so, she assumed the ambiguous position of a child-citizen with little proof of citizenship, making her vulnerable to additional questioning and violence during her return to the United States.

Esther accompanied Elisa and me to the border. As we waited in line on the Tijuana side, they hugged and wept quietly until we reached the turnstiles to cross to the United States. They said their goodbyes and we walked on. We ended up in a line where the agent left for a few minutes and returned apologetically, "Sorry folks." He then tried to process us quickly. When we walked up to his booth, Elisa told him that she did not have her birth certificate or passport. She handed him an envelope with her student identification, an expired California identification, her Social Security card, and a notarized paper signed by her *nina* authorizing Elisa to travel to Los Angeles to visit family friends. The agent opened the envelope, took out the notarized paper, and said, "What is this? This doesn't mean anything here! I don't know why you are giving me this!" I rushed to explain that Elisa had placed the letter in the envelope because it was where she kept her important documents, but before I could finish he interrupted and began to ask Elisa questions. The following conversation took place as the agent apparently looked up Elisa's information on the computer:

AGENT: Why were you in Mexico?
ISABEL. My mom got deported, so I came to see her.
AGENT. When did this happen?
ISABEL. Three months ago.
AGENT. Who is she? (referring to author)
AUTHOR. I'm a family friend.
AGENT. Where is your dad?
ISABEL. I don't have a dad.
AGENT. Who are you going to stay with?
ISABEL. With my aunt in Union City.
AGENT. Okay, go . . . and be a good citizen.

While relieved that Elisa was not going to face additional questioning, I left the agent's booth upset at his attempt to discipline her. In my mind, with that one phrase, "be a good citizen," he inadvertently devalued Esther and others like her. One, she is not a US citizen and will never be able to assume this identity. Two, "good citizen," as I have argued thus far, implies individuals who are self-reliant and without any criminal record. Given the conditions of the neoliberal global economy and the centrality of criminalization in organizing society, very few people can assume this "good citizen" identity. The officer's statement to Elisa erased these facts.

After the interaction with the Border Patrol officer and our arrival on the US side, Elisa and I drove to my apartment, and later that day, she boarded a bus to return home.

Esther attempted to cross the border in late September 2008. During her crossing, she landed in a muddy swamp where, in a matter of seconds, she was engulfed up to her chest. The group of (im)migrants traveling with her reacted immediately and pulled her out using a thick log. The swamp had consumed all her clothes, leaving her completely naked and covered in mud. One of the men was wearing shorts beneath his clothes and he offered them to Esther. Another man gave her his shirt. She was in such poor physical condition that the group sought out the Border Patrol to obtain medical attention for her. She was taken to the emergency room and then transported to the county jail. Afterward, she was transferred to the Western Region Detention Facility in San Diego, a private prison run by the GEO Group Inc., which is a transnational corporation dedicated to the private warehousing of bodies and formerly known as Wackenhut Corrections Corporation.

Esther was held in (im)migration detention for six months while she awaited her trial. During this time, her lawyer requested to have the charges of crossing the border with a felony dropped, which they were, leaving only the charges of crossing the border undocumented. Both Esther and her lawyer expected the judge to release her since the average sentence for crossing the border undocumented is six months. She gathered documents for her trial that addressed her character, including a brief letter that stated that she was a person of good moral character who volunteered at Casa Refugio Elvira. Esther always carried the letter with her while in Tijuana so that, in the event that she faced harassment by police, she could demonstrate that she was not transient. Elvira Arellano had signed the letter. Elvira is a well-known (im)migrant activist who took sanctuary in Chicago, Illinois, between August 2006 and August 2007, to condemn the separation of (im)migrant families by US (im)migration control policies. During Esther's trial in February 2009, the prosecutor used this letter to argue that Esther, through her association with Elvira Arellano and the (im)migrant advocacy work she performed, was involved in encouraging (im)migrants to cross the border illicitly. Arguing that Esther advanced criminal acts against the United States, the prosecutor asked the judge to sentence her to forty-eight months in prison. Completely dumbfounded, Esther's lawyer was unable to respond. According to Esther, he was taken aback by the new charges made by the prosecutor. Esther was unsure why this was the case. She felt that he had her best interest in mind and actually tried to provide her support. However, in this moment, for whatever reason, he failed to do so. Instead, Esther argued against the prosecutor's claims as best she could. The judge in turn sentenced her to twenty-six months in prison.

The irony is not lost in this part of Esther's narrative. Her lawyer was able to get the charges of crossing the border with a felony dropped, but Esther's return to prison was secured by her work as an (im)migrant rights activist. Her association with criminalized (im)migrant activist Elvira Arellano and her alleged organizing with (im)migrants to illicitly cross the border justified Esther's imprisonment. Her story highlights what (im)migrant rights discourse does not acknowledge: how the definition of criminality shifts and changes to adapt to particular situations. In this case, advocating for (im)migrant rights is constructed as a criminal act and worked to sentence Esther to more than two years in prison. This underscores how the subject of the advocacy carried out by the (im)migrant rights movement cannot be Esther, or anyone like her.

## Conclusion

The (im)migrant rights efforts to dislodge criminality from the (im)migrant identity are in large part responses to the criminalization, policing, and violence that (im)migrant communities increasingly encounter. While these efforts seem imperative given the current anti-(im)migrant climate, it is important to recognize the ways in which (im)migrant rights discourse participates in reinforcing racial and gender power relations. In the previous chapter, I considered how, historically, criminality helped to construct Blackness. One key area in which this occurs is the targeting of Black women's reproduction as criminal. I demonstrated that this patriarchal white supremacist discourse is re-mapped onto Latina (im)migrants' bodies through the logic of gendered (il)legality.

This re-mapping process is essential to neoliberal social organization. Since undocumented (im)migrants are the ideal neoliberal workers, given their undocumented and thus flexible status, relegating them to the space of criminality maintains their flexibility. As in the case of Black women, (im)migrant women's reproduction is targeted to contain their criminalized reproduction, resulting in separating their reproduction from their productive capabilities and advancing their role as workers. The (im)migrant rights discourse that attaches the identity of (im)migrant to hard worker ultimately re-masculinizes (im)migration, reinforces the exploitability of (im)migrant bodies, and thus participates in the regulation of both Black and brown women's productive and reproductive labor. The current (im)migration debate shapes and limits the (im)migrant rights discourse to a binary framework that weds the identity of (im)migrant to the masculine identity of worker and allows the criminalization of women's reproduction to go unchallenged.

I also discuss how the efforts of (im)migrant rights advocates to claim (im)migrant innocence is ultimately a negotiation between racial Blackness, perpetually detached from the American identity, and racial whiteness, a defining characteristic of "American." By reinforcing American-ness, as is done with the claim "(im)migrants are not criminals, (im)migrants are hard workers," patriarchal white supremacy essentially remains unchallenged and the expendability of Black and brown bodies is perpetuated. To more effectively organize against the violence to which (im)migrant communities are subjected, (im)migrant rights advocates need to move away from the idea "no one is illegal" to "no one is criminal." This statement challenges the state's ability to categorize bodies as criminals and, as such, challenges patriarchal white supremacy. It underscores the fact that a great amount of ideological and material labor goes into making "criminals." Challenging the state's ability to criminalize bodies directs our attention from individual acts of "crime" toward the ways that the creation of "crime" serves social and political purposes. This does not mean that individuals who harm others through their actions should not be held accountable. Rather, it means shifting the ability to maintain accountability from the punitive state to other entities.[29]

Whereas this chapter focused on the (im)migrant rights movement and how it participates in constructing some (im)migrants as irrecuperable, the following chapter shifts attention toward states (in this case, the United States and Mexico) and indicates their responsibility in perpetuating heteropatriarchal violence against (im)migrant women. I also analyze the collaboration between states and individuals. The analysis contributes to the mapping of racialized patriarchal formations that contribute to the violence undergone by (im)migrant women.

CHAPTER 3

# Violent Formations: Criminalizing and Disciplining (Im)migrant Women

According to social theorist Michel Foucault, the disciplining of the body is the process through which social subjects are formed, and these practices of subject formation are inherently spatialized (1978, 144; 1995, 141–142). The control of bodies and their spatial movement become places and moments for the exercise of power. For modern nation-states, the control of national boundaries, especially the movement of bodies, affords their legitimacy. Each (im)migration becomes a moment and site of political agency that threatens and simultaneously provides an opportunity to assert nation-state sovereignty and legitimacy. As such, (im)migration is central to the (re)production and maintenance of the nation-state. The violence confronted by (im)migrants in the US-Mexico borderlands highlights their centrality in the nation-building projects of both the United States and Mexico.[1]

In this chapter, I consider the stories of detained, imprisoned, and deported (im)migrant women. I examine the heteropatriarchal relationship between individuals and the state responsible for shaping (im)migrant women's lives. (Im)migrant women's movements through the borderlands signal a socio-political transformation of gendered and racialized relationships on multiple levels. Women's (im)migration destabilizes their historical relegation to the domestic sphere, both at the level of the home and of the nation. The initial moment of agency—as marked by (im)migration—brings (im)migrant women into a co-constitutive relationship with the public, socio-political sphere. (Im)migration then becomes a complex negotiation to redefine women's social and spatial location in relation to the nation. As a result, the destabilization of gender norms generates possibilities of intervention by individuals and the state in the lives of (im)migrant women.

Furthermore, in terms of US policing of the border, it is critical to read this connection within the larger historical context linked to the role that ideologies about race play in the design of the nation. US (im)-migration policy has served and continues to serve as an instrument that affects the racial makeup and design of the nation (Glenn 2002; López 2006; Luibhéid 2002; Ngai 2004; Hing 2009; Zolberg 2006). However, today the use of (im)migration policies to design the nation largely operates through non-racial language, such as controlling (il)legality, crime, and terrorism (Dowling and Inda 2013; Gonzales 2014; Menjívar and Kanstroom 2013). Consequently, the violence encountered by (im)migrant women in the US-Mexico borderlands—as carried out by both individuals and state representatives—must be examined as moments that form part of a larger gendered and racialized political struggle to construct history.

As I conducted my research and read through the many stories, it became evident that interpersonal and state modes of violence go hand in hand in determining experiences for (im)migrant women. Initially, I read this interconnection as one form of violence feeding into the other. However, a closer examination revealed that, rather than just informing each other, the boundaries between these modes of violence become blurred to the point that they become indistinguishable. These changes are in part produced by the presence of the US-Mexico border.

Beyond its physical and formal presence, the border ideologically serves to construct and assign meaning to bodies. It participates in fashioning the United States as a white nation while assigning foreignness to non-white, mainly brown bodies. This foreignness is further complicated as notions of "appropriate" national femininity and sexuality are contested in this space.[2] The ideological work produced at the border and the social meaning created are assigned to (im)migrant bodies. Depending on the period, different social meanings are attributed.[3] For (im)migrant women, the entrance into the borderlands, which begins upon their initial arrival and remains with them throughout their travels, transforms them individually and with respect to their relationship to global society. This process blurs the lines between the public and the private. At this vital instant, the border and what it represents—geopolitical sovereignty and racial, cultural, ethnic, heteronormative, and classed boundaries—marks (im)migrant women's bodies. From that moment on, (im)migrant women's violability is cemented through their assumed violation of the nation-state, constructing them as a public enemy who needs to be disciplined and, in some cases, killed.

In the case of Mexican (im)migrant women, they do not just pose a threat to the United States, but are also an ideological threat to the Mexican nation-state. Their female bodies in public, especially at the periphery or actually outside the national domestic space, signify the inability of the Mexican state to fulfill its masculinized role as the nation's provider and protector. This is especially the case for women traveling without a patriarchal figure. They represent the disintegration of the Mexican family structure, either by not reproducing Mexico's next generation or by leaving children behind to be cared for in arrangements that deviate from the normative family. Thus, their presence in the US-Mexico borderlands ideologically constructs their bodies as threats to both the United States and the Mexican nation-states. These ideological constructions render the boundaries between interpersonal and state violence unintelligible.

## Road Map

I begin this chapter by addressing the significance of Latina (im)migrants to modern forms of governance. I make use of Michel Foucault's (1978 and 2008) concept of biopolitics (politics over life) and Achille Mbembe's (2003) concept of necropolitics (politics over death) to examine the ways in which Latina (im)migrants are not only made expendable, but also killable. In other words, I argue that their (im)migration processes and experiences are informed by a collaboration of biopolitics *and* necropolitics. I expand on this insight by focusing on women's experiences, and I employ a feminist analysis that demonstrates how gender and sexuality, as axes of power, interconnect with race and inform the politics over life and death that shape (im)migration experiences. I draw from feminist women of color scholarship on gender violence to make this connection.

Then I present stories of imprisoned (im)migrant women whose children are placed in the foster care system, illustrating one of the ways that social irrecuperability is carried out through the separation of mothers from their children. Together, these stories reveal how the boundary between states—in this case, between the United States and Mexico—is blurred when Mexican social services are enlisted to perform the labor of the US welfare state.

I end with an analysis of four additional stories of (im)migrant women that highlight the role that some individuals perform in the policing of borders and in doing so, participate in designating (im)migrant women violable subjects. The analysis underscores the unintelligibility of the boundaries between state and interpersonal forms of violence.

## Racialized Gendered Violence as a Politics of Life and Death

To examine the experiences of (im)migrant women, I explore some of the ways in which boundaries between different modes of violence are distorted and argue that this development is necessary for the legitimization of the state as the benevolent protector of the nation's inhabitants, rather than as a site of violence. In other words, the role of the state in creating the conditions that not only make possible, but also probable, the violation of (im)migrant women gets erased when individuals carry out the violence. I argue that this violence needs to be conceptualized as a fundamental condition of the US nation-building project.

I turn to the work of INCITE! Women of Color Against Violence (2006), which asks the question, "What would it take to end violence against women of color?" Central to INCITE!'s critique is the understanding that the anti-violence against women movement that increasingly relies on the state tends to bolster the criminal legal system and causes additional violence to communities. INCITE! compels us to move beyond this model given that, for women of color, the role of the state is often not that of the benevolent protector, but rather of a perpetrator and enabler of violence.[4] In addition, INCITE! maintains that struggles for racial justice silence women of color around issues of domestic violence in order to "maintain a united front against racism" (1). INCITE! encourages society to rethink strategies so that rather than contribute to the strengthening of the state, as is often the case with the anti-violence movement that relies heavily on the criminal legal system, we engage in strategies that work *against* the state and create safe communities for women of color.[5]

The experiences of (im)migrant women require us to complicate the relationship between interpersonal and state violence against women of color by expanding the understanding provided by INCITE! Women's (im)migrant status prompts individuals and nation-states to help police and enforce not only territorial, but also the racialized and gendered boundaries of the United States. Ruth Wilson Gilmore, in discussing prisons within the United States, defines racism as "the state-sanctioned and/or extralegal production and exploitation of group-differentiated vulnerability to premature death" (2007, 247). The development of the policing of US territorial borders has its roots in a history of white supremacy in which groups racialized as non-white are constructed as threats to the nation and systematically targeted. Employing Gilmore's conceptualization of racism to the policing of the nation-state's boundaries makes clear that the production of the social irrecuperability of (im)migrant women is a vital component of the labor of violence that individuals and states carry out.

(Im)migrant women are rendered vulnerable to violence and premature death through a racialized and gendered combination of biopolitics *and* necropolitics. According to Michel Foucault (1978, 135–159), biopolitics, or the politics over life, centers on modern governments fostering life considered worth living (normative), while simultaneously letting other forms of life (non-normative) die (135). This requires processes of differentiation and valuing. The norm, which is valued, is constructed by deploying notions of pathology, deviancy, and abnormality (Foucault 1972 and 1978). As discussed throughout, in the United States, the national life that is valued is white, and other forms of life are measured against this norm.

In the case of (im)migration, Latina/o (im)migrants are marked as especially threatening to the welfare of the (white) nation. While (im)migrants, in particular undocumented (im)migrants, provide an important source of labor within global neoliberal capitalism, most Latina/o (im)migrants and their families are not desired as citizens.

While Latina/o (im)migrants in general are perceived as threats, fears over (im)migration are largely fueled by racial understandings of Mexican (im)migrants. These notions are often applied to Latinas/os in general. The geographic position of Mexico coupled with the racialization of ethnic Mexicans as foreign and culturally different from white America, their assumed inability or unwillingness to assimilate, and their supposed inclination to criminality, to name a few factors, generate fear over Mexican (im)migration.[6] These racialized nativist discourses, mainly articulated through the paradigm of culture, provide a demarcation between lives that are considered worth living and lives that are unworthy and thus can be allowed to die. Latina (im)migrants make up an important part of (im)migrant labor, especially in the service sector, but their reproduction is particularly undesirable. Latina (im)migrant life is marked as distinctly dangerous. Ideologically, their "hyper-fertility" threatens to take resources from and, eventually, out-live white life. This renders them not only expendable, but also violable.

Social policies directed at (im)migrant women's reproduction—in-cluding policies such as the 1994 California ballot initiative Proposi-tion 187; the Welfare Reform Act and the Illegal Immigration Reform and Immigrant Responsibility Act, both enacted in 1996; and legisla-tive attempts to amend the Fourteenth Amendment of the Constitu-tion to deny birthright citizenship to children of undocumented (im)-migrants—exemplify the work of biopolitics.[7] In these cases, the intent is not to kill but, rather, to deny resources that make life livable.

However, simply "allowing to die" is sometimes not enough, and it becomes politically possible to engage in what postcolonial scholar Achille Mbembe (2003) terms "necropolitics"—politics as a "work of death" (12). Race is central to society's ability to construct the norm against that which is considered pathological, deviant, and abnormal. Non-white bodies were objects against which the modern universal Subject was constructed. Since this is an essential condition of moder-nity, their bodies cannot be disciplined and normalized, and thus re-main permanent potential threats.[8] The permanency of such threats makes possible the production of what Mbembe terms "death-worlds," spaces where the political objective is the maximum destruction of non-normative life (40). The militarization of the US-Mexico border, for example, renders this space a death-world. While not officially stated policy, moving (im)migrant bodies into more isolated and dangerous terrains directly produces deaths, all in the name of protecting the (white) nation. This is not letting people die, but actually determin-ing and reproducing death. Thus, as argued by Mbembe, the sovereign right to determine who dies remains an important technique of modern governance. In the case of the US nation-state, its legitimacy and sover-eignty are secured and expressed by the reproduction of Latina/o (im)-migrant death.

As demonstrated, biopolitics *and* necropolitics are implicated in the management of Latina/o (im)migrant life. As I argue throughout, (im)migration processes and experiences, including life and death, are not only racialized, but also gendered. Feminicide in the US-Mexico borderlands speaks to this fact. The mass deaths of young, poor, brown women—especially women working in maquilas, which provide wealth for both the US and Mexican nations—exemplify how the borderlands have become death-worlds. Feminist scholars Rosa Linda Fregoso and

Cynthia Bejarano (2010) provide a useful definition of feminicide as not only the patriarchal murder of women, but also as

> gender-based violence that is both public and private, implicating both the state (directly or indirectly) and individual perpetrators (private or state actors); it thus encompasses systematic, widespread, and everyday interpersonal violence . . . [it is] systematic violence rooted in social, political, economic, and cultural inequalities. (5)

Similar to the work of INCITE!, Fregoso and Bejarano contend that gendered violence—in this case, feminicide—is systemic and implicates private individuals as well as states. Furthermore, gendered violence functions concurrently with other relationships of power, including racial and economic injustices. In the case of feminicide in the borderlands, the US and Mexican states are marked as responsible for creating the conditions where the mass deaths of these women are generated. Not only have they collaborated in producing the detrimental conditions of the borderlands, but these states, and specifically Mexico, are also held responsible for institutionalizing misogyny through its dismissive and inadequate treatment of feminicide. Fregoso and Bejarano mark the state as a perpetrator of violence and warn against strategies that lead to the "reempowerment of the state" (21). One way to limit its power is to re-define violence, especially gender violence. The authors propose defining these actions as violations of human relationships, rather than as offenses against the state. Ideologically, this re-definition is useful because it displaces the state as the violated body, which limits the state's power, and demands alternative responses.

The violence experienced in the US-Mexico borderlands is in part informed by the historical construction of this space as a zone of "sexual excess," which serves to signify women at the border as not only sexually available, but also marked as sexual excess and thus, expendable (Fregoso 2007, 43). Women's (im)migrations to and through the border—a space constructed as a zone of sexual excess—disrupts their heteropatriarchal confinement to the domestic sphere and places them outside of patriarchal state protection. Once in this space of excess, women themselves are judged expendable and violable. As a society, we need to conceptualize the violence and death lived by women in the borderlands as racialized, classed, and gendered forms of "state-sanctioned terrorism" (Fregoso 50–54). This violence and these deaths are produced by the very states that purport to police such exceptionality, which exemplifies Mbembe's conceptualization of necropolitics but also centers gender in understanding modern governance.[9]

## Incarceration and the Separation of Latina (Im)migrants' Productive and Reproductive Labors

Latina (im)migrant women's bodies are particularly targeted for biopolitical state intervention. The discourse of criminality that the United States, including the state and civil society, developed in relationship to Black motherhood gets re-mapped onto (im)migrant women's bodies and contributes to their racialization. This re-mapping occurs in great part through negative media representations of Latina (im)migrant women and state policies that target their reproductive capabilities. This resulted in constructing notions of them as entering the United States to obtain welfare, failing to pay taxes, draining resources, and being too different and thus unassimilable.

(Im)migrant women, particularly women who assume the identity of mothers, pose a distinct problem because they do not quite fit the categories of ideal laborers or ideal women. Ideal (im)migrant labor in the United States is traditionally defined as sojourner and exploitable, meaning that they (im)migrate, labor for a while, and return to their home countries. (Im)migrant women's presence disrupts this ideal since their bodies represent reproduction and settlement. Despite the second-wave feminist movement, the identities of "ideal" laborer and "ideal" mother—for many women, especially non-whites—are incompatible. The idealized mother, responsible for reproducing the future citizens of the nation, remains in the domestic sphere while the ideal laborer cuts domestic ties to serve in the public sphere.

For a long time, (im)migrant laborers represented the personification of the ideal laborer because their (im)migration across national borders forced them to temporarily sever domestic ties, including family and nation. (Im)migrant women's ability to have children, and thus create connections to the United States, goes against the conventional (im)migrant labor model. Rather than cutting domestic ties, (im)migrant women are imagined to be able to create these social connections through their children. However, at the same time, they remain outside of ideal womanhood. Traditionally, women have been considered important within their roles as mothers and wives of "ideal" citizens, an identity limited to white middle- and upper-class people and, more specifically, men (Mink 1990, 93; Glenn 2002, 41–45).[10] (Im)migrant women are positioned outside of this ideal because their social function is primarily to perform particular forms of labor. Their non-white racialization informs this labor arrangement. In short, Latina (im)migrant women, particularly Mexican, do not fit the categories of ideal laborers or ideal women, but their presence is tolerated because they perform important labor functions.[11]

In order to manage the dilemma (im)migrant women pose, the state targets their reproduction, perceived as threatening to the nation's ethno-racial makeup (Chavez 2007; Collins 1999; Fujiwara 2008; Inda 2007; Lindsley 2002; Ono and Sloop 2002; Park 2001 and 2011; Roberts 1996). Targeting their motherhoods reveals assumptions about the worth of (im)migrant mothers and, by extension, their communities. Their undesirability to contribute to the citizenry of the nation and the attempts to curtail their reproduction show the gendered and racialized biopolitical logic of modern governance. Anthropologist Tamar Diana Wilson argues that anti-(im)migrant policies and practices are related to "the desire to re-separate the generational and daily reproduction of labor force, including its maintenance during times of unemployment, illness, and retirement (processes which represent a cost to any society) and of productive activity (a process which represents a gain to any society)" (2000, 192). In other words, there is a concerted effort to separate women's productive and reproductive labors, privileging their exploitability as workers and investing energies into restricting their mothering. These practices highlight some of the ways in which the United States manages its economic and racialized nativist desires. The criminalization that (im)migrant women confront needs to be placed within this context and understood as a form of population control enforced through biopolitical logic.

In chapter 1, I discussed the historical and social process of the criminalization of Latina (im)migrants and demonstrated that this resulted in the increased incarceration of this group. This has severe consequences, particularly in terms of family separations. Losing their children to the state is too often a reality for women in prison (Bortner 2002; Enos 1998 and 2001; Gabel and Johnston 1995; Golden 2005; Johnson and Waldfogel 2002; Sharp and Eriksen 2003; Simmons 2000). Under changes implemented in 1997 federal legislation, the Adoption and Safe Families Act (ASFA), parental rights termination must be initiated by social workers when children are in foster care for fifteen of the previous twenty-two months.[12] Given requirements set by child welfare policies, the placement of children with families or friends has proven to be increasingly difficult. While ASFA is federal legislation, how the needs of children in foster care are addressed differentiates by state.

In California, requirements for placing a child in a home include: conducting criminal background checks on everyone in the home, demonstrating the ability of the tentative guardian(s) to provide a safe and stable environment, and assuring that the necessities of the children are met. No more than two children can share a bedroom in the home; children over the age of five and of the opposite sex may not share a bedroom; with the exception of infants, children cannot share a bedroom with an adult; and no room commonly used for other purposes may be used as a bedroom (Child Welfare Information Gateway 2011, 26). The requirements are applied to all the children in the home, including those of the caregivers. Given such standards established by child welfare policies, the placement of children with relatives or friends is very difficult for anyone in prison, but especially for (im)migrants (Escobar 2011).

Their legal status also contributes to incarcerated (im)migrant parents being unable to place their children with family or friends. An undocumented person can, and often is, denied custody because their undocumented status represents instability for children since deportation can occur at any moment. One option that the state offers (im)migrants is to have their children placed in their country of origin. However, home evaluations must also be carried out, and the home must meet the same standards as homes in the United States.

In the case of Mexican (im)migrants, the US child welfare services enlist the Mexican social services to conduct home evaluations. With respect to the six (im)migrant women I interviewed who attempted to have their children placed in Mexico, none of the homes were able to meet these standards. These stories highlight how the state, under the disposition of benevolent protector, separates (im)migrant families and erases its responsibility in their separation. Under the current logic of (im)migration, the violence (im)migrant communities undergo is conceptualized as of their own making since they presumably chose to enter the United States, more than likely undocumented. Their apparent (il)legality represents them as enemies of the nation and constructs the violence they encounter as logical.

Separating (im)migrant women in prison from their children is further rationalized by signifying them as "bad" mothers through their imprisonment and then through their inability to secure "adequate" caretakers. The role of the welfare state in causing these separations is veiled upon the recruitment of the Mexican state to perform the home evaluations on behalf of the US social services. This process creates an impression of objectivity. I present Lupe's and Carmen's stories to show how this process operates.

## Structural Separation of Captive (Im)migrant Families: Lupe and Carmen

Lupe and her husband, Salvador, are undocumented (im)migrants who were both imprisoned for drug-related charges. Upon their imprisonment, the couple asked to place their six children with Alberto, the children's paternal uncle. Lupe and Salvador signed forms giving power of attorney and temporary guardianship of the children to Alberto. They also requested that, in the event that the children could not be placed with Alberto and his wife, custody should be granted to Roberto and Berenice, close family friends. In a letter to Justice Now, the organization where I interned and where I met Lupe, she wrote:

> But if you can talk with them [Roberto and Berenice] and orient them on how they can do it so that the children can be placed with them until I get out. On September 20 at 8:30 I have an appeal for my children and I have to have who they are going with, but I in no way want my children to be placed for adoption. Or have them send them to my mother in Mexico. She has also asked for them. I want to be sure that I am not going to lose my children.

Both couples, Alberto and his wife and Roberto and Berenice, were denied custody of the children because their homes were found to be inadequate. Lupe's lawyer filed a complaint on her behalf, arguing that the court had erred in the children's placement. In a case report, the San Diego County Health and Human Services Agency (hereafter "Agency") responded to her complaint by defending their position:

> The agency investigator believed the children could not be placed with Alberto and Lucha because they lived in a two-bedroom apartment

with one other adult and three children and did not meet the criteria
for foster care licensing regulations. Further, Alberto had not obtained
the necessary supplies to take care of six more children, refused to be
fingerprinted, and was an undocumented illegal alien. (2004)

The court used these factors to argue that the parents had not made
suitable arrangements for the care of their children during their incarceration. The blame was placed on Lupe and Alberto, and the result was
the removal of their children. Her inability to make "suitable" arrangements for them, rather than the standards enforced by child welfare services, was cited as the cause for the children's foster care placement. It
is meaningful that foster parents who are not related to the children receive more financial support than relatives, which indicates a willingness to separate children from their families. Logically, if the families
were offered similar support, fewer family separations would take place
(Raeder 2003, 181).

In addition to the two couples named as viable options, Lupe submitted several names of relatives in Mexico as potential caretakers, including her mother. The Mexican social services evaluated the children's grandparents' home and found it inadequate for placement. For
(im)migrants such as Lupe, with children in foster care, child welfare
policies, which are standards formed by white middle-class ideals, serve
to violate their families, as people on both sides of the border are required to meet these standards. While the intent of the process may be
to conduct a thorough investigation and to make a genuine attempt to
place the children with family members, the standards themselves serve
as mechanisms that separate families. Rather than considering the difficulty in meeting these requirements, the state places sole responsibility on the parents. The agency cites that "the arrangements made by the
parent must be suitable or adequate" and that the purpose of dependency law is to "ensure the safety and well-being of children." In Lupe's
case, the agency argued and the court agreed, the arrangements presented by Lupe would put the children's welfare at risk. Lupe, and every (im)migrant woman I interviewed who was either separated or faced
separation from her children, said that, if her children were taken, she
would return to the United States, even if it meant more prison time
or the possibility of taking her children forcibly from a foster home or
adoptive parents.

I met Carmen while conducting research at Instituto Madre Assunta (hereafter "Instituto"), an (im)migrant shelter in Tijuana. Carmen (im)-migrated to Tijuana from Guadalajara to find work. Like Lupe, Carmen had been imprisoned in the United States, which resulted in permanent separation from her son. The following includes an excerpt from our conversation:

> CARMEN. I was sent to prison in '98 and was there for three years. I needed money, and they offered to pay me well if I delivered two pounds of drugs. It was meta . . . meta . . . something like that. It ended up that the person that was going to pick up the drugs was a cop and a bunch of them surrounded me with pointed guns and arrested me. They gave me three years. I had my two-month-old son with me, and they took him from me. I lost my son. When I was in prison, they would sometimes take me to custody court hearings, but people in prison don't have a voice in that. As if I wasn't even in the room. I don't speak English.
>
> AUTHOR. Did you have a social worker?
>
> CARMEN. No, I never saw one. If I did, I don't know.
>
> AUTHOR. Did you have a lawyer?
>
> CARMEN. No, nothing. They didn't help me in anything that had to do with my son's case. After prison, they deported me but I crossed back to look for my son. I wasn't going to let them take him from me. When I arrived, I joined many programs.
>
> AUTHOR. What kind of programs?
>
> CARMEN. Parenting programs, drug programs, anything to get my son back. I had gained visits with him and everything, but someone called immigration, and they caught me again. That time they put me in jail for seven months, and then they deported me. Now my son is ten years old.
>
> AUTHOR. Do you know who called immigration?
>
> CARMEN. I think it was a neighbor, but I'm not sure.
>
> AUTHOR. Do you know where your son is?
>
> CARMEN. They sent me a letter to Guadalajara letting me know that he was adopted, I think by a Japanese woman. But I have no contact. I still have faith that I will find him. I have two sons and a daughter that are grown up. I want them to meet their brother, to look for him.
>
> AUTHOR. And why didn't they place him with a family member?
>
> CARMEN. The Mexican government went to my parents' house and evaluated it, but I do not know what happened.

Carmen's narrative is reflective of the many stories I witnessed through my advocacy work for (im)migrant mothers in prison. Multiple factors were consistently cited as playing a role in the separation between imprisoned mothers and their children. This includes the lack of support from lawyers and social workers, the limitations that not knowing the English language imposes on their ability to fight for their children, and the inevitable fact of deportation.

Carmen's efforts—returning to the United States to claim custody of her son, even if it meant risking additional time in prison, and joining various programs to demonstrate her aptitude as a mother—were invalidated when immigration enforcement authorities were called and deportation ensued. Her story shows how racialized nationalism works to justify violence against people constructed as "enemies of the nation." Immigration authorities informed Carmen that someone had called to report her as an undocumented (im)migrant. In her case, an individual's actions—calling immigration authorities to report her as an undocumented person—resulted in Carmen losing complete custody of her son. This occurred despite the fact that she was meeting the requirements imposed by child welfare policies, which allowed her to attain visitation rights with her son. Carmen's story illustrates how state mechanisms can be used by individuals to inflict violence on people under the premise of protecting the nation. Legal residents and citizens are allowed, and at times called upon, to police the nation through the naturalized logic that undocumented (im)migrants are automatic threats to the nation. As a result, the violence that occurs from such an action is rationalized as an act carried out against an enemy on behalf of the nation. Simultaneously, the Mexican state participates in imposing this violence, as is the case with Lupe, Carmen, and other imprisoned (im)migrant mothers. This occurs in part through the home evaluations that it conducts on behalf of US child welfare services.

The nation-state mainly defines women within the concept of motherhood; the responsibility of the state is widely imagined as the protector of the national family, and thus of mothering. For women in prison, separation from their children denies their value as mothers and secures their worth as ideal neoliberal laborers by separating their productive and reproductive labors. For imprisoned (im)migrant women, separation from their children reinforces their status as irrecuperable subjects. They are denied their worth as mothers and laborers due to current laws that permanently ban them from re-entering the country. The physical presence of (im)migrant women's bodies challenges and shatters the account of the state as protector when, to defend the racialized white nation, it renders them socially irrecuperable through the negation of their mothering and through the threat of re-imprisonment if they are caught crossing the border. The act of deportation disposes of any evidence and liberates the state of moral responsibility.

However, for many of the deported (im)migrant women forced to leave their children behind, the border follows their bodies. Some decide to travel back to the United States, as Carmen did, and attempt to re-enter the nation-state in search of their children. While Carmen was the only individual I met who returned specifically to recuperate her child, as noted above, several of the women maintained that they would return if their children were taken. Despite the barriers that combine to structure (im)migrant family separations, for many, their connection to their children surpasses US sovereignty claims. For those who do return, once again, the nation-state has to contend with their presence as they refuse to disappear and leave their children behind.

The role of the Mexican state in perpetrating violence against Mexican (im)migrant women must be part of the conversation. This role begins long before the individual's (im)migration. It commences with the neglect and inability of the nation-state to create and provide the resources needed to ensure that (im)migration is not perceived as the only option people have to secure their livelihoods. Rather than displacement structured by a person's positionality, (im)migration should be one among other options. Not only do many Mexicans become exploitable labor for the United States and other wealthier nation-states, their (im)migration is also constructed as a benefit to Mexico. This is demonstrated, for example, through remittances sent by Mexican nationals.

However, Mexico's role does not end there. As Lupe and Carmen's stories illustrate, the relationship that has developed between the United States and Mexico includes managing the return of those deemed unfit by the US nation-state. Both Lupe and Carmen's imprisonment and deportation present the additional challenge of managing their children's social belonging, whether they remain in the United States or are sent to Mexico. The US welfare system demands that Mexico apply regulations produced in the United States, which privilege white middle-class standards, to presumably protect the children. Ultimately, the United States frees itself from responsibility for the severance of families by enlisting the Mexican state to act on behalf of the US welfare state, thus blurring the lines between the two nation-states. Accordingly, blame is placed on (im)migrant mothers and families for their inability to meet the requirements.

## Blurred Boundaries of Violence: Dariela and Elizabeth

In the stories above, I discussed the experiences of imprisoned (im)migrant women whose incarceration labeled them as bad mothers, which resulted in separation from their children and reinforcement of their social irrecuperability. Both the United States and Mexico participate in constructing their irrecuperability. The following story reveals how women who deviate from "proper" femininity can be punished by the state. It exemplifies how individuals can exert control over others by deploying and making use of notions of deviancy.

Dariela (im)migrated from Honduras and arrived in the United States in 1999 undocumented. She was involved in an abusive relationship with Maria, a US-born citizen. The couple lived in Hanford, California, approximately thirty miles southeast of Fresno. Maria threatened Dariela with deportation if she did not have sexual relations with her and/or if she left their home. Dariela's mother (im)migrated from Honduras to search for her daughter, who, because of her abusive relationship, had ended communication with her family. After a jealous episode in which Maria accused Dariela of sleeping with her own mother, the abuse escalated. In a letter Dariela writes:

> One day I told her, "I don't care anymore, go ahead and call INS. Do whatever you want." I was very tired of all of it. She hit me until she broke the t.v. control and then she called the police, and they took me to jail for domestic violence, and I was the one that was abused. But that is how the law is . . . she is American, and I did not speak English, and I am an immigrant, things went bad for me. I spent thirty days in county jail and then she got me out with "house arrest." After that, I stayed there for a couple of months and then I told her "I am leaving to Los Angeles with my mother." She couldn't believe it, but that's what happened. She would stalk me. She would call me every hour and tell me that if I had another partner that I should choose between death or prison.

After a while, Maria's obsessive tendencies mitigated and Dariela believed that they could be friends. In February 2002, Maria invited Dariela to celebrate Maria's birthday. According to Dariela:

> I went to her house and once there she went to the store with her eldest son and she left me with her three other children, two girls and a boy. Everything went well until I told her that it was time for me to leave to

my mother's. I returned to Los Angeles on February 8th. When I arrived she told me that Maria had been calling and at that moment the phone rang and when I answered she said, "Dariela, what do you prefer, jail or death? because I am going to kill you. If you are not mine, you are no one's. I prefer you jailed or buried." I told her that she was crazy. Then she asked me why I had abused her children. My mouth was wide open. She had reached a limit. I told her to do what she needed to do and she asked me, "Are you sure? Because I am going to call the police." I told her to do it because I had nothing to fear.

Maria called the police, and Dariela was consequently investigated and accused of sexual abuse, during which time Maria continued to visit Dariela. After a monthlong investigation, Dariela was arrested, taken to the county jail, and incarcerated for four months until the conclusion of her trial. Dariela wrote the following account:

> By August 8th of that same year, they sent me to prison with a forty-five years to life sentence. In court, I had a public lawyer who did not speak Spanish and never interviewed me. He would just talk with me five minutes before going into court. I was an immigrant and also a lesbian. They gave me an interpreter who would only tell me about half of what was being said. I had many people on my side but during court they did not let me have any witnesses. During court they would say that Maria was my roommate and I would tell them that she was my partner. There were some friends that wanted to go into court and they didn't let anyone in. It's very difficult, especially when I think of all the sacrifices I did to try to get to this country and to end up in prison for life without being guilty.

In prison, Dariela received several letters from Maria, apologizing for what she did. In a letter to Dariela, Maria wrote that she had asked the children's social worker if it was possible to take her children to visit Dariela. However, the social worker denied her request because Dariela was imprisoned for sexually abusing the children. In 2013, the Innocence Project accepted Dariela's case.[13]

Dariela's story reinforces my argument that interpersonal violence and state violence enable each other. Initially, Maria enlisted Dariela's undocumented status, a state construct, to secure control over Dariela. When Dariela defied Maria and threatened to leave, Maria used the state to discipline Dariela, enabling state control over her. She was incarcerated for thirty days on charges of domestic violence and then she was released on house arrest to Maria's home, which further secured Maria's power over Dariela. When Dariela finally left, Maria again resorted to the state to punish Dariela, this time employing notions of sexual deviancy already attributed to Dariela due to her lesbian identity. The relationship that developed between Maria and the state—as reinforced by the ability to discipline Dariela—is produced through the complex intersections that compose Dariela's positionality. This includes her undocumented status, inability to speak English, and sexuality—all factors constructed as deviant that allow the state's intervention. Maria made use of these notions of deviancy to secure control over Dariela. As much as state mechanisms participated in the disciplining of Dariela, the individual's agency, in this case Maria, is essential to securing domination.

Dariela's example expands the work of scholars who examine the situation of Latina (im)migrant women in abusive relationships (Menjívar and Salcido 2002; Reina, Lohman, and Maldonado 2014; Salcido and Menjívar 2012; Villalón 2010). This scholarship largely focuses on heterosexual relationships and the abuse that (im)migrant women endure at the hands of their male partners.[14] In addition to structural issues of poverty, institutionalized misogyny, and racism, which often configure relationships of domestic violence for women of color, undocumented (im)migrant women also contend with vulnerabilities produced by their lack of legal status. Individuals are able to make use of undocumented status to control intimate relationships. Dariela's case not only exemplifies this point, it also provides insight into the ways that non-heteronormative sexuality, which is constructed as deviant and abnormal, informs her relationships with Maria and the state. For Dariela, and others like her, their social positionality allows the blurring of lines between the state and individuals to discipline people constructed as socially deviant.

Elizabeth's story further demonstrates the way the border follows (im)migrant bodies and enables violence by individuals. During one of my visits to Instituto, I met Elizabeth, who was originally from Guadalajara, Jalisco, but, given her English-speaking abilities, appeared to have lived many years in the United States. Elizabeth suffers from schizophrenia and was taken to Instituto after she was found roaming the streets in Tijuana. Her speech was incoherent. She shared how she had been away from her family, but was unsure as to how long it had been. Together, Mari, Instituto's social worker, some of the other (im)-migrant women, and I attempted to converse with Elizabeth in order to figure out details regarding her situation. According to Elizabeth, she had nine sons, her mother's name was Antonia, and she had lived in Watts, California, but she was unable to give a definitive last name. Along with a photograph, Mari sent her information to authorities in Guadalajara. At the same time, I contacted an office for missing persons in Los Angeles and provided Elizabeth's information to a detective, who never returned my phone calls.

As the days passed, Elizabeth had moments of clarity, and in one of those instances she provided an address in Los Angeles. It was largely due to Lucia, an (im)migrant woman at Instituto whose story concludes this chapter, and her insistence that I devoted so much time and energy to locating Elizabeth's family. As I arrived at the shelter one day, Lucia insisted, "You have to help her. She is incoherent, but she gives a lot of information about her past. You have to find her family." Lucia's insistence in part marked my many privileges. As a US citizen, I could travel across the border. Some of the (im)migrant women at Instituto often remarked upon this fact, jokingly asking me to take them over the border in my bag. I was also capable of carrying out a search for Elizabeth's family due to my bilingual and technological abilities—skills that limited others involved, including the Instituto social worker.

Through an online search of the address provided by Elizabeth, the name "Antonia Hernandez" appeared. Since Elizabeth had noted that her mother's name was Antonia, I was confident this was her mother. There were no phone numbers listed for the home, and I obtained a service to provide the names of the people who had lived in the address stated by Elizabeth along with their listed phone numbers. As a result, I obtained the records for a total of twenty-three people and more than one hundred telephone numbers. When I reached entry number twenty on the list, a woman answered. I shared Elizabeth's story, and she recalled that she had rented a room from a woman named Antonia whose daughter had gone missing several years back. She was able to contact Elizabeth's family and provided them with my information. Elizabeth's sister, Denise, called me that same day and, as I shared what I knew of Elizabeth, she began to cry. Mari e-mailed Denise the photo of Elizabeth to confirm her identity. That same day, Denise and Antonia drove to San Diego, picked me up, and together we drove to Instituto in Tijuana. We learned that the name Elizabeth had provided was actually not her birth name. She also did not have nine sons; instead, several of her sons had middle names, which she counted as additional children.

It was an extremely emotional reunion even though Elizabeth did not seem to comprehend how much time—eight years—had elapsed.

Elizabeth's disappearance, as shared by Denise and Antonia, makes evident the violent relationship that develops between the state and individuals. As a result of Elizabeth's schizophrenia, she periodically disappeared for one or two days at a time, but always returned. After she had given birth to her last son, her mental state deteriorated. Elizabeth's family shared that she had many problems in her relationship with her abusive husband. At one point, he called the police and accused her of trying to stab him. Consequently, she spent six months in jail and was then transferred to a mental health institution. At first, she appeared to be improving, but her health significantly deteriorated after she was transferred to another institution. Antonia then decided to take her daughter home. When she improved, Elizabeth returned to live with her husband, and shortly after, she disappeared. According to Denise, Elizabeth's husband laughed as he informed the family that Elizabeth had once again disappeared, and within a week, another woman was living with him in their home. While they had no concrete evidence, Elizabeth's family highly suspected that he had transported her to Tijuana. If this is the case, it demonstrates how the border was used as a mechanism to enable patriarchal violence. However, even if he did not physically transport Elizabeth to Tijuana, her story highlights how he made use of her mental illness to discipline her by drawing the state into their relationship and having her arrested.

Furthermore, Elizabeth's story brings light to a related issue—how mental or physical illness can contribute to the situation of (im)migrants. Although the details surrounding how Elizabeth left the United States and ended up in the streets of Tijuana remain unclear, what is unmistakable is that her mental health contributed to her separation from her family for eight years. This issue of (im)migrants' illnesses contributing to their expulsion from the United States and their repatriation to their home countries has received some scholarly attention. For example, a joint report by the Center for Social Justice and the Health Justice Program (New York Lawyers for the Public Interest 2012), "Discharge, Deportation, and Dangerous Journeys: A Study on the Practice of Medical Repatriation," documented more than eight hundred cases between 2006 and 2012 where public and private hospitals, most often without the collaboration of the federal government, forcibly or coercively repatriated undocumented (im)migrant patients. Individuals unable to cover their medical expenses were expressly targeted. Attempts to repatriate are not limited to undocumented (im)migrants. These practices extend to citizens, as in the case of a two-day-old US citizen born to undocumented parents, and a nineteen-year-old permanent resident legally in the United States (6).

Notions of dependency and public charges work together to remove hundreds of (im)migrants, removals made possible through their (im)migrant status and presumed (il)legality. As with Elizabeth's story, physical and mental illnesses add a dimension where private and public entities make use of the geopolitical border to discipline (im)migrants and, in the process, inflict violence. In these cases, removal separates (im)migrants from families, communities, and the lives they made for themselves in the United States. In Elizabeth's case, it appears that patriarchal violence informed her expulsion. In the case of (im)migrants repatriated by hospitals, gendered notions of dependency and public charge inform the understanding of (im)migrants' use of public resources, including health care, and categorize them as undeserving. This biopolitical logic contributes to their removals. Private and public hospitals make use of (im)migrants' non-citizen status and illnesses to repatriate them in order to ameliorate the financial situations of the hospitals. Meaningfully, the precarious conditions of public services, including health care, are in part produced by the neoliberal retrenchment of the welfare state.

## Gendered Border Violence: Jesusa and Lucia

In the previous section, I mainly discussed violence against (im)migrant women in the United States, but it is also necessary to examine the violence lived by (im)migrant women attempting to cross the border. In these stories, it is much more difficult to locate the role of the state because individuals often carry out violence against (im)migrant women. However, this difficulty precisely indicates the importance of understanding the patriarchal relationship that develops between individuals and states.

Taking up Rosa Linda Fregoso's (2007) call to understand how both Mexican and US states create the climate of violence that enables the expendability and violability of women in the borderlands, and using the framework provided by Sylvanna Falcón in "Rape as a Weapon of

War: Advancing Human Rights for Women at the US-Mexico Border" (2001), I consider in this section how the state's border militarization contributes to the violability of (im)migrant women. In her article, Falcón argues that rapes at the border are one outcome of border militarization. Far from being random acts by individuals, they are instead systematic acts that participate in marking relationships of power through the dehumanization of women (31), essentially constructing them as a racial enemy of the nation (34). The logic of the militarization of the border constructs this space as a war zone where the state wages wars against alleged threats to the nation.

Falcón draws from Timothy Dunn's analysis of the Low Intensity Conflict (LIC) military doctrine, which includes three aspects:

> an emphasis on the internal defense of a nation; an emphasis on controlling targeted civilian populations rather than territory; and the assumption by the military of police-like and other unconventional, typically nonmilitary roles, along with the adoption by the police of military characteristics (Dunn 1996, 21). (32)

Building on Dunn's work, Falcón provides an analysis of various cases of rapes against (im)migrant women by Border Patrol agents. She demonstrates how the climate generated through the militarization of the border is conducive to these gendered forms of violence. Falcón cites the following factors that contribute to the pervasiveness of militarized border rape: "unaccountability, abuse of power, ineffective hiring protocols, minimizing human rights standards, and a culture of militarization" (42). Sexual violence was an issue prior to the militarized buildup initiated primarily in 1993 with Operation Blockade in Texas.[15] However, border militarization served to move (im)migration paths into more isolated areas, increasing (im)migrants' vulnerability, including greater susceptibility to sexual violence.

Falcón's work demonstrates how border militarization makes (im)migrant women vulnerable to gendered violence. In addition to producing the situation in which state representatives perpetrate gendered violence against (im)migrant women, the border-crossing conditions to which (im)migrant women are subjected enable individuals' ability to exert power against (im)migrant women. Thus, in addition to considering the violence carried out by state agents against (im)migrant women, how personal relations participate in enabling and/or perpetuating violence against (im)migrant women must also be considered. I now turn to the stories of Jesusa and Lucia, two (im)migrant women who attempted to cross the US-Mexico border and failed for different reasons.

I met Jesusa at Instituto. She attempted to (im)migrate to the United States together with her two children in order to reunite with her husband, who had been residing there for the previous four years. The two children crossed the border on the first try, but Jesusa's six attempts were all unsuccessful. On her fifth attempt, she almost drowned in a water canal, and on her sixth attempt, the person smuggling her into the United States tried to rape her. At this point, she decided to end her journey and return home. However, they had already spent part of their savings, paying for the children's border crossing, and her husband refused to return the children to Mexico. Instead, he informed Jesusa that if she wanted to see her children, she had to cross the border. The shelter's social worker presented the option of having the Mexican consul retrieve Jesusa's children for her, but warned that her husband might be arrested.

I am unaware whether her husband returned with her children or sent them back to Mexico, whether she opted to have the Mexican consul retrieve her children for her or she attempted to cross the border to reunite with her family. I concluded my research at the shelter while Jesusa was still there. However, her story exemplifies how individuals—in this case, her husband and the individual who attempted to rape Jesusa—perpetrate and enable violence against (im)migrant women. Although Jesusa had already been confronted with the possibility of death and sexual violence, her husband insisted that she cross the border. The violence that Jesusa and other (im)migrant women suffer at the border is a production and an expected outcome of state practices that stem from border militarization, which functions to police racialized and gendered boundaries of belonging. Gilmore's definition of racism as "the state-sanctioned and/or extralegal production and exploitation of group-differentiated vulnerability to premature death" applies in this example. Her husband's insistence that she cross the border, despite the risk of it resulting in the violation of Jesusa, enables the work of the state in making certain bodies violable and vulnerable to violence and premature death. If she decided not to cross the border, or if her husband refused to return her children, then, as in the cases of Lupe and Carmen, Jesusa would be separated from her children and her motherhood would be negated. This negation is a production secured by state border enforcement policies. In this case, Jesusa does not even have to cross the territorial border of the United States to be violated by the state. Her presence in the borderlands and status as an (im)migrant mother are sufficient.

Lucia's story is unlike those discussed thus far, which are largely limited to the notion of social irrecuperability. Her irrecuperability materialized at the border upon her death. I met Lucia at Instituto. She, as noted earlier, insisted I find Elizabeth's family. Originally from Mexico, she (im)migrated to the United States where she married an (im)migrant man from Peru. After having three children, they left for Peru, where they lived for a short period. During this time, Lucia suffered physical and emotional abuse from her husband, and she decided to leave with her children, a boy and two girls all under the age of six. They traveled to Tijuana to cross to the United States. The children are US citizens and family members transported them across the border. In contrast, Lucia had to confront the dangers of the geopolitical border. According to her, during one of her attempts, the guide wanted the (im)migrant group to travel down El Espinazo del Diablo, the Devil's Spine. Lucia refused because of the steepness of the cliff, and, as a result, the group was immediately detained by the Border Patrol. After this incident, she decided to try crossing through a different area, the Douglas-Agua Prieta border crossing. About a month before ending my research at the shelter, I was informed by one of the staff that Lucia's body was found in Agua Prieta, Sonora, a border town adjacent to Douglas, Arizona. Apparently, she was killed during one of her attempts to cross the border. According to an Instituto staff member, Lucia was found shot to death.

Although I am unaware of who killed Lucia or why, what I do know is that she died trying to enter the United States to escape violence from her husband. Her death is the materialization of racist, white supremacist, and heteropatriarchal policies implemented by the US nation-state to secure its boundaries, and it speaks to Mbembe's conceptualization of necropolitics. Whether state agents or other individuals carried out her killing, the responsibility lies with both the United States and Mexico for producing the very possibility of Lucia's death, and the deaths of thousands of (im)migrants. Lucia's account complicates our understanding of the patriarchal relationship that develops between interpersonal and state modes of violence. In Lucia's case, one did not inform the other, but rather her husband's abuse and the individual(s) who killed her performed the necropolitical work of the state by contributing to and bringing about her death. This serves to distort the boundaries between interpersonal and state violence. The social irrecuperability that occurs with the deportation of (im)migrant women and the severance from their children is often contested when the mothers return to reclaim their children. In these cases, the state has to contend with the physicality of their presence, even if it means engaging in the biopolitics of re-imprisoning or detaining and deporting them. In Lucia's case, we have to ask, "Does she disappear?" Her example, contextualized within the long history of deaths at the border, reinforces Mbembe's contention that the politics of death is very much a contemporary technique of modern governance, especially when bodies racialized as non-white are concerned.

## Conclusion

The stories presented in this chapter reinforce the argument of INCITE!, Fregoso and Bejarano, and so many others that new strategies are needed to move beyond reliance on the state for protection. As the stories in this chapter demonstrate, it is the very state that enables and perpetrates violence against women of color. For (im)migrant women, the border imprints their bodies as enemies of the nation who need to be punished, and in some cases, killed. This transformative moment obscures the lines, not only between the interpersonal and the state, but also between nation-states. The transnationality of the experiences of (im)migrant women—in particular, the way that one state is deputized to carry out the labor of violence of the other—compels us to rethink the state beyond the boundaries of the nation, which is a conversation that I continue in the next chapter. Furthermore, these experiences force us to expand the understanding that INCITE!, as well as Fregoso and Bejarano, provide of the patriarchal relationship between interpersonal and state violence by exploring the ways in which the interpersonal blends with the state, moving us closer to answering the question: What would it take to end violence against women of color?

# Domesticating (Im)migration: Coordinating State Violence beyond the Nation-State

*One of the major risks that hundreds of immigrants deported daily to Tijuana confront is illegal arrest by the city police and, with the pretext of "not having an identification," they are interrogated, mistreated verbally and on occasion physically, and in other cases robbed, only to be subsequently transferred to face a city judge who, invariably, will give the victim up to 36 hours of lockup in the City Institute for Offenders.*
VICTOR CLARK-ALFARO (2008, MY TRANSLATION)

The above quote is taken from "Migrantes Repatriados: Arresto y De-tenciones Arbitrarias. Derechos Humanos: Derechos Violados" ("Repa-triated Migrants: Arbitrary Arrests and Detentions. Human Rights: Vi-olated Rights"), a report from a study conducted by Victor Clark-Alfaro, researcher at the Centro Binacional de Derechos Humanos, located in Tijuana, Baja California. The study spans August 21, 2007, through April 18, 2008, and documents more than 187 cases of repatriated (im)migrants arrested by Tijuana police for not having identification.

(Im)migrants' vulnerability, produced in part through their displace-ment and lack of resources, makes them easy targets for scapegoating in efforts to legitimize the state. Clark-Alfaro's study highlights Mexi-co's active participation in the criminalization of (im)migrants. It dem-onstrates how their criminalization serves as a fundamental mechanism of global governance.

Many arrests were made under the pretext of (im)migrants lacking proper documentation. Several detained (im)migrants had one or more identifying documents, such as deportation forms, detention wrist-bands, and/or identifications provided by either (im)migrant shelters or the government office Desarrollo Integral de la Familia (DIF). However, these were often not considered valid by Tijuana police and other legal authorities. The following are quotes from arrested (im)migrants cited in Clark-Alfaro's study:

> (053) The police ripped my deportation documents when they detained me.[1]
> (052) I only have my deportation papers, which I showed the judge, and [she/he][2] said that it was going to be 24 hours.
> (020) The police arrested me because I did not have an identification, but I do, the one from the Casa del Migrante (Scalabrini), but they said it was not valid, that it wasn't good.
> (013) I had my deportation documents and the police took them from me, and they took me to jail for not having identification.
> (080) I showed the police the identification from Casa del Migrante, and they told me it wasn't good, and up I go, the same with the judge.
> (079) I showed the judge the ID from Casa del Migrante, [she/he] saw it and didn't tell me anything, [she/he] gave me 24 hours [jail time].
> (063) I showed the police the identification from Casa del Migrante and they told me it was not valid, and they took me with the judge and I showed it and [she/he] said the same thing and gave me 10 hours.
> (071) I had the American identification wristband and the police took it and detained me.
> (116) At the time when I was deported the police detained me, asked if I had identification, and I did not, but I did have the wristband, but they didn't care and put me in the police car.
> (119) The police detained me because I did not have identification, I explained to the judge, I showed my wristband, and [she/he] told me "that is not valid," and gave me 16 hours.
> (018) They arrested me because they said that the DIF identification was not valid, they took the 100 pesos that I had, and they took me to the judge who said my identification was expired and gave me 36 hours.

These quotes demonstrate the pervasiveness of (im)migrant arrests by Tijuana police as social performances in an attempt to demonstrate publicly that the government is combating crime. Interviewed police agents are noted stating that they have daily quotas to meet. Arresting (im)migrants to meet quotas makes their bodies the raw material through which the state legitimizes itself not only to its citizens, but also to the rest of the world, particularly the United States. Ironically,

Mexican (im)migrants in the United States are often elevated to the status of heroes by Mexican politicians as remittances represent a very significant part of the Mexican economy. Mexico's behavior toward (im)migrants, as indicated by Clark-Alfaro's study, reflects a contradiction:

> In the US, immigration authorities detain undocumented Mexicans for not having "papers"; in Tijuana, city police detain repatriated immigrants for "not having identification documents." Whereas the US has immigration authorities and anti-immigrant vigilante groups that attempt to control and criminalize (im)migrants, Tijuana has the local police who perform as "migrant hunters."

Clark-Alfaro notes that at the same time that the Mexican government presents itself to be indignant at the anti-Mexican (im)migrant discourse and treatment in the United States, "when the same immigrant is classified as a deportee, the government (conveniently) forgets its discourse and becomes a violator of immigrant rights."

Displacement and homelessness require (im)migrants to search for resources and employment in the public sphere, rendering their bodies publicly available for arrest. All too frequently, the location of (im)migrant shelters concentrates (im)migrants in these spaces, which are often accompanied by a heavy police presence. As cited in Clark-Alfaro's study:

> Directors of the immigrant shelter, Salvation Army, complain about the constant police presence outside of their location with the purpose of arresting (im)migrants sheltered there: "We have confronted the police to demand that they not take immigrants" (personal communication, Director of the Salvation Army Migrant Shelter 2008).

There are many examples of the Mexican state making use of (im)migrants, particularly deportees, to present itself as combating crime and delinquency. For instance, on August 5, 2013, federal, state, and municipal authorities destroyed (im)migrant makeshift homes at El Bordo, the Tijuana canal. El Bordo serves as shelter for many deportees who are unable to secure work and housing. Residents of El Bordo dig holes underground or create improvised homes with discarded materials to shelter themselves from the environment and interpersonal harassment and violence. Many have drug addictions, a central reason provided by Tijuana authorities to rationalize the raid and destruction of residents' homes. In addition, many were arrested. As part of the strategy to clear out the area, a steel fence was constructed and divides El Bordo from Zona Centro (downtown Tijuana). As one of the residents noted, "They built another wall! . . . It's like they've deported us again! What are we supposed to do?" (Florido 2013).

The documentary *Deportee Purgatory*, produced by Laura Woldenberg (2013), depicts the situation of deportees living in El Bordo. Victor Clark-Alfaro is profiled. The documentary corroborates his study of police criminalization of (im)migrants, especially deportees. In the documentary, Armando Rascón Guevara, technical deputy director of the Tijuana Municipal Police, is interviewed about the situation of residents of El Bordo. He is filmed as he guides a tour through Tijuana, including El Bordo. He attributes 86 percent of crime in Tijuana's Zona Centro to the residents of El Bordo. According to Guevara, the role of the Tijuana police is to protect Tijuana citizens, tourism, and commerce, and he marks El Bordo residents as threats to these. To reduce delinquency in Tijuana, Guevara proposes deporting (im)migrants via air transportation into the interior of Mexico. As a representative of the Mexican state and a key figure in the Tijuana police, Guevara's interview exemplifies the ideological and material criminalization of deportees.

This criminalization is further made evident in Guevara's claims that many El Bordo residents were involved in US gangs. He contends that deportations are used as a solution for US jail overcrowding: "[T]hey are saturated. What do you do? You take all Mexicans and deport them back to Mexico. The problem is, they don't tell us if they are ex-convicts. So we take them in as deportees" (Woldenberg 2013). Guevara's statement underscores how US criminalization of these individuals extends to Mexico and the relationship of the Tijuana police with residents of El Bordo in general.

Guevara goes on to state that, while El Bordo residents are undesirable, it is best to have them located in the enclosed area of the canal because the police are able to secure greater control over them. He describes police operatives meant to capture these individuals. He directs attention to a yellow line that divides Mexico from the United States and notes that, since Tijuana police are unable to enter that area, when being rounded up, residents move toward the US side. Guevara states, "It's like we're playing a game. We go over there, and then the Border Patrol helps us, and pushes them over to this side. It's like we're playing ping-pong" (Woldenberg 2013). This last statement keenly illustrates a collaborative relationship between Mexico and United States in criminalizing and disciplining these particular (im)migrant bodies.

In this chapter, I draw from the framework provided by historian Kelly Lytle-Hernández, whose work shifts the analytical lens to Mexico's active, and at times enthusiastic, participation in the policing of the US-Mexico border. She maintains that border policing is a collaborative project between the United States and Mexico. I examine Colonia Postal, an area in Tijuana where (im)migrants are hyper-visible, and I analyze their gendered criminalization and disciplining by Tijuana police. While the criminalization of (im)migrant men is explicitly evident through their everyday arrests by Tijuana police, as evidenced in Clark-Alfaro's study and Woldenberg's documentary, it is more complicated to decipher how (im)migrant women are criminalized. Part of my objective lies in understanding how women experience border policing in Tijuana. In other words, if the (im)migrant body being *seized* by Tijuana authorities is predominantly male, how do women experience (im)migrant criminalization in this space? Are they arrested, like men, or do they have particular gendered interactions with authorities? I not only reinforce Clark-Alfaro's argument that Tijuana police function as an extension of US border enforcement, I also examine how gender and sexuality differentially shape (im)migrants' experiences. The analysis of (im)migrant women's experiences in Tijuana demonstrates that the local police participate in disciplining (im)migrants into heteronormativity. In this sense, I respond to Lionel Cantú's (2009) challenge to make visible "regimes of normalization" by highlighting how gender and sexuality, as axes of power, inform processes of migration (21).

## Road Map

Historically, Mexico has not engaged the issue of (im)migration in a singular way. Its development and positioning in the global political-economic field, especially its relationship to the United States, has influenced Mexico's internal response to (im)migration (Andreas and Biersteker 2003, 38; Delgado Wise and Márquez Covarrubias 2005; González Gutiérrez 2006; González Ortiz and Rivera Sanchez 2004; Imaz Bayona 2003; Vila Freyer 2007; Isacson, Meyer, and Morales 2014). I begin this chapter with a discussion of Mexico's relationship with the United States in terms of border control by highlighting Mexico's active participation in the criminalization of (im)migrants. I note that Mexico is located in an in-between positionality in relationship to the United States and other Latin American countries. While Mexico actively polices both its northern and southern borders and participates in the criminalization of (im)migrants, it simultaneously must respond to civil society's demands to protect vulnerable (im)migrants, specifically women and Mexican nationals.

I then shift the analytical lens to Colonia Postal in Tijuana and examine how the significant presence of (im)migrants in this space enables local police to make use of their bodies as evidence of their delinquency-fighting efforts. I then focus on the experiences of some (im)migrant women who inhabit this space. Specifically, I highlight the contradictory responses that the Mexican government offers (im)migrants and how the gendered criminalization of the border that is mapped onto (im)migrant bodies results in local police authorities functioning as an extension of US border control. The policing and incarceration of (im)-migrants in these border areas function as additional sites of carcerality. This distends our understandings of (im)migrant imprisonment and detention as occurring solely in the United States. It demonstrates how (im)migrant incarceration operates as a transnational phenomenon in direct and indirect collaboration with the US and Mexican nation-states.[3] This perspective is significant given the dearth of scholarly attention afforded to the role of the Mexican nation-state in the criminalization of (im)migrants on its northern border. I simultaneously discuss the many responses afforded by (im)migrants to secure protection for themselves and others. These responses often include strategically performing heteronormative familial formations in public spaces, which speak to (im)migrants' resourcefulness, as well as the disciplinary power of heteronormativity.

I conclude by discussing how the developing relationship between the United States and Mexico to "secure" the border results in the institutionalization of violence. Both states perform this through the policing of national borders. It demonstrates the way in which the notion of criminality is employed to organize relationships of power in ways that are not limited to the nation, but instead extend beyond its borders. The analysis highlights the transnational implications of the construction by the United States of (im)migrant women as irrecuperable subjects.

## Mexico's In-Between Global Positionality

While Mexico benefits from emigration and actively participates in generating and furthering these movements, it also participates in and contends with the criminalization of the border and of the bodies that find themselves in the borderlands. At present, a significant portion of the scholarship dedicated to the history of border militarization—some of which I discuss throughout—focuses on the United States and its state representatives as originators of violence (Andreas 2000; Brownell 2001; Dunn 1996; Falcón 2001; Nevins 2002; Palafox 1996 and 2000; and Dunn and Palafox 2000). I complicate these dominant narratives by, in part, drawing from the analysis of Lytle-Hernández, whose works (2006 and 2010) turn attention from the United States toward Mexico and its central role in determining border policing.

Mexican and US histories are interrelated and contradictorily embedded in conflict and collaboration, as most prominently characterized by the US-Mexican War of 1846, which ended in 1848 with the signing of the Treaty of Guadalupe Hidalgo. The treaty granted the United States more than five hundred thousand square miles of Mexican territory. It is within this critical context that the US-Mexico border takes physical shape. The establishment of national borders creates the possibility for their control, implicating bordering nations in a bilateral negotiation of what control looks like. While (im)migration control along the US-Mexico border is mainly socially regarded as actions performed by the United States, Mexico plays a vital role in this process (Lytle-Hernández 2006 and 2010).

Mexico has a long and active history of intervention in matters of (im)migration. Mexican emigration scholars Raul Delgado Wise and Humberto Márquez Covarrubias (2005) cite Jorge Durand's chronology of Mexican emigration policies, which underscores Mexico as an active border-policing agent. Durand divides his chronology into the following:

> i) 1910–1940, a time period when migration is conceived negatively and thus attempts to dissuade it are made; ii) 1942–1964, migration as a bilateral negotiation through the Bracero Program; iii) 1964–1986, the politics of no politics shaped by the criminalization of migration; iv) 1987–2000, a politics of attention and closeness towards immigrants given the visibility of the phenomenon, and v) 2000 onward, the failed attempt to negotiate an immigrant agenda and continued politics of attention and closeness. (14)

Whereas Durand extends the third phase to 1990, Delgado Wise and Márquez Covarrubias limit it to 1986 to recognize the impact of the passage of the Immigration Reform and Control Act (IRCA) in the United States, as well as to account for neoliberal policies that guided the economic integration of Mexico and the United States.[4] Although this overarching chronology underscores the actions of the Mexican government in influencing emigration, this reading needs to be complicated to account for Mexico's paradoxical behavior toward emigration within and across these different eras.

While appraising this entire history is outside the scope of this chapter, Lytle-Hernández (2006) provides a reading of one key period, 1940–1954. Highlighting the contradictory, and in this case punitive, nature of the Mexican government's politics toward emigration, Lytle-Hernández focuses on the bilateral collaboration between the United States and Mexico with respect to border policing, revealing Mexico as a dynamic actor responsible for affecting how the US-Mexico border has been domesticated. Her work provides a framework to think through the contemporary relationship between Mexico and the United States in terms of border policing. Lytle-Hernández analyzes Operation Wetback, an (im)migration law enforcement initiative that targeted people of Mexican origin and others who "looked Mexican" for repatriation. Through her analysis of this operation, Lytle-Hernandez demonstrates that the United States and Mexico developed a binational relationship of control. According to Lytle-Hernández, this relationship generated new forms of policing and enabled "coordinating state violence beyond the limits of the nation-state" (438). The analysis that Lytle-Hernández affords to the period leading up to Operation Wetback not only disrupts the understanding of the 1942–1954 era as a time of collaboration defined through the Bracero Program, but also demonstrates Mexico's active participation in the criminalization of (im)migrants.

Mexico's participation in the criminalization of (im)migrants is in part informed by its relationship to the United States, particularly the cross-country collaboration to manage the geopolitical border. Because the border defines the limits of the territorial nation, it forms part of the domestic sphere. However, at the same time, it also forms part of the international public sphere as a central space where Mexico negotiates its relationship to the world in general and to the United States in particular. This relationship constructs this space as a "historiographic surface," which, according to political theorist Allen Feldman (1991), "is a place for reenactment, for the simulation of power and for making power tangible as a material force" (2). The US-Mexico border functions as a space where history is written, particularly by and through the bodies of (im)migrants.[5] The narrative afforded by Mexico professes to protect the feminized domestic sphere, and, at the same time, it writes the public sphere through neoliberal logic as the space of rationality where free-choice and personal responsibility govern.

(Im)migrant women who transgress the boundaries of heteropatriarchy, for example, by (im)migrating—moving from the private to the public—are often made responsible for what happens while they inhabit this space. The stories of (im)migrant women reveal the involvement of the nation-state in reinforcing heteropatriarchal relations between individuals and the nation. Furthermore, the punitive response by the Mexican government to (im)migrants renders it a key participant in the construction of (im)migrants as criminals. This is reflected through increased policing and border militarization, which further naturalizes violence against (im)migrant bodies. By participating in the criminalization and containment of (im)migrant bodies, the Mexican government operates as an extension of US (im)migration control practices that constitute (im)migrant women as violable. These practices speak to the institutionalization of violence performed by both states to police national borders and reflect some of the ways criminalization functions to organize global racialized and gendered relationships of power.

Expanding on Lytle-Hernández's framework that labels Mexico as an active agent in the criminalization of both the border and Mexican (im)migrants, I consider in the following section the ways in which gender informs the Mexican nation-state's response to (im)migrants. I now turn to discuss the experiences of (im)migrants in Colonia Postal, an (im)migrant concentrated space. The discussion highlights Mexico's policies in disciplining (im)migrant women while also collaborating with the United States in racializing (im)migrants as criminals, engaging in the process that Lytle-Hernández describes as "coordinating state violence beyond the limits of the nation-state" (438).

## Domesticating and Disciplining (Im)migrant Bodies in Colonia Postal

Colonia Postal, a busy neighborhood located one-and-a-half miles from the US-Mexico border, sits atop one of Tijuana's many populated hills and is home to two shelters—Casa del Migrante (Casa) and Instituto Madre Assunta (Instituto). Established by Scalabrinian missionaries, their objective is to provide social, cultural, and spiritual guidance and support to (im)migrants.[6] Casa, established in 1987, and Instituto, established in 1992, are two (im)migrant shelters that exist in Tijuana.[7] Casa provides temporary shelter and services to (im)migrant men, while Instituto was created to address the particular needs of (im)migrant women and children. Although both shelters are located on a fairly quiet street, Calle Galileo, two blocks away from the main street, Avenida Defensores de Baja California (Avenida Defensores), their presence produces an effect that resonates beyond the immediate walls of the shelters and transcends the boundaries of Colonia Postal. (Im)migrant women recounted time and again how they found themselves with nowhere to go and recalled news and personal stories of shelters dedicated to (im)migrants. If they are fortunate enough to have money on hand, they can ask a taxi driver to take them to Casa.[8] However, in some cases, women do not have this option and instead walk to the shelter. For some, this means an all-day journey. In other instances, taxi drivers or other individuals offer to take them to the shelter free of charge, or people along the way provide them with money for bus fare. Widespread support of (im)migrants and the knowledge of these shelters and their location highlight the significance that these two shelters have assumed in this transnational city and beyond. Their presence and the mobilization that takes place in general to provide support for (im)migrants provide a complex picture of the Mexican government and community. While, as I argue in this chapter, Mexico participates in criminalizing (im)migrants, which includes Mexican nationals and non-Mexicans, the Mexican government and Mexican communities simultaneously engage efforts to address the violence experienced by (im)migrants at both the northern and southern borders.[9]

For more than six months, I conducted research at Instituto.[10] Once a week, I would walk across the US-Mexico divide, board a bus, and travel from the San Ysidro crossing to the corner of Calle Galileo and Avenida Defensores in Colonia Postal. During my numerous two-block walks to and from the shelter, I witnessed (im)migrant men waiting for employment at this main intersection, men talking about their (im)migrations, and many (im)migrants, men and women, walking along the streets with small bags of belongings.

I also witnessed police drive by with men handcuffed in the back of their trucks. The adjacent location of Casa and Instituto concentrates (im)migrants in this area and creates an acute perception of Colonia Postal as an (im)migrant space. The presence of (im)migrant bodies carries with it meanings that are ideologically fused to the border, including criminality. Beginning in the 1970s with the deployment of the US war on drugs, concerns about the border increased for both the United States and Mexico. More and more, the border is imagined as a hub of criminality that includes "illegal" border crossings and drug trafficking (Dunn 1996; Andreas 2000; Payán 2006). Efforts to control the border region are driven by the law-and-order logic that drives national and international politics, which centers on border militarization as the main response to these perceived threats. What often results is the conflation of the (im)migrant figure with crime. Part of the ideological labor carried out in US politics and media is to present (im)migrants as threats to the United States by portraying them as drug traffickers, gangsters, and breeders. Moreover, through its law-and-order response to their bodily presence, the Mexican government also participates in the criminalization of (im)migrants as reflected by the concentration of police where (im)migrant bodies are hyper-visible.

Colonia Postal epitomizes the contradictions that (im)migration poses for the Mexican nation-state. It actively participates in the production of this (im)migrant space through economic and institutional support for shelters such as Casa and Instituto, but the constant *seizing* of (im)migrants—whether through arrest and/or separation from a would-be place of protection—by Tijuana police highlights the government's active role in containing individuals present in these spaces. Witnessing the *seizing* of suspected (im)migrant men by local police reveals the Mexican government's criminalization of and punitive response toward (im)migrants. The construction of social irrecuperability of (im)migrants in the United States carries into Mexico as state agencies—in this case, the local police—re-criminalize and target their bodies.

The criminalization of (im)migrants by Tijuana police is evident in the following narrative of Javier, a Mexican deportee in Colonia Postal:

> The police come by once in the morning and once in the afternoon. Sometimes we can get away. I've been taken a few times. They probably think I'm selling drugs or something because they see me all tattooed. They need to meet their quota to show that they're doing their job. If we don't have an identification they take us in and we either have to pay a fine or they keep us for up to seventy-two hours. I had one from the shelter at the beginning but it's only good for the first few days. I don't know what the shelter did that for a while the cops couldn't come by here and pick up people like that, but they started doing it again. It's all about the money. I was deported five months ago and I've tried crossing five different times. One time I tried to cross through Arizona and

I was put in immigration detention for a few weeks. I'm going to try again this weekend . . . we'll see how it goes. I need to get back because I have my four little girls over there. I'm not with my babies' mom, but I don't ask them for anything because I don't want to take anything away from my girls. It's hard to get a job here. They ask for references, which I can't give them, and they look at you all dirty and they don't want to give you a job. People used to come by and pick up groups of people to go work, but since the cops started rounding people up they almost don't come no more . . . once in a while. We eat mostly bread because a Christian brother comes by every Tuesday night with a bunch of bread for people here. Some of it is good. Sometimes we eat because we wash cars and get some money that way.

Javier is an undocumented (im)migrant who spent most of his time in the Colonia Postal while he attempted to return to Oxnard, California, his hometown where his family resides. The police harassment that Javier shares is a common phenomenon in Colonia Postal. During one of my visits to the Instituto, Leti, an eight-year-old girl staying at the shelter with her mother and sister, spent much of her time looking out the window toward the shelter's gate. One day, Leti entered the garage/meeting room where some of us were sitting and approached her mother, "Look Mami, they are taking them again. They are picking them all up. Poor things." When I asked Leti who was being taken, she responded, "The police are outside picking up the men. They come a lot and take them away."

During another visit to the shelter I met Ilea, Ilea's mother-in-law Ana, and Juan, Ilea's fifteen-year-old son. Together, they attempted to cross the border with Ilea's husband, David, but the entire group was caught, with the exception of the person guiding them. David was arrested by the Border Patrol and accused of human smuggling. American authorities deported everyone but David, and the family was left with no means of communicating with him. Juan was fifteen at the time but looked older and Sister Orilla, the shelter's director, informed them that the shelter was for (im)migrant women and young children, which meant that Juan could only stay for a couple of days. However, the shelter's staff supported Juan and his family in transferring to another shelter where they could stay.

Ana and Juan related their story and their encounter with Tijuana police. One day, during their stay at the shelter, Ilea left to work to clean a house while Ana and Juan left to wash clothes at a local laundromat.

As he was waiting for the laundry to finish, Juan sat down on the sidewalk, drinking a soda. Two police officers asked him for his identification. Juan answered back saying no, that he was not doing anything wrong. The police told him to go with them and started to grab him by his shirt. Alarmed, Juan called for his grandmother. His grandmother yelled at them not to take him, that he was her grandson. In response, the police yelled back at her, stating that it was not true and continued to pull him toward the police truck. The ordeal went on for a few moments until Ana realized that Juan had her wallet, and she took it from him to show the police her identification. They hesitantly let him go. After that event, Ana and Juan decided not to go outside the shelter unless it was necessary.

Both Javier's and Ana and Juan's stories reveal that policing and arrests by Tijuana police are deliberately directed toward (im)migrant bodies. Often, (im)migrants attempt to avoid being identified by the Border Patrol by traveling without identification. In addition, several (im)migrant women recounted that the (im)migration authorities did not return their belongings when they were deported, often leaving them without identification. Consequently, the police's insistence that they show their identification, despite the high likelihood that they will not have any with them, illustrates a deliberate attempt to detain (im)migrants. Similar to the United States, the Mexican state manages the mass deportations through the policing and incarceration of (im)migrants. This demonstrates the systemic logic of (im)migrant criminalization and incarceration carried out by both US and Mexican state authorities: deported (im)migrants are not only denied legal status in the United States, but also, for Mexican (im)migrants, the withholding of their identification documents serves to deny them legitimate status in their country of origin—Mexico—and results in their detention. This reflects the larger dynamic of how being designated "criminal" makes them socially irrecuperable. (Im)migrant criminalization also extends to Tijuana residents who are harassed by the police because they *look* transient, attesting to the generalized criminalization of the borderland spaces. At the time the research was conducted, deportees were often put to work on local city projects.[11]

The criminalization to which (im)migrants are subjected is not uniform; instead, it is very much gendered. Part of the ability to target (im)migrants directly relates to the physical access Tijuana police can secure over (im)migrant bodies. At Instituto, (im)migrant women and children are allowed to stay throughout the day. In the case of (im)migrant men at Casa, they are allowed to spend the night, but have to leave the shelter early in the morning. Thus, gendered ideas of domestic femininity afford (im)migrant women a level of protection not extended to (im)migrant men. That Juan was let go only after Ana showed the police *her* identification and their mutual decision to remain inside the gates of the shelter for the rest of their stay highlight this fact. However, for Juan, his physical appearance—looking older than his actual age—along with his gender limit the protection the shelter extends to him and his family since the director informed them that he could only stay a couple of days.

For (im)migrant women, the response by Mexican police reveals a series of contradictions. In some cases, the status of being a woman affords some insulation from being targeted by local police. For example, several of the women at the shelter were directed, and in some cases driven, to the shelter by Tijuana police. According to the shelter's social worker, men do not receive similar attention and are more often left to find their own way to shelters through organizations and agencies, including Grupo Beta,[12] or through other means. However, in other instances, (im)migrant women, like men, face arrest, which functions as a form of gendered state control enabled by one's (im)migrant status. In other words, women face arrest for performing an action considered traditionally performed by men—(im)migration. In both cases, the police serve as a disciplining mechanism that regulates gender norms. This disciplining occurs either by providing a form of protection to women often not afforded to men, which occasionally includes transportation to shelters, or by treating women *like men* by arresting them when they violate heteropatriarchal definitions of femininity.

The following stories demonstrate the gendered disciplining of (im)-migrants that happens in this border area. I not only consider how Tijuana police serve as a disciplining mechanism, but also, where possible, I account for the ways in which (im)migrants themselves engage in gender constructions—particularly with respect to the heteronormative nuclear family—to secure some degree of protection. While it is important to be mindful of how, in the desire for pragmatism, such efforts reinforce heteronormativity, it is also essential to understand how (im)-migrants are compelled to draw from normative disciplinary discourses.

In this section, I consider how (im)migrants make use of, and in many cases *perform*, normative familial formations in efforts to guard themselves and others against state violence. For undocumented (im)-migrants in the borderlands, whether they are attempting to cross the border and/or are later deported, their illicit (im)migrations across national boundaries construct them as violable. While the trope of family sanctity is difficult to access for many, I highlight how (im)migrants in the borderlands make use of this trope by creatively fabricating kinships to present themselves and others as deserving of protection. I read the attempts by (im)migrants to perform normative familial formations as decriminalizing strategies. Drawing from Monisha Das Gupta's notion of unruly (im)migrants, which she defines as (im)migrants who "struggle for rights in the face of their formal/legal and popular codification as noncitizens" (2006, 4), I present the stories of (im)migrants who engage in what I term "unruly (im)migrant kinships"—constructed kinships among (im)migrants that are meant to disrupt and defy the ability of the state to inflict violence, especially to other (im)migrants. The narrative highlights how US criminalization of (im)migrants transcends national boundaries as Mexican authorities—in this case, Tijuana police—further criminalize the very same bodies. I also indicate the significance of (im)migrants' resourcefulness in performing unruly (im)-migrant kinships and the limitations as many (im)migrants are unable to access such tropes.

During one of my visits to Instituto, Celia and Vicky arrived. Celia had previously spent time at the shelter, and Vicky was a fairly new arrival to Tijuana. They came to Instituto with the hope of obtaining assistance for Vicky. Celia had been imprisoned in Central California Women's Facility (CCWF), where she met Vicky. Celia was deported, and after staying at Instituto, she secured a place to live in Tijuana. During a trip to Tijuana's downtown, Celia came across Vicky. "As soon as I saw her I remembered her from prison," Celia said. "She never spoke and always kept to herself. When I saw her, she was so dirty. I could tell she was living on the street. I took her home with me to see what I could do for her. I wasn't going to leave her out on the street." Even though the two had never spoken to each other while incarcerated, the shared experiences of incarceration and deportation were enough for Celia to take Vicky into her home to provide some protection from the dangers she potentially faced living in the streets.

Vicky, a woman in her mid-fifties, was born in Los Angeles, California. For years, she used drugs, which led to her incarceration. Her difficulties in communicating, both in English and Spanish, led in part to a misunderstanding over her citizenship, and she was deported to Mexico. Vicky notes, "I am going to court hearings about my citizenship. I don't have an i.d., so I got deported. I need an i.d. to go to court." She was in the process of trying to obtain identification to deal with her deportation case. She also noted the importance of having her identification on hand in order to deal with Mexican police: "I need an identification because of the police. They stop me all the time and ask me 'Are you selling drugs?' 'Are you using drugs?' Water is hard to find here in Tijuana so the police see you dirty, and they pick you up." Vicky's story shows how the racialization of (im)migration informs US border control. Vicky asserted her US citizenship to (im)migration enforcement authorities. However, the combination of her lack of *proper* documentation, racialization as Mexican, criminalized appearance, and difficulty in communicating in either English or Spanish led to her deportation.

Her gendered criminalization continued in Tijuana. In addition to being unable to remain clean—which represents her as transient— her manner of dress signals masculinity. At the time, she wore brown baggy shorts below her knee, a large beige t-shirt, white socks, and tennis shoes, and her body was marked by old faded tattoos. The police harassment described by Vicky reveals how women who transgress the boundaries of heteronormativity are targeted for disciplining. Her forced deportee status made her vulnerable to the violence endured in the borderlands, including having to live on the streets, merging with her masculinized appearance and resulting in her arrests. In this case, the Tijuana police's harassment of Vicky served to discipline and punish her for physically signaling masculinity. Although Celia's efforts to extend Vicky some level of protection does not explicitly speak to my argument that (im)migrants perform normative familial formations to secure their safety, it does highlight Celia's attempts to disrupt both the state's and individuals' ability to inflict violence on Vicky and extend domestic protection to her by allowing her to stay in her home. Vicky is one of the many individuals unable to draw from heteronormativity to elicit protection.

Esther's story, which I discussed in chapter 2, also reveals the involvement of Tijuana police in disciplining (im)migrant women into heteronormativity. Esther was imprisoned in the United States for five years and then deported to Mexico. In a letter, Esther wrote of her experiences, including her deportation. Addressing the moment when she was deported, she wrote:

> I walked across the rails and walked towards where the taxis were. I was putting the laces on my shoes because in immigration detention they take them off. I didn't know where to go. I was thinking, when a Mex-

ican policewoman told me, "What are you doing mami?" In that instant, she grabbed me and put handcuffs on me. I could not believe it. "This cannot be happening." She put me in a truck full of drunk homeless men, and it smelled horrible in there. She took us to the police station and they lined us up there. We were in front of a man's office where we were going to get a fine for not having an i.d. with a picture. I showed him my paperwork for my deportation and he let me go. I left there around 10 [in the morning] and I asked for directions to downtown.

During a conversation, Esther discussed her deportation and subsequent arrest:

The night that I arrived here, thank God that I was picked up by the police. What if I was taken by a couple of, a couple of bad men? . . . I was deported at three in the morning . . . I don't know why they don't put a better time. Really . . . I would really like Mexico . . . okay, they are going to deport my people, but you know what? Deport them in the morning. Why do they have to throw us out exactly at midnight? one in the morning? three in the morning? Why?

Esther's arrest was directly correlated to her status as a deportee, given the fact that she was seized at three in the morning, near the border crossing, while placing the laces on her shoes. It is common knowledge that while in (im)migration detention, (im)migrants' shoelaces are removed for security reasons. Arresting Esther was a punitive act since the police did not even ask for her identification. At the same time, her appreciation for her arrest highlights some of the challenges (im)migrants face at the border. Even though her arrest functioned as a violent act in and of itself—the fact that individuals with a badge can seize a person at any moment for any reason—Esther perceived this as the lesser of two evils because, had she not been arrested, she would have faced potential danger from other individuals on the streets. Her narrative reveals how one state action, in the form of her deportation, enables another state action—in this case, her arrest. This illustrates the punitive nature of official (deportation) and unofficial (arrest of (im)migrants in Mexico) (im)migration enforcement policies.

Esther's masculine and disheveled appearance also contributed to her arrest. When non-citizens in California prisons are deported, they are not given new clothes, shoes, or the two hundred dollars that US citizens are provided. Instead, Esther was deported in her prison clothes, which consisted of baggy light blue denim jeans, a large gray t-shirt, and tennis shoes. Her hair was shaved on the bottom half of her head, and she tied the remainder in a tight ponytail. Cognizant of how her appearance transgressed social norms of femininity, Esther attempted to fit herself into these norms: "When I was going to get out I started letting my hair grow, because I said, 'I am going outside to a society' . . . I have my daughter. But I would shave all of this [signaling the lower half of her head]." When I asked Esther about the possibility of returning to the United States, she responded, "I don't want to go back just like that. Right now if they [Border Patrol] pick me up this nervous. . . . Look how I am [noting her shaking hands]. No, besides, I want my hair to grow out for my daughter." Esther was aware that her appearance contributed to labeling her as socially deviant, and she attempted to comply with normative femininity and gain social acceptance by trying to change her appearance. However, her hair did not grow out soon enough, and her prison clothes further denoted her as deviant, which factored into her arrest. The arresting policewoman's comment, "What are you doing, *mami*?" (emphasis added), served to re-signify Esther as female, which underscores how her arrest essentially performed as a gendered disciplining act.

Not only did Esther face disciplining by authorities, but civil society also participated in this process. During one occasion, Esther and I were riding a bus to downtown Tijuana. A male passenger, apparently intoxicated, aggressively approached Esther. He yelled obscene comments about sexual acts he was going to perform to her to stop her from being a lesbian, an assumption he made based on her appearance. I, as a female body that signaled heterosexuality, and thus not the target of this person's aggression, attempted to intervene. Meanwhile, Esther remained silent for fear that the situation would escalate. The verbal aggression went on for a few minutes until he got off the bus. It is significant that, while there were several other passengers on board, they did not get involved, thus sanctioning this individual's actions.

In both Vicky and Esther's cases, their non-gender-conforming appearances played a central role in their (im)migration experiences, including their interactions with Tijuana police. Esther could not discipline her body into femininity before being deported, which ideologically enabled the police to take on the role of disciplining her into heteronormativity. Their experiences also speak to the fact that sexual identities are produced and policed at the US-Mexico border (Luibhéid

2002; Luibhéid and Cantú 2005; Cantú 2009). Vicky and Esther's accounts show the active role of the Mexican state in practices of policing (im)migrant sexualities.

Other ways that police regulate (im)migrant sexualities is through the policing of sex work. There is an area in Tijuana, Zona de Tolerancia (tolerance zone), where sex work is lawful and intended for a US clientele. However, sex workers must obtain legal permits and submit to, and pay for, monthly health checkups. At Instituto, I met Suly, a young woman fleeing from her home state of Michoacán with her toddler son. She was attempting to (im)migrate to the United States because her child's father had initiated a legal case to claim custody of their son and she did not have the economic means to fight the case. Suly's intent was to cross to the United States, but family members who had agreed to pay for their crossing declined once Suly and her son were in Tijuana. She left the shelter and rented a small room. I came across Suly during one of my walks to Instituto. I had learned from other women at the shelter that Suly had begun engaging in sex work. During our encounter, Suly shared that when she found herself without any financial support, she considered sex work to be the quickest way of obtaining money to provide for her son. I am unaware of whether she knew of the ability to work in the Zona de Tolerancia, but given her economic situation, this may not have been an option. She feared being jailed for the sex work, and she was also afraid that authorities would take her son. However, she did not see other alternatives.

Suly's account addresses another dimension of how (im)migrant sexualities are produced and disciplined in the borderlands. Her inability to cross the border and her lack of resources placed her in a situation where sex work readily became a means to sustain her son and herself. Her vulnerable (im)migrant identity directly contributed to her assuming the identity of sex worker.[13] Her fear of being caught and having her child taken away by authorities shows the punitive treatment of this identity. The sexual formation of this border area contributes to Suly's experiences. The fact that there are specific areas in Tijuana legally designated for this type of work and regulated by authorities, and that it is largely intended for people from the United States, underscores some of the structural forces that make situations such as Suly's predictable. Drawing from an established form of labor directly structured by the presence of the US-Mexico border, Suly made use of her female sexual body to obtain money to sustain her son and herself.

In a different case, Nora, a forty-three-year-old (im)migrant woman, made use of her feminine body in attempts to secure safety for her husband. The couple migrated to Tijuana in hopes of crossing the border. She was three months pregnant but miscarried during one of her attempts to cross the border. Her husband stayed at Casa, and she stayed at Instituto. While Nora remained predominately inside the shelter, her husband spent most of his time on the street, looking for work. In addition to temporary housing, (im)migrant women are provided three meals a day. In contrast, (im)migrant men receive coffee and some bread in the morning and a meal in the evening, but they have to find additional sustenance throughout the day. When possible, Nora would give some of her food to her husband.[14] Through a government rent subsidy program, she received approximately one hundred and thirty dollars to secure a place to live. The couple then moved to their new home, but they remained determined to cross the border. A few weeks after they left, I ran into Nora on the street near the shelter. By that time, her husband was working as a mover at a furniture store near the shelter, and she accompanied him to work. Although Nora did not get paid, she went with him anyway because, since arriving in Tijuana, he had been stopped by the police on eight occasions and arrested three times for not having identification. She hoped that her presence would provide her husband some protection from further police harassment.

Nora's story highlights how gender affects (im)migrant experiences. She was allowed to stay in the shelter and had access to three meals a day. In contrast, her husband was made vulnerable to the violence of the borderlands, which sometimes included going hungry and being taken by local police. Nora decided to accompany her husband to work, essentially using her feminized body to afford him some level of protection. Even when (im)migrants fit into the model of the heteronormative nuclear family, as do Nora and her husband, they sometimes have to exceedingly perform this relationship in public to secure protection. This highlights the ways in which (im)migrants creatively make use of the limited resources available to ensure their well-being and that of others. In essence, Nora subverted heteronormative ideas of gender by taking her feminine body into public space to provide a level of safety to her husband, who otherwise remains outside of feminized domestic protection. As noted through the notion of unruly (im)migrant kinships, (im)migrants at times strategically *stretch* heteronormativity to fabricate an appearance of relative normalcy.

Stories of women using notions of femininity to provide some protection to (im)migrant men are not uncommon. Their work to protect others seems to stem from their experiences of (im)migration and a shared understanding of the difficulties that this process entails. The story of Reyna and Linda demonstrates this point. Reyna was imprisoned for five years in Central California Women's Facility. Linda attempted to cross through the Nogales border crossing and was given a seventy-five-day sentence for attempting to cross the border undocumented. She was sent to the Federal Correctional Institution in Dublin, California. Reyna and Linda were deported to Tijuana around the same time and met at Instituto. While outside the gates of the shelter, Reyna and Linda observed as the police arrested several (im)migrant men. As Linda described the scene:

> We started to tell them, "Why are you taking them? They are not doing anything! They don't do anything to anyone." And they told us that the men were disturbing the public and to shut up, or they'd take us, too. I told them that we are running away from those racists over there, but they are worse because they are treating their own people like that. Now we have to run from them, too. They are more racist. Then the police started to leave, and Reyna tells me so that they can hear, "Leave them alone already, can't you see that they need the money for their lunch?" And the police come back and tell her to get on the truck, and she asks them, "Why aren't you taking her, too? She was telling you things as well," and the police tell her, "Yeah, but you said we needed money for lunch. Now for that you are going with them," and they took her, too. Later in the day Reyna arrives outside singing, "I've arrived from where I was."

Linda marks an important connection between US authorities and Tijuana police in the treatment afforded (im)migrants. She notes that racism comes from multiple fronts: not only do (im)migrants have to evade US authorities, they also have to run from Mexican police. This is important in that she regards the capturing of (im)migrants on both sides of the border as essentially forming part of the same larger structure of racism. Tijuana police, similar to US authorities, contribute to the racialization of (im)migrants as criminal. As Linda notes, this racialization is gendered. The presence of (im)migrants in Tijuana specifically, but the border area in general, is a production founded on the protection of the US nation-state from foreign racial threats. Women are particularly regarded as threats due to their reproductive capabilities, which represent permanent settlement. In these border spaces, ideas about gender influence interactions with local police as (im)migrant women who perform normative femininity—including remaining within the confines of the shelter, dressing femininely, and leaving the masculine authority of the police unchallenged—lower the likelihood of an arrest.

Like the (im)migrant men, Reyna and Linda were both on the street. However, unlike the men, they did not immediately face being arrested. It was not until Reyna and Linda confronted the police in efforts to defend the (im)migrant men that they became targets. The police attempted to discipline both women by warning them to "shut up" or else face being arrested. While both defied the police's attempts to discipline them into feminized silence, Reyna disrupted their legitimacy by characterizing their actions as corrupt, and the police arrested her.

I observed a similar situation with Noemi, an (im)migrant woman who had attempted to cross the border on three different occasions. Noemi befriended one of the (im)migrant men outside the shelter. A group of us observed as the police arrested several (im)migrant men and ordered them on the police truck. Noemi rushed to the shelter's gate and told them, "Don't take him! He's my husband, and we have to leave to Mexicali in a little while. Let him go!" A police officer responded, "We'll let him go at the station, but right now we have to take him." About thirty minutes later, her friend arrived at the gates and we heard him call out, "Noemi, they let me go! I'm here already." According to Noemi, her friend told her that he was let go at the police station immediately because of her interaction with the police officer. In this case, Noemi's use of her status as his "wife" ensured that he would not spend time in jail, which is what men in his situation are usually subjected to.

The cases of Nora, Linda and Reyna, and Noemi demonstrate how some (im)migrant women attempt to make use of notions of heteronormativity to secure the protection of (im)migrant men. Coyotes, the individuals who guide undocumented (im)migrants through the border, also understand the power of the heteronuclear family and how it can afford some amount of protection. Ofelia's border-crossing experience as a young Mexican (im)migrant woman makes this evident. During an attempt to cross the border through Mexicali, one of the guides told her group to immerse themselves into a water canal where they would remain under a palm tree. For sixteen hours, they stayed in water up to their chins until finally the Border Patrol left, and the guides told them to get out and start walking. Eventually, they were caught by the Border Patrol and deported. In a separate attempt, one of the guides told Ofelia that, if they were caught, she should say that he was her husband so as to avoid being accused of human smuggling. She agreed, she noted, because she knew that if he was legally tried the entire group could be detained until the conclusion of his trial. According to Ofelia, the trial could take up to three months.

Simultaneously, as (im)migrants perform normative familial formations, often deploying the trope of the heteronormative nuclear family to protect themselves and others, feminized bodies are often what make women the targets of violence. The group of which Ofelia was part was composed of several men, as well as Ofelia and Susana, a sixteen-year-old woman. When they were spotted and detained by the Border Patrol, Susana was ordered by one of the agents to undress Gustavo, an (im)migrant man whom the Border Patrol assumed to be the guide. Antonio, another (im)migrant, offered to do so himself, but the Border Patrol insisted that Susana undress Gustavo. Antonio's attempts to protect Susana were ineffective. Ofelia stated that Susana was traumatized from this occurrence and did not want anything else to do with crossing the border. The group was taken into custody by the Border Patrol and they gave their official declarations, which were to be used in the trial against the guide. Unlike most cases where (im)migrants are transported by bus to the San Ysidro border and released into Tijuana, Ofelia and two of the men, who were brothers, were taken and transferred directly from the Border Patrol into the hands of Mexican police. The group was driven to the police station in Tijuana to have their declarations taken again, now by Mexican authorities. The ordeal ended at two in the morning when they were finally told they could leave. Given the time and the danger they potentially faced on the streets, the group asked to stay in the police station. Instead, they were told, "This is not a shelter and that is not our problem. You have to leave." Ofelia, who had met the two men during the trip, was forced to leave with them. The men had a distant uncle in Tijuana and they called their mother and obtained his number. They then called their uncle and took a taxi to his house. The following day, Ofelia was taken to the shelter.

There are several significant factors to be noted in her narrative. In addition to Ofelia's case of performing heteronormativity, several (im)migrant women at the shelter related how border-crossing guides had also instructed that, if caught, the women should state that they were a married couple. If successful, this performance affords the guides protection from being prosecuted for human smuggling. It simultaneously prevents the detainment of the group of (im)migrants. Thus, this heteronormative performance obstructs the state's ability to convict and detain (im)migrants. However, (im)migrant women transgress the boundaries of heteronormativity when they (im)migrate, especially if they (im)migrate unaccompanied. The Border Patrol forcing Susana to undress the guide functions as a violent sexual act, inflicting a trauma that stopped her from attempting to cross the border again. This violent act essentially disciplined her into hegemonic femininity.

Sexual violence thus functions as a tool for (im)migration control by deterring women from (im)migrating and punishing those who do.[15] In Ofelia's case, the Mexican police further exposed Ofelia to violence by sending her away in the middle of the night with two strangers into the streets. Fortunately for them, they were able to secure a safe place to stay. Finally, Ofelia's story exposes one of the ways in which the Mexican state—in this case, the police—involves itself in the management of (im)migrant bodies and labors by policing (im)migration to the United States. The fact that the US Border Patrol handed Ofelia and the two men directly into the hands of Mexican police in order to take their declarations in effect makes Mexican police participants in US criminal investigations. This serves to construct the Mexican police as an extension of the US Border Patrol. Ofelia's story signifies the gendered bilateral labor carried out to *secure* the US-Mexico border.

The story of Rita and Mari further exemplifies the notion of unruly (im)migrant kinships. Rita, an (im)migrant woman from Oaxaca, Mexico, lived undocumented in the United States for more than eighteen years. She married, had children, and started a printing business in Los Angeles with her husband. In 2009, Rita returned to Oaxaca because her mother was very sick. Before leaving, Rita was in the process of legalizing her status; by leaving the country and trying to re-enter the United States, she lost her opportunity to obtain legal residency. While she was in Oaxaca, her mother died and Rita stayed for a while to keep her father company and make some final arrangements.

On her trip back to the United States, Rita boarded a bus that would take her to Tijuana where she would try to cross the border once again. Another woman sat with Rita on the bus, and they struck up a conversation. According to Rita, Mari is a woman from Guatemala, and she was (im)migrating to the United States. Rita asked her how she planned to travel through Mexico without proof of Mexican citizenship. Mari asked Rita what she should do, and Rita responded, "pray." During their trip, Rita took it upon herself to coach Mari on what to say if Mexican (im)migration authorities asked her questions. They agreed that they would say that they were cousins and that Mari would claim that she was from the southern Mexican state of Puebla, had never gone to school, and did not know that she needed an identification. Rita prepared Mari with possible questions that the Mexican (im)migration authorities would ask, including the town she was from, the national anthem, and the Mexican flag. When an agent boarded the bus, he asked Mari several questions, including where she was from, where she was going, and her reasons for travel. At one point, Rita responded, "She's with me . . . she's my cousin." The women's responses did not convince the officer, and he took Mari off the bus. Rita followed them and said that if they took Mari, she would get off, too. The agent took them into an office where another agent questioned them. He said to Mari, "Let's see, if you are from Puebla, this is going to be easy. Who was the Mexican president who was an Indian and from your state?" Rita intervened, "Who is not going to know who Benito Juarez was?" Rita's intervention freed Mari from answering. The agent asked Mari to point out where Puebla was on a map on the wall. To stall, Rita commented on how Mari would get nervous because she had never gone to school and asked how they could expect Mari to know. In the meantime, Mari found Puebla on the map and pointed it out to the agent. Finally, he asked Mari to sing the national anthem and Rita responded, "Can't you see that she can't even sign her name? I don't know the anthem either." The agent finally let them get back on the bus.

Rita and Mari's story highlights how the Mexican state participates in policing the border not only in the north, but also through border enforcement in the south that is targeted specifically at Central American (im)migrants. Their story demonstrates the on-the-ground work carried out by individuals to secure others' freedom. Rita's own (im)migration history connected her to the experiences of Mari and informed her decision to risk punishment from the state to help Mari avoid being taken, detained, and deported to Guatemala. Not only did they construct a family history, but Rita also went to the extent of getting off the bus and interfering with the agent's questioning of Mari. Rita made use of stereotypes of older Mexican women as uneducated and thus unintelligent to outwit the agent, which succeeded since he allowed them both to get back on the bus. Their story underscores the fact that (im)migrants engage in creative forms of resistance, including creating what I term "unruly" (im)migrant kinships to disrupt and defy the ability of the state to carry out different forms of violence. Without knowing Mari, Rita worked toward Mari's freedom because, according to Rita,

"I could not leave her behind." Rita worked against the state and toward Mari's freedom because of her understanding of (im)migrant policing as a violent process and the role of the state in creating and enforcing this violence.

I share a final story that highlights the collaborative relationship that the United States and Mexico have formed to manage and control (im)-migration at the border. I initially met Gabriela at Instituto. A young (im)migrant woman in her early twenties, she is originally from the Mexican state of Michoacán. On two different occasions, she unsuccessfully attempted to cross the border, and she planned to try again. The week after I met Gabriela, as I returned to the shelter, I walked through the turnstiles that served as the US-Mexico divide.[16] On the right was a parked Border Patrol bus and several (im)migrants lined up against the wall. On the Mexican side of the border, a Grupo Beta member called out their names one by one and directed them toward the Grupo Beta station. I caught a glimpse of a person who looked like Gabriela, but I was unable to call to her because she entered the station. A while after I arrived at the shelter, Grupo Beta dropped off Gabriela, who was returning from an unsuccessful border-crossing attempt. This brief experience demonstrates the relationship of collaboration that Mexico and the United States have formed on the issue of (im)migration. Grupo Beta in general appears to have a positive image among deportees. Many of the (im)migrant women at Instituto showed appreciation for the agency's immediate support after their deportation and the fact that it provides them discounted bus fares to their hometowns. However, it is still important to note that the collaborative relationship between the United States and Mexico in managing deportees enlists Grupo Beta in the deportation process.

### Conclusion

In this chapter, I centered on Colonia Postal, a predominantly (im)migrant space in the border city of Tijuana, and on the gendered criminalization of (im)migrants. The analysis of this space reveals the conflicting relationship that the Mexican government shares with (im)migrants. While the Mexican government responds to some of their needs—for example, by providing support for (im)migrant shelters such as Instituto and Casa and the creation of government bodies such as Grupo Beta—it also contributes to the criminalization of (im)migrants by concentrating police in (im)migrant spaces. The strategies of policing employed by local authorities are directly related to (im)migration control. By asking for identification and targeting individuals who "look" transient, the authorities make (im)migrants direct targets for harassment and arrest. Women who embody masculinity are targeted and punished like men, revealing how heteronormative and patriarchal policing serves to discipline their bodies.

I also presented the notion of unruly (im)migrant kinships to highlight the productiveness of (im)migrants' deployment of normative familial formations to disrupt the state's ability to exert violence. However, it is also important to mark the limitations of such strategies. Many individuals find themselves isolated in their (im)migrations and are not able to perform familial normativity, which increases their vulnerability. This is the case, for example, in instances that I witnessed in which Tijuana police disproportionately targeted (im)migrant women whose bodies signified masculinity, such as Vicky and Esther. Thus, while performing normative familial formations can provide some protection from state violence, not everyone can or should have to engage in such strategies of resistance.

Finally, the collaboration between the local Mexican authorities and the US Border Patrol speaks to the issue of "coordinating state violence beyond the limits of the nation-state." Lytle-Hernández argues that this practice developed between Mexico and the United States to secure the interests of both nations. This collaborative relationship attempts to discipline (im)migrant women into normative sexual and gender norms as part of nation-building projects and thus should be understood as what Cantú (2009) terms "regimes of normalization."

In the previous chapters, I focused on understanding formations of violence that are gendered and racialized and result in criminalizing and disciplining (im)migrant women. In this respect, relationships among the state, advocates, and individuals develop and result in violence against (im)migrant women. These relationships participate in the separation of (im)migrant women's productive and reproductive labors. I take the following chapter as an opportunity for self-reflection and consider some of the ways that even the most progressive spaces can reinforce relationships of power. It provides a critique of advocacy work within prison abolition and suggests a reflection of this work that, at various moments, participates in passing judgment over who does and does not deserve to be advocated for.

## CHAPTER 5

# Emancipation Is Not Freedom:
# A Reflection and Critique of Advocacy Abolition

Throughout this book, I focused my analysis on a range of factors responsible for the criminalization of Latina (im)migrants and the ways in which this criminalization contributes to rendering them vulnerable to various forms of marginalization and violence. I have largely drawn from the prison abolition movement's vision of creating a world without prisons where someone's freedom and life are not dependent on the captivity and death of others. As part of the prison abolition movement, many individuals and organizations engage in advocacy work along with and on behalf of people in prison. This work attempts to address immediate concerns that include issues of physical and psychological violence, health care, family separation, education, and "unjust" sentences.[1] However, at the same time, I am deeply cognizant of the many structural limitations presented to the prison abolition movement, and I am critical of many of its strategies, particularly in relation to advocacy abolition.

I take this chapter as an opportunity to reflect on my involvement in prison abolitionist efforts, particularly advocacy abolition, and my observations of the limitations this type of organizing encounters. Rather than argue against this work, I am driven to carry out this analysis as a way to reflect on Derrick Bell's notion of Racial Realism (1992). Bell, and critical race theorists in general, posit that the promise of racial equality, particularly for Blacks, is not a realistic goal. From its very foundation, the juridical construction of the United States was inherently white supremacist. Any legal successes that appear to further the goal of racial equality are appropriated by the systems being challenged and often are used to maintain white dominance (373). According to Bell, acknowledging the permanency of racialized subordination, "*en-*

*ables us to avoid despair, and frees us to imagine and implement racial strategies that can bring fulfillment and even triumph"* (374, emphasis in original). It is worth citing Bell at length:

> While implementing Racial Realism we must simultaneously acknowledge that our actions are not likely to lead to transcendent change and, despite our best efforts, may be of more help to the system we despise than to the victims of that system we are trying to help. Nevertheless, our realization, and the dedication based on that realization, can lead to policy positions and campaigns that are less likely to worsen conditions for those we are trying to help, and will be more likely to remind those in power that there are imaginative, unabashed risk-takers who refuse to be trammeled upon. Yet confrontation with our oppressors is not our sole reason for engaging Racial Realism. Continued struggle can bring about unexpected benefits and gains that in themselves justify continued endeavor. The fight in itself has meaning and should give us hope for the future. (378)

Here, Bell maintains that not only is transcendent change probably not going to occur, but also that those who struggle for change and their efforts may be appropriated and coopted to maintain white dominance. Bell suggests that the realization that communities of color are unable to escape subordination may open up new possibilities for struggles. However, the struggle in itself is worth the effort because, according to Bell, "struggle for freedom is, at bottom, a manifestation of our humanity that survives and grows stronger through resistance to oppression, even if that oppression is never overcome" (378).

In this chapter, I reinforce Bell's arguments and note that while the advocacy abolitionist work in which many of us engage will probably not bring about freedom from oppression, it does provide alternative visions and understandings of how to be with one another. Furthermore, our resolve to resist *is* a manifestation of our humanity—despite the fact that we know that we will more than likely fail, we continue to struggle.

## Road Map

I begin this chapter by engaging with scholarship on social movements and advocacy work to contextualize the limitations encountered by the prison abolition movement and specifically nonprofit advocacy organizations. I then offer my story of how I became involved in prison abolition as it provides a direct link to the development of the contemporary prison abolition movement. This is followed by a discussion of the theoretical work of Joy James and her critique that, rather than freedom, advocacy abolition mainly offers emancipatory opportunities.

The core body of the chapter is then divided into two main parts, which primarily draw on my experiences with Justice Now and California Coalition for Women Prisoners (CCWP). I address the structural limitations encountered by advocacy abolition by engaging in critiques of prison reform as serving to further institutionalize prisons in society. Mainly, I highlight how even though a vision of creating a world without prisons drives advocacy abolition, it is restricted. The restrictions on advocacy abolition include inadequate resources, the sheer number of people in prison, and the constant response to the transformations that prisons undergo. All of these factors place structural limitations on this work and make it largely emancipatory since it fundamentally involves engaging the state on behalf of people in prison.

I then shift the focus to individual advocates, especially myself. I highlight how, even with the best of intentions, advocacy work can result in additional pain, both for the person being advocated for and the advocate. I provide specific examples of how advocates are able to exert power over people in prison, noting this as emancipatory since it is up to the advocate whether to provide such support. In addition, I also discuss the structural constraints that this work presents in cases where advocates write letters of support for trials and parole hearings. In these letters, supporters reinforce the legitimacy of the state while simultaneously attempting to demonstrate the merit of the person being advocated for. Finally, I share my experiences with Nyla, a woman incarcerated in Central California Women's Facility (CCWF) and eventually deported to Mexico. Our interactions and my attempts to provide hope for Nyla resulted in contributing to the pain she was already enduring.

I conclude the chapter by drawing parallels between the strategies of the (im)migrant rights movement and those of advocacy abolition. Advocacy abolition, which is largely emancipatory, often has to engage the state on behalf of people in prison and, in doing so, demonstrate their deservingness. This resembles the efforts of (im)migrant rights advocates who are at pains to demonstrate the deservingness of (im)migrants to civil society and the state.

## Social Movements, Nonprofits, and
## the Potentialities of Transformative Change

In significant ways, the challenges encountered by advocacy abolition are characteristic of the dilemmas transformative social movements face overall.[2] In order to address social problems, long-term solutions are necessary. However, this suggests that social movements need to find ways to sustain themselves over long periods of time. Long-standing sustainment often implies resorting to private and public funds, which generates a relationship where outside forces, through their contributions, exert some control over the trajectory of these movements.

The retrenchment of the welfare state shifted the responsibility for people's social well-being from the public to the private, and nonprofit organizations are central to this equation. Movements often form nonprofit organizations as a means to address social needs and create change (Rudrappa 2004, 6). In *The Revolution Will Not Be Televised: Beyond the Non-Profit Industrial Complex* (2009), INCITE! Women of Color Against Violence discusses many of the limitations that structure the work of nonprofit organizations. It argues that while there is significant support to fund projects that serve as safety valves to maintain the status quo, little support exists for efforts that target structural disparities. Furthermore, the work of running nonprofits, even if they begin as radical projects, often converts individuals from radical activists into bureaucrats, consumed with the everyday labor of sustaining their organizations and maintaining their positions.

Several scholars who, as part of their research, participate in advocacy efforts make critiques similar to that of INCITE! (Garfield 2005; Rudrappa 2004; Villalón 2010). For example, Rudrappa (2004) addresses the role of nonprofit organizations working to address ethnic and racial inequalities. She argues that in the post-1970s age of multiculturalism, the celebration of "difference" serves to obfuscate social disparities. Ethnic and racial nonprofit organizations often participate in these celebratory projects. Rudrappa examines two particular ethnic organizations and argues that they "intentionally and involuntarily articulate with the late-twentieth-century American nation state in particular ways whereby race resistance is smoothly cleansed into ethnic assimilation" (6). Rudrappa terms this "benign incorporation" and argues that it ultimately functions as a politics of containment that limits the work of these nonprofits (7).

Garfield (2005) and Villalón (2010) examine organizations that attempt to address violence against women. While Garfield focuses on the experiences of Black women, Villalón addresses Latina (im)migrants. Both authors consider the mainstream anti-violence against women movement and highlight some of the drawbacks in its strategies. They both argue that by using the broad category of "women," this movement constructed women as a homogenous group and failed to consider the particular contexts and histories that shape lives differentially. Other social markers—including race and ethnicity, sexuality, and class—form women's experiences of violence. The erasure of differential subjectivities resulted in this movement seeking a standardized solution to the issue of violence against women. A central response was turning toward the state to make men accountable for their violent actions against women, a model that Harris (2011) and Law (2014) term "carceral feminism." The result was an increased punitive presence of state authorities in the lives of women of color and their communities. Furthermore, this strategy did not reduce, but actually increased, the violence against women of color.[3]

Differential subjectivities shaped in important ways how the state responds to the violence encountered by women. For example, both Garfield and Villalón examine the 1994 Violence Against Women Act (VAWA), which is understood as a victory of the anti-violence against women movement. VAWA largely placed the responsibility of addressing violence against women in the hands of the state. Garfield maintains that this shifted the production of discourse over violence against women from the social movement to the state; in other words, government-sponsored discourse replaced advocacy-led discourse (2). As a result, the organizing logic of VAWA is that it is the state's responsibility to punish men in order to secure women's safety. In this sense, "justice" for women is equated with punishment against men. Furthermore, government-sponsored discourse limits the understanding of violence to interpersonal forms, mainly domestic violence and sexual assault, and erases both the role of the state in structuring these relationships and its role as primary perpetrator.

Villalón demonstrates that while VAWA and the Victims of Trafficking and Violence Protection Act (VTVPA) have the potential to benefit undocumented Latina (im)migrants affected by interpersonal violence by providing means to legalize their status apart from their male partners, women who are perceived as less worthy of citizenship encounter barriers to obtaining such benefits. She highlights the role of nonprofit organizations in passing judgment over individuals' worthiness. For example, she notes that employees at the organization where she was an advocate admitted that they were pressured by grant requirements to process large numbers of applications, which limited how much time they could spend on cases. Individuals who were "difficult," including people who could not produce documents quickly, had difficulties securing childcare during their appointments, and were emotional during their meetings, were undesirable. Furthermore, Villalón demonstrates that individuals who are perceived as normative, including people who appear to adhere to heteronormativity, tended to be prioritized and fared better in the process. The available means to address the situation of undocumented Latina (im)migrants in violent relationships provide incomplete and problematic solutions to what are structural problems.

In this chapter, I consider some of the limitations encountered by advocacy abolition. Similar critiques can be advanced of advocacy abolition as those discussed above of social movements, particularly social movements that resort to creating nonprofits. These critiques include how the pressures created by a lack of resources for transformative work shape the efforts of prison abolition advocacy organizations. Also included are the constraints of being consumed with the everyday maintenance of nonprofit organizations, the cooptation by the state of the discourses of social movements, the necessity to turn to the state for remedies, the erasure of the role of the state in creating conditions of violence and perpetuating violence, the involvement of the state in processes of social valuing, and, often, the inability to implement structural change.

## The Origins and Significance of Critical Resistance

In part, my critique of advocacy abolition has been informed by my personal involvement in the prison abolition movement, which I initially became involved in as a student activist. In what follows, I present the origins of my involvement. These details not only provide a context for my experiences but also serve to bridge the early foundations of the prison abolition movement's critique of the Prison Industrial Complex (PIC).

In the United States, prison abolition is not a new issue. It has roots in the movement to end slavery, as well as other forms of unfreedom, such as segregation.[4] During the 1970s, critiques of prisons as sites of repression flourished as incarceration rates increased. The growing number of political prisoners served to highlight the repressive nature of prisons. This in turn ignited demands for reform and, in some cases, the end to the prison system.[5] Due in part to the neoconservative backlash of the 1970s and 1980s, prison abolition efforts waned for a time. In the late 1990s, the movement ascended again. Critical Resistance: Beyond the Prison Industrial Complex, a conference held in Berkeley, California, in September 1998, brought together more than thirty-five hundred scholars and community/student activists. Attendees engaged in a dialogue centered on the issue of prisons. The conference provided a critique of the US prison system as a profit-driven hybrid of public and private interests that targets poor communities of color for imprisonment, labeling this development the "Prison Industrial Complex." As a whole, the conference served to re-invigorate prison abolition efforts nationwide and inspired the creation of several prison abolition organizations, including Critical Resistance (CR). As an organization, CR continues the labor that the conference incited.

The analysis provided by the CR conference was adopted by youth and used to organize against California's Proposition 21, the Gang Violence and Juvenile Crime Prevention Initiative, on the March 2000 ballot. Proposition 21 expanded the criminal legal system's reach into communities of color by intensifying the criminalization of youth of color as gang members.[6] Anti-Proposition 21 organizing highlighted how the energy of the 1998 CR conference transcended its three-day trajectory. Employing the critique introduced at the conference, especially with respect to the notion of the PIC, youth across California waged the "Schools Not Jails" campaign. They demanded that resources be invested in education rather than in their criminalization and incarceration. The Schools Not Jails campaign of 2000 functioned as my introduction to prison abolition, a movement in which I continue to be involved. My participation with prison abolition efforts include an internship with Justice Now in the summer of 2004, membership in the California Coalition for Women Prisoners (initiated in 2008), and involvement with the organization Critical Resistance, specifically, the Los Angeles chapter of Critical Resistance and their Leadership, Education, Action, and Dialogue (LEAD) project. LEAD provides educational workshops through a reentry program for women leaving prison. Together, these experiences are responsible for providing critical insight into some of the dilemmas presented to the prison abolition movement.

In this chapter, I draw from my experiences as a participant observer, holding to the vision of radical freedom provided by prison abolition. However, I simultaneously consider some of the ways that advocacy work, under the charge of bringing relief to people in prison, reinforces relationships of power and oftentimes unintentionally extends some of the pain that people in prison already experience. My intent is not to argue that these efforts should not be carried out. Rather, I am driven to engage in this self-reflection and analysis because if we are serious about social justice struggles, we have to examine power relations, including our potential complicity.

## Emancipation and Freedom

Prison abolition scholar Joy James greatly informs my critique of prison abolition advocacy. In *The New Abolitionists: (Neo)Slave Narratives and Contemporary Prison Writings* (2005), James draws connections between enslavement and the current US prison regime, as well as slavery abolition and prison abolition movements. James links narratives of imprisoned intellectuals by providing visions of freedom beyond our current carceral state. Through an assemblage of experiences and voices of people in prison, she points to not only a vision of a world without prisons, but also a radical definition of freedom.[7] Most significantly, James provides a critique of advocacy abolitionism that differentiates between *emancipation* and *freedom*:

> Advocacy abolitionism and its narratives by nonprisoners—like state narratives—grant only "emancipation." Neither advocacy abolitionism nor state abolitionism can control or create "freedom" for the captive . . . we can note that despite the common assertion that "Lincoln 'freed' the slaves," the President issued proclamation and legislation to establish emancipated people. Emancipation is *given* [emphasis in original] by the dominant, it being a legal, contractual, and social agreement. Freedom is taken and created. It exists as a right against the captor and/or enslaver and a practice shared in community by the subordinate captives. . . . Freedom is an ontological status—only the individual or collective—and perhaps a god—can create freedom. (xxii–xxiii)

According to James, advocacy abolition remains coercive because it relies on emancipation and can only be granted by others, particularly the state.[8] In other words, the state can recognize and allow imprisoned people to be regarded as something beyond that of criminal. Advocacy abolition attempts to demonstrate the humanity of imprisoned people to the state by advocating for forgiveness, clemency, mercy, and justice—all acts that may or may not be afforded, depending on the state's judgment. Advocacy abolition relies on civil society to pressure the state to create changes to ameliorate the conditions for people in prison. This implies that advocacy abolition does not only have to show prisoners' deservingness to the state, but also has to make this case to civil society.

## Structural Limitations of Advocacy Abolition

One of the fundamental issues with regard to prison abolition focuses on the effectiveness of the movement's strategies and, more specifically, the question of reform versus abolition. Many scholars make the argument that prison reform tends to contribute to the expansion of prisons. As Michel Foucault noted: "One should recall that the movement for reforming the prisons, for controlling their functioning is not a recent phenomenon. It does not even seem to have originated in a recognition of failure. Prison 'reform' is virtually contemporary with prison itself: it constitutes, as it were, its programme" (1995, 234). Prison abolitionist and philosopher Angela Y. Davis makes a similar critique: "[P]rogress in prison reform has tended to render the prison more impermeable to change and has resulted in bigger, and what are considered 'better,' prisons" (Davis and Rodriguez 2000, 217). In this sense, reform serves not only to solidify prisons in society, but also, significantly, to expand the prison system itself.[9] In response to this phenomenon of prison reform, anti-prison scholars and activists put forward the notion of prison abolition—the idea of crowding out prisons to the point of their obsoleteness (Davis 2003).

Prison abolition organizations that do advocacy work, such as Justice Now and CCWP, face a conundrum. While the vision and mission of these organizations is to struggle toward a world without prisons, they attempt, at the same time, to address the immediate concerns of people in prison, and, in these particular cases, women. Essentially, they simultaneously engage in abolitionist and reformist efforts. These organizations are acutely mindful of the critique of prison reform as further socially expanding and entrenching prisons. However, they are also driven by a sense of urgency caused by the situation of people in prison.[10]

Key concerns faced by advocacy abolition are linked to the structural limitations placed on this type of work. In part, the ideological construction of people in prison as undeserving criminals limits the amount of resources that advocacy abolition organizations can obtain for their efforts. Consequently, they are constantly struggling to sustain their efforts financially.[11] Furthermore, both the mass number of people in prison and their needs far surpass the resources and abilities of these organizations. These facts, coupled with the decades of law and order, hard on crime, and zero tolerance policies, make advocacy abolition a continually arduous battle. In this section, I discuss the structural limitations advocacy abolition organizations confront. The examination reinforces James's critique of advocacy abolition because, structurally, this work is mainly limited to emancipation.

My first experience in advocacy efforts within the prison abolition movement was an internship in 2004 with Justice Now, which provided insight into the relationship between (im)migration control and incarceration. Justice Now is a prison abolition organization that provides advocacy for people in women's prisons.[12] At the same time, it engages strategies to create a world without prisons, in part by organizing to prevent the creation of additional carceral sites. Part of their mission is to address the immediate needs of people incarcerated in women's prisons, including parental rights terminations, poor health care, and sexual violence.[13]

During my first weeks as an intern, I vividly remember how taken aback I was by the sheer number of letters addressed to Justice Now from incarcerated people asking for assistance. The first task of interns was to filter the letters and assess the appropriate response. This included responding to individuals to let them know that the organization was unable to address their particular needs, referring them to other potential resources, requesting additional information in order to further assess their cases, or sending them forms for legal visits. In many respects, we had to pass judgment over who would receive our attention. The need was so great and our resources were insufficient. I remember the feeling of extreme debilitation at having to send letters informing people that the organization could not provide them with support.

As the only Spanish-speaking intern that summer, I was assigned to advocate for five Latina (im)migrants in prison with parental rights termination cases. Because my role was that of an advocate, I was involved in obtaining information on their cases in order to adequately advocate for them. In most cases, the organization had to know the facts of their criminal case in order to provide support. This meant building their file and acquiring as much information as possible, including the facts leading up to their imprisonment, their particular (im)migration history, the type of relationship they had with their partners and children, and the names and addresses of relatives. When I was not researching policies around their cases, I was writing letters to judges and contacting lawyers, social workers, and family members. Although this was my responsibility as an intern, I also felt personally driven as our actions within the organization could affect whether these individuals lost their children to the state.

One of the most memorable moments of the internship was a conversation with a social worker who informed me that the children of Laura, one of the people for whom I was advocating, had been adopted. Informing Laura of this news was one of the most difficult things I have ever had to do. Despite the fact that the children had been in the adoption process long before I came into the picture, I felt guilt for not being able to help Laura keep her children. It seemed to me that, as advocates, we served as a valve to mitigate anxiety by providing desperate individuals with some hope, most likely preventing many from having complete breakdowns. Ultimately, the illusion that someone was advocating on their behalf helped to keep them going during very difficult times. I use the word "illusion" because for many, given the structural conditions of their incarceration, very little could be done, as exemplified by Laura's case. During this internship, I learned that, although the individual needs of people in prison should be addressed to attempt to end or mitigate violence, especially with respect to the destruction of their families, the transformation first and foremost *must* be structural.

Another important limitation presented to prison abolition organizations—particularly those involved with advocacy work—consists of responding to the prison system and the various transformations it undergoes. For example, in May 2011, the Supreme Court ruled the overcrowding in California's prisons unconstitutional. In part, the ruling reaffirmed the critiques that prison abolitionists and reformers had been advancing for many years: mainly, how overcrowding has dire effects on people in prison, including a significant increase in mental and physical health problems.[14] Here the work of advocacy abolition makes evident how the state's appropriation, in this case through the Supreme Court, functions to reform the prison system, while simultaneously socially engraining it even further.

To meet the prison reduction requirements ordered by the Supreme

Court, Governor Brown signed Assembly Bills (A.B.) 109 and 117, known as Public Safety Realignment (Realignment). Multiple strategies are employed in Realignment to reduce the number of people incarcerated, including maintaining custody of people convicted for non-violent, non-serious, non-sex offenses in county jails rather than placing them in prison. Another strategy is the transformation of Valley State Prison for Women (VSPW) into Valley State Prison (VSP) (CDCR 2012, 26). VSP became what the California Department of Corrections and Rehabilitation (CDCR) terms a "Level II Sensitive Needs Yard (SNY) institution" for individuals vulnerable in men's prisons. Beginning in October 2012, transfers took place: people incarcerated at VSPW were transferred to other women's prisons and people marked as vulnerable in men's prisons were transferred to VSP (*Correctional News* 2013).

People considered vulnerable in men's prisons include individuals leaving a gang; people who have been raped, especially if they identify as openly gay or gender non-conforming; people convicted on charges of child molestation; and former cops. While the process was designed to address the needs of these vulnerable groups, it made the women's situation worse, according to some of the individuals at VSPW. CCWF, located across the street from VSPW, was the only women's prison that initially received individuals carrying out life sentences. The first concern among the people with whom I worked rested on the complete destruction of the life created in VSPW. Although the transfer does not seem significant compared to other aspects of prisons, the conversion participates in the dehumanization of those most affected—people incarcerated at VSPW. The conversion meant separating people who had created relationships, removing all possessions that were not registered under the person's name, as well as the burden of starting anew at another prison. As Clara, who had been incarcerated at VSPW noted, prisoners are not treated as humans, but rather as state property.

Some people at VSPW held enemy concerns toward individuals housed at CCWF—meaning that documented evidence exists that there are disagreements between people in prison that may result in threats or violence. Several individuals at VSPW feared being transferred to CCWF and instead requested a transfer to other facilities, particularly California Institution for Women (CIW) in Corona. However, because claiming enemy concern presented obstacles for CDCR in the VSP transition, several individuals reported that their counselors deterred them from making these claims. According to some individuals, their counselors would inform them that if they claimed enemy concerns, they would be assigned to administrative segregation (AdSeg), which is solitary confinement. For individuals with upcoming parole hearings, being placed in a space where they have enemy concerns could easily result in disciplinary punishments that could ultimately contribute to being denied parole. Simultaneously, being placed in solitary confinement could potentially be noted as a sign of lacking rehabilitation and also be used to deny parole. In addition, while VSPW had dozens of programs for people to demonstrate their rehabilitation to the parole board, CCWF's minimal programming further worsened their possibilities for parole. Many reported that, due to the stress that the conversion placed on them, including the upheaval of their communities and lives, they had mental breakdowns, panic attacks, and were in an overall crisis.[15]

The city of Chowchilla, home to both prisons, responded negatively to the transition. In large part, in contrast to the families of people incarcerated in women's prisons, the families of people incarcerated in men's prisons tend to move closer to the prison where loved ones are held. The city of Chowchilla expressed great concern about the consequences associated with the introduction of these families to the area due to the stigma associated with the families of incarcerated men.[16] In January 2012, as a result of the legal battle carried out by Chowchilla, a judge placed a restraining order against the CDCR that prevented it from making any of the changes needed to transition VSPW to a men's prison. Although several extensions were requested and granted for the restraining order, a judge suspended the order during a hearing in October 2012, allowing the CDCR to begin the transition. The battle to stop the transition of VSPW into VSP consumed energy from Justice Now and CCWP. Justice Now submitted an amicus brief for a December 2012 hearing to make the point that the transition had tremendous negative consequences for people in prison, including significant overcrowding. Other organizations, including CCWP, signed on to the brief.

There are several key issues that bear greater scrutiny in relation to California's Realignment plan. First, maintaining custody of incarcerated people in county jails does not address the issue of prison overcrowding. Instead, the use of county jails simply shuffles people from one carceral space to another while failing to reduce the overall number of people held.[17] Second, while the conversion of VSPW to VSP was intended to address the particular needs of vulnerable groups of people incarcerated in men's prisons, individuals imprisoned at VSPW faced detrimental consequences as a direct result of the conversion. Society must ask why women and gender non-conforming individuals incarcerated at VSPW were sacrificed during the transition and ask what the long-term consequences of this strategy entailed. Furthermore, California's Realignment highlights the critique that prison reform expands and further institutionalizes prisons in society.[18] By transforming VSPW into VSP, and thus a sensitive-needs institution, the CDCR appears to reform itself by addressing the needs of groups considered vulnerable in men's prisons, but it worsens conditions in women's prisons.

Society witnessed the strategy of legitimizing the prison system through reform on previous occasions when incarcerated women and advocates argued that prisons were designed with men in mind and thus, the particular needs of women were not met. The CDCR reacted by creating gender-responsive carceral sites.[19] Prison abolitionist Rose Braz addresses this in "Kinder, Gentler, More Gender Responsive Cages: Prison Expansion Is Not Prison Reform" (2006). Braz discusses Governor Arnold Schwarzenegger's plan to expand the prison system by creating community correctional facilities to house women convicted of non-violent offenses. Braz examines some of the texts produced by the state in relation to this proposal and demonstrates that the state couched the proposed changes within a feminist rhetoric and presented them as prison reform intended to address women's specific issues. Braz maintains, "The biggest pitfall of gender responsiveness in relation to imprisonment is that gender responsiveness fails to challenge the notion of prison as an institution that can effectively 'address the issues of women'" (87). What appears as prison reform essentially serves to make prisons more impermeable. This is the case with the 2006 CDCR plan cited by Braz, and it is the case with the Realignment process.

Justice Now, CCWP, and other prison abolition organizations make the critique that reform tends to expand the prison system. However, as the example of the transition of VSPW to VSP demonstrates, advocacy abolition is structurally limited. The struggle to prevent the transition is essentially a request that the state keep VSPW as a women's prison. Prison abolitionists are placed in a position where they are compelled to organize for things to stay as they are. It is important to underscore that this is a decision that ultimately rests in the hands of the state, thus rendering this work emancipatory.

Together, the examples of the advocacy work that I carried out with Justice Now, coupled with the battle against the prison Realignment project in California—particularly the conversion of VSPW to VSP and the attempts to make prisons more responsive to women's needs—demonstrate the structural limitations imposed on advocacy abolition struggles. The advocacy work that I carried out during my internship with Justice Now in 2004 provided the illusion that the needs of incarcerated Latina (im)migrants were being addressed. Fundamentally, however, the organization could provide very little support. The Realignment project—in part informed by the critique of prison abolitionists and reformers marking prison overcrowding as a serious risk for people in prison—results in an increased level of violence faced by the individuals transferred from VSPW to CCWF and CIW. It also serves to legitimize California's prison system by appearing to reduce prison overcrowding while simultaneously addressing the vulnerability of particular groups of people in men's prisons. Similarly, the state appropriated critiques advanced by prison abolitionists and reformers that prisons were modeled around men's incarceration, and the response was the creation of additional carceral sites that are allegedly created on a gender-responsive model. These examples speak again to the critique that prison reform, even if driven by a vision of abolition, often serves to expand the prison system. Collectively, they underscore how the structural limitations faced by advocacy abolition organizations dramatically affect their work and restrict their ability to further the goal of ending incarceration. Even with an abolitionist vision, these efforts are often restricted to emancipatory work.

### The Power and Pain of Advocacy Efforts

From the internship with Justice Now, I began to recognize the importance of bridging the relationship between prisons and (im)migration, and thus I set out to provide this understanding in this book. I expanded my knowledge of the experiences of incarcerated Latina (im)migrants through my involvement with California Coalition for Women Prisoners (CCWP), a prison abolition organization that provides advocacy for people incarcerated in women's prisons, which has a similar vision as that of Justice Now. I joined their Compañeras Project in May 2008. CCWP created the Compañeras Project in 2005 as a way to address the particular challenges and needs of incarcerated Latina (im)migrants. Chiefly, language barriers and (im)migrant status presented distinct conditions of imprisonment. Accessing adequate health care and/or legal services becomes a difficult challenge that is further complicated when the person cannot communicate with service providers. Almost immediately, the situation intensifies when (im)migrants have to contend with placing their children with family members who may be undocumented and may lack English-speaking skills. Their almost inevitable deportation at the end of their sentence also presents significant obstacles. In an effort to address these challenges, the Compañeras Project aims to create strong relationships between Latina (im)migrants in prison and people on the outside. It attempts to do this by building leadership skills for people in prison and project volunteers as well as providing education and a knowledge base on their rights so that they can exercise some control over their situation. My involvement in the project provided me with the opportunity to examine the racialized and gendered intersection of (im)migration control and incarceration, insight that integrally informs this project and, ultimately, my critique of advocacy abolition.

In this section, I present various examples that I witnessed or in which I participated where the efforts of advocating for people in women's prisons reinforced relationships of power between the "free" and the unfree, even if unintentionally. In these cases, advocates were not only unable to create freedom for captives, but, as a direct result, the emancipatory work either resulted in advocates exerting direct power over the individual they were advocating for or, due to structural constraints, it served to legitimize the prison system, thus intensifying the pain already felt by people in prison.

In chapter 2, I presented Esther's story and demonstrated how the (im)migrant rights movement negotiated the belonging of "good" (im)-migrants. I argued that this negotiation results in the re-criminalization of "bad" (im)migrants, which Esther automatically forms a part of, given her imprisonment and identity as "criminal." I initially met Esther at a shelter in Tijuana where I conducted part of my research and developed a long-term working relationship with her. Often she would speak to me of Sonia, her partner, whom she was forced to leave behind at VSPW upon her deportation. When I informed her about my initial visit to VSPW with the Compañeras Project, she became excited and hopeful that Sonia would be part of the group. Sonia was not among the individuals I met during my first visit, but I asked about her and was informed that, although she at some point was part of the group, this was no longer the case. The following day, as I read through the Compañeras Project files, I saw her name listed on a file under "OUT," meaning that she was released from prison. However, I knew that this was not the case because, according to Esther, Sonia had some years left before her first parole hearing. I inquired and learned that a past coordinator of the project had taken Sonia off the visitation list.

According to Sonia, she and the previous coordinator disagreed on an issue, and after that, she was never called for visits again. Xiomara, who was then the volunteer coordinator for the Compañeras Project, was upset that Sonia would be taken off the list for disagreeing with the advocate and immediately added her back to the list of Compañeras to be visited. In a subsequent visit, I was able to meet Sonia. In part, the advocate's action of removing Sonia from the visitation list highlights the coercive nature of advocacy work. It reflects a relationship of dependence between advocates and those being advocated for. When Sonia disagreed with her advocate, she was dropped from the project. It is important to note that there are differences between the actions of individuals and actions that are representative of entire organizations. The examples that I provide in this section are of individuals' actions and not necessarily supported by the organization.

I witnessed a similar dynamic when Xiomara and I conducted bimonthly visits to VSPW from July 2008 through September 2012—up until the facility was transformed into VSP.[20] Throughout the visits to VSPW, additional volunteers in the Compañeras Project joined Xiomara and me. During a prison visit that I did not attend, Clara, one of the Compañeras for whom we sought to advocate, was evidently very upset and loud, particularly toward the guards. Although I am unclear about the actual details surrounding the incident, it appears that a new volunteer suggested taking Clara off the list, and by the next visit, we did not see her. Xiomara and I discussed the situation and added Clara to the list once again. At our subsequent visit, Clara shared some specifics, noting how she was upset and depressed because her sister had been recently killed in her apartment in Los Angeles by a police officer responding to a domestic violence call. Clara's behavior during the previous visit was thus related to the news of her sister's passing. Removing her from the visitation list functioned as a form of disciplining Clara, whose reaction "jeopardized" the efforts of the Compañeras Project. Both Sonia and Clara's cases highlight some of the problems of advocacy abolition in that individuals in prison must rely on their advocates to find them worthy of their efforts. Again, drawing on James's critique, this speaks to emancipation as something granted by others. In both Sonia and Clara's cases, their advocates deemed them unworthy.

However, even when individuals are deemed worthy of advocacy, as discussed in the previous section, structural limitations significantly shape abolition advocacy. In some cases, the work required of advocates means legitimating the prison system, as best exemplified by Esther's story. As noted in chapter 2, Esther was deported to Tijuana after being incarcerated in California for five years. Upon attempting to return to the United States, she was caught and detained by the Border Patrol and held in (im)migration detention for six months while she awaited a criminal trial. She was accused of crossing the border after being deported under the category of "criminal alien."

Esther requested that I write a letter to the judge on her behalf, and she asked that I address her good moral character in order to demonstrate her deservingness. Consequently, I conducted research on how to write strong letters of support for individuals facing criminal trials. One of the central recommendations made by various blogs and informational websites conveyed the importance of focusing on the individual's character, rather than on the criminal legal system. In other words, including judgments over the racism and/or classism of the criminal legal system could harm the individual's case. In Esther's letter, I could not write how race, class, gender, sexuality, and legal status informed her experiences. I could not discuss either the violence that she underwent at the border upon her deportation or the violence she experienced when she attempted to return to the United States. Nor could I write about the years of separation between Esther and her daughter caused by her incarceration and later deportation. As a result, Esther's incarceration foreclosed her permanently from ever legally reentering the United States, and thus the battle was not about claiming belonging to the United States, but rather fighting against her re-incarceration. Instead, my letter inscribed Esther within narratives of deservingness. For example, I wrote of our initial meeting:

> I found several things inspiring in Esther. Although Esther was just beginning to resettle in Mexico, she had great plans for her future, including reuniting with Elisa, her fifteen-year-old daughter. The same day I met her she secured a job working as a cook at Ocean City, a Mexican and Chinese restaurant where she worked until she attempted to come to the US. Throughout our conversation, she talked about her excitement since now she would be able to provide for Elisa, something she regretted not being able to do from prison.

In this paragraph, I present Esther as a "good" mother, trying to reunite with her daughter. I also present her as a "good" worker in an attempt to further exemplify her role as a supportive mother because her job would allow her to support her daughter. While I felt greatly compelled to provide a critique of the circumstances that led to Esther's incarceration, I was simultaneously pressed to present her within hegemonic heteronormative narratives, given that the letter could potentially contribute to Esther's tentative release. Again, this was an attempt at emancipation since, ultimately, the result of Esther's case rested on the decision of the state, personified by the judge who heard Esther's case.

In the letter, I went on to write about Esther's work at two different (im)migrant women's shelters and how the community she built among staff members reflected her good moral character. I concentrated on Esther's volunteer work at these shelters. I also wrote about how I observed her send a seventy-dollar money order to a friend in prison, asking her to purchase food and other essentials to distribute among incarcerated individuals who did not receive outside support. While this was true, I could not include the fact that her "friend" was Sonia, the intimate partner she had left behind in prison, or anything about their struggle to remain connected. The letter went on to describe the many ways that Esther supported my work, and I concluded by writing, "I end this letter with great hopes that you will consider not only Esther's criminalized act of crossing the border while undocumented, an act that she performed to reunite with her daughter, but also consider her strengths as a person. Thank you for your time in reading this letter." As noted in chapter 2, the judge sentenced Esther to twenty-six months in prison, not for having crossed the border with an aggravated felony on her record, but for the (im)migrant advocacy work she carried out in Tijuana—as presented by the prosecutor who accused her of conspiring to commit crimes against the United States. After her trial, Esther wrote and thanked me for my support, especially with respect to the letter that I submitted on her behalf. She wrote that the judge stated that the letter spoke well of her character, and, in part, influenced his decision to sentence her to twenty-six months, and not the forty-eight months sought by the prosecutor.

In many ways, my advocacy work functioned as a double-disciplining act. It forced Esther into a narrative where I attempted to present her as deserving, by stressing her "good" mothering, her work ethic, her desire to help others, and her support for me. Just as significant is what I did not write about Esther: I did not include details of what led to her incarceration, nor did I address the difficulties presented by living in (im)migrant shelters. I also did not include the fact that she was in a non-heteronormative relationship. Instead, her deservingness was predicated on representing her within heteronormative narratives of belonging. The judge could provide emancipation for Esther, if she was considered deserving. At the same time, writing the letter also served to discipline me. My work centers on providing a critique of various forms of oppressions, specifically, the criminal legal system; advocacy efforts for individuals, such as Esther, discipline what I can and cannot express in relation to the state. In order to advocate for her, I placed attention on Esther's individual merit, and the state remains uninterrogated.

Over the years, I found myself in similar situations. As part of CCWP's Compañeras Project, I worked with a group of Latina (im)-migrants incarcerated at VSPW and subsequently at CCWF. Several are carrying out life sentences and have already had or are awaiting parole hearings in the coming years. Individuals seeking parole rely on the subjective decisions of the board. During these hearings, the board takes for granted the individual's guilt. Instead, their responsibility is allegedly to make decisions about the incarcerated person's suitability to re-enter society.[21] Factors taken into consideration include:

> Counseling reports and psychological evaluations; behavior in prison (i.e., disciplinary notices or laudatory accomplishments); vocational and educational accomplishments in prison; involvement in self-help therapy programs that can range from anti-addiction programs for drugs and alcohol to anger management; and parole plans, including where an inmate would live and support themselves if they were released. (CDCR 2011)

During these hearings, individuals must demonstrate remorse by taking responsibility for their actions. Some of the people with whom I worked maintain their innocence. If they argue that they were wrongfully convicted, they are more than likely going to be denied parole because, according to the board, they lack remorse and insight. However, if they maintain their innocence at one parole hearing and later accept "their guilt," they can also be construed as deceitful. This was the case for a few of the people with whom I worked.

Part of the parole process entails providing evidence of the individual's rehabilitation. This includes family, friends, and advocates providing letters of support that speak to the individual's moral character and the impact that their release will have on loved ones and the larger community. My relationship with the Compañeras Project placed me in a situation where several of the individuals with scheduled parole hearings requested that I write letters of support for them. As in the case of Esther, I wrote these letters with their freedom in mind, which now I understand and define as emancipation. As part of their requests, the individuals provided me with the guidelines for the letters. Again, the letters needed to address the individuals' character and the positive impact they could potentially make on the community if granted parole. However, as noted earlier, letters could not speak to any critiques or injustices in the individual's case or with respect to the larger criminal legal system. Here I use a letter I wrote for Joana Blanco to demonstrate the requirements. Joana, an (im)migrant woman brought as an infant to the United States, was incarcerated in 1995 and had been denied parole on several occasions.[22]

The guidelines, which are distributed throughout the prison by incarcerated people themselves to be given to potential supporters, instruct the letter writers to state their credentials and relationship to the individual in the first paragraph. In the letter, I stressed my academic credentials and my three-year collaborative relationship with Joana as part of the Compañeras Project. In order to write her letter, I asked Joana to provide me with a detailed list of her various activities throughout her incarceration. In the second paragraph of the letter, I wrote:

> My support for Ms. Blanco's parole stems from the commitment she
> expresses to self- and social transformation. Throughout her time in
> prison she participated in various types of programming to assist her in
> her rehabilitation. Once she obtained the various skills to help with her
> own transformation, she took it upon herself to support other women
> in prison. For example, Ms. Blanco served as a Spanish Domestic Vio-
> lence Facilitator when she realized the need to have such programming
> available for the many monolingual Spanish speakers. She also forms
> part of the Narcotics and Alcohol Anonymous panel; she is a member
> of the Coalition for Cultural Awareness, which attempts to bridge cul-
> tural differences to ameliorate some of the cultural challenges that can
> lead to problems among imprisoned people; and she is also a member
> of the Longtermers' Organization, which works to provide positive op-
> tions for women imprisoned, including preparing women with long-
> term sentences to learn to cope with their situation and engage in char-
> itable events that contribute to the outside community. These are a few

of the countless examples of Ms. Blanco's services to the prison and outside community.

I cite the letter in detail because it demonstrates my effort to represent Joana as rehabilitated. This narrative, however, does not allow for a critique surrounding the circumstances leading to Joana's incarceration with respect to how race structures incarceration so that women of color are incarcerated at a higher rate than white women. It also does not allow a critique of how the parole process itself is carried out so that people of color are denied parole at a higher rate than whites (Huebner and Bynum 2008). My letter instead centers on demonstrating to the board, which represents the state, Joana's merit in the hope that I can convince them of her deservingness.

Following a discussion of the individual's merit, the guidelines instruct the letter writer to address how they will support the individual to avoid recidivism. This dynamic demonstrates how the idea of the state granting freedom is simply conditional emancipation because the previously incarcerated person can easily be re-incarcerated.

The experiences of (im)migrants seeking parole highlight the unsoundness of the parole hearing process. Faced with deportation at the end of their sentence, they are "encouraged" to provide two parole plans—one for the United States and one for their country of origin.[23] Parole plans should include a potential job and housing. Many people seeking parole have sometimes spent decades in prison. Therefore, their ability to develop parole plans poses an extreme challenge because maintaining a connection with family and friends over such an extended time, coupled with long distances, proves trying. However, the two plans requirement adds barriers for incarcerated (im)migrants because they have to create a parole plan for another country where they often have few connections.

In Joana's letter, I wrote that I could offer her practical support during her deportation. The support included meeting her at the Tijuana-San Diego border, taking her to a shelter, and connecting her with individuals who could help her secure housing and employment. I also made myself available for advice and encouragement. I concluded by stating, "I end this letter by thanking you for your time and consideration. I am positive that, if given the opportunity, Ms. Blanco will demonstrate that she is not only capable of social reintegration, but even more, she is ready to contribute greatly to the outside community."

Similar to Esther's case, Joana noted that the board was impressed with the letter during her hearing. However, again like Esther, Joana was confronted with the bad news that the state denied her parole and emancipation. Here again, there was a double-disciplining that takes place. Although I represented Joana as a rehabilitated individual who had first addressed her own problems and then took it upon herself to help others, the narrative reinforces the idea that the individual's faults led to incarceration—a model that erases structural inequalities. In the same letter, I could not address how board members are assigned the responsibility to ultimately pass judgment on who is morally worthy of being granted release; how problematic it is that the majority of board members, appointed by the governor, have a history in law enforcement, prosecution, or prison administration; or how the "encouragement" to have parole plans functions as a predictable obstacle to people's release, especially in the case of (im)migrants facing deportation who are "encouraged" to provide two plans. Most important to this conversation, however, is that Esther and Joana's cases highlight the limitations of advocacy abolition since it relies on the state to grant their release—the very state that participated in creating the conditions leading to their incarceration and structuring the parole process that maintains incarcerated individuals' need for rehabilitation.

Why do I spend so much energy addressing the letter-writing aspect of advocacy abolition? Is this the best place to address questions of justice? I decided to include this aspect of advocacy efforts because it is representative of the kind of work in which abolition advocates consistently engage. Making a written case of the deservingness of people in prison—writing letters to the state and its representatives on behalf of individuals or collective groups, submitting editorials to news outlets to bring attention to a particular situation in prison, or publishing reports and articles on their findings—consumes abolition advocacy organizations' time and energies. Thus, in providing this reflection and critique, it is significant to address this aspect of advocacy abolition efforts.

Despite the drawbacks of advocacy work, it is difficult to resist the impulse to respond when advocates witness people in situations of vulnerability. However, advocates' responses can have unintended consequences that, rather than provide relief, ultimately make them participants in the pain suffered. That is the case for Nyla and me. Nyla was on the initial list of Compañeras to be visited by the group of volunteers. When I first joined the Compañeras Project in 2008, I wrote to everyone on the list, introducing myself and letting them know of our visit.

The letter to Nyla was returned since she was transferred to CCWF. I wrote to Nyla at CCWF, and she was very excited to hear from someone. She had (im)migrated to the United States from Mexico in 1968 as a child and had never returned. She spent almost eight years in prison, beginning in 2001, and she was later deported to Mexico in June 2009.

Through letters, Nyla shared her fear of being deported. "I have to admit I am a little afraid of my future. I have no family in Mexico. I would very much like to know what's in store for us immigrants as far as (the) INS goes." I wrote to Nyla and told her what I had observed of other people leaving prison and facing deportation. I noted that I could provide her with information of possible shelters where she could stay following her deportation. In response, Nyla wrote, "I don't really know too much about what's going on out there, I just know that INS is picking me up, and I will be deported. To be honest instead of being happy because I will be getting out, I am dreading it. I've been told that the detention centers are hell." Nyla's fears had some bearing on her interactions with her family. She noted:

> I really haven't mentioned it to them that I will be deported. I just can't bring myself to telling them I won't come home. My youngest son has mentioned it, but then I tell him not to worry. When I try to talk to my mom about it she tells me they can't do that, that I been here all my life. All she tells me is don't sign anything. All I know is that I don't want to stay in the detention center longer than I have to.

Nyla tried to comfort her son by telling him not to worry, while Nyla's mother attempted to comfort Nyla by telling her that she could not be deported because she had been in the United States all her life.

In her letters, Nyla wrote her story, sharing details about why she was in prison and what had motivated her to do what she did. Our relationship, even though limited to correspondence, centered not on providing actual advocacy, but instead on my offering Nyla hope. She wrote, "Can you tell me any success stories about some of the women that have been deported? Like, are they living and adjusting well to living in Tijuana. I need to hear something positive. That will keep my negative thoughts from thinking I will end up homeless under some bridge in T. J." Responding to the advocate's impulse to provide some form of relief, I initially wrote of Esther, who was deported after being in prison. At the time, Esther found herself in a good place as she had obtained a place to live, secured a job, and was active in organizing for (im)migrant rights. Toward the end of her sentence, Nyla asked me how Esther was doing; she wanted to hear how well she was. I had to respond to Nyla to let her know that Esther was caught after trying to cross the border and placed in (im)migration detention. I could not provide Nyla with the story she hoped to hear. While not officially that of an advocate and an incarcerated person, our relationship was one based on offering Nyla information on the outside world; she depended on me to offer hope. By initially responding to her appeal and writing about Esther's achievements, I set us both up for disappointment. It was a hope short-lived as Esther was re-imprisoned. Nyla's response was one of disappointment to know that Esther, who found herself in a similar situation as Nyla, did not "make it."

My efforts to provide relief for Nyla resulted in furthering her pain as I relayed the additional violence inflicted onto Esther by the state. Esther's narrative reminded Nyla of the conditionality of her *freedom*, especially if she attempted to re-enter the United States. Nyla and I remained in contact after her deportation. Although she was in a relatively comfortable situation since her family lived in San Diego and helped her secure a place to live in Tijuana where they were able to visit consistently, she shared how difficult it was to live by herself away from her family and friends. She often contemplated crossing the border illicitly. However, Esther's experiences of re-incarceration served as a reminder of the potential consequences.

In this section, I discussed various examples that demonstrate some of the dilemmas that advocacy abolition presents, and particularly ways that advocates themselves participate in relationships of power and, at times, in furthering pain. I discussed Sonia and Clara's examples, which underscore the role of advocates as judges who decide whether the captive being advocated for is worthy of their efforts. Again, this is emancipatory work that is *given*, rather than freedom, which according to James is created and taken by captives themselves. I also presented examples that demonstrate the structural limitations imposed on advocates who, in order to advocate on behalf of individuals, often participate in legitimating the prison system. This is particularly noted in the letters of support requested during criminal trials and parole board hearings. Finally, I note some of the unintended consequences of offering hope to captives when, structurally, all advocates can attempt to do is support them in obtaining conditional emancipation.

## Conclusion

In this chapter, I advance that self-reflection needs to be central to anti-prison organizing efforts by remaining cognizant of how advocacy abolitionists reify relations of power. Doing so moves society closer to the abolitionist objective, which James advances as freedom rather than emancipation. In chapter 2, I provided a critique of the (im)migrant rights movement, which reinforces racialized and gendered boundaries of belonging by claiming that "(im)migrants are not criminals, (im)migrants are hard workers." I demonstrate that this utterance deploys the disciplinary discourse of "good" (im)migrant, which does not transform hierarchical relations of power. Rather, it attempts to expand and limit who can and cannot access power—a process that innately deems some bodies as irrecuperable. Likewise, advocacy abolition participates in similar maneuvers that rely on emancipatory methods to advocate for people in prison. I suggest that prison abolitionists need to recognize that, in many instances, advocacy abolition is coercive since it often relies on the advocates' and the state's recognition of the humanity of people in prison.

Returning to Joy James's distinction, freedom, unlike emancipation, "is taken and created" and does not rely on the dominant for recognition. The question remains, how is freedom taken and created within a carceral society? Given the various limitations discussed throughout this chapter, should there be no advocacy abolition? This last question is extremely challenging to address. While keenly in tune with James's critique of advocacy abolition as restricted to emancipation, I found that witnessing the incomprehensible situation of people in prison makes it difficult to argue against such work. I opt to view this situation through Derrick Bell's perspective and maintain that the very act of resisting oppression, recognizing well in advance that we are probably going to lose, still has value because it is a manifestation of our humanity. To not resist, knowing what we know, is to participate in our own dehumanization and that of others. However, as people and communities engaged in struggle, we also have to be mindful and self-reflective to appreciate when, and to what extent, we are being complicit, whether intentionally or not, in reinforcing relationships of power.

In the conclusion, I turn toward A New Way of Life (ANWOL), a re-entry program dedicated to providing resources for women leaving prison. Its aim is not only to prevent their re-incarceration, but also to provide them with the resources necessary to thrive socially and, in doing so, address the fundamental concern in locating ways to end violence against women of color, both inside prisons and in the communities they come from. In other words, ANWOL is involved in struggles to bring about structural changes. I believe this program is a significant model of prison abolition on the ground. ANWOL engages the notion of radical freedom, by which I mean a collective struggle, defined, created, and carried out by former captives, with a vision that resists processes of valuing between deserving and undeserving bodies.

CONCLUSION

# Envisioning and Performing Freedom

*What would it take* to end violence against women of color?
INCITE! WOMEN OF COLOR AGAINST VIOLENCE (2006)

*We call on social justice movements to develop strategies and analysis*
*that address both state AND interpersonal violence, particularly violence*
*against women. Currently, activists/movements that address state*
*violence (such as anti-prison, anti-police brutality groups) often work*
*in isolation from activists/movements that address domestic and sexual*
*violence. The result is that women of color, who suffer disproportionately*
*from both state and interpersonal violence, have become marginalized*
*within these movements. It is critical that we develop responses to gender*
*violence that do not depend on a sexist, racist, classist, and homophobic*
*criminal justice system. It is also important that we develop strategies*
*that challenge the criminal justice system and that also provide safety for*
*survivors of sexual and domestic violence. To live violence-free lives, we*
*must develop holistic strategies for addressing violence that speak to the*
*intersection of all forms of oppression.*
INCITE! WOMEN OF COLOR AGAINST VIOLENCE AND
CRITICAL RESISTANCE (2006)

This study is my struggle to engage the discussion generated through
the efforts of organizations such as INCITE! Women of Color Against
Violence and Critical Resistance. I attempt to contribute to the discussion of state and interpersonal violence lived by women of color and
our communities by considering the experiences of criminalized Latina
(im)migrants. My first step is to place the (im)migrant rights movement

in conversation with the prison abolition movement. The next step is to maintain the engagement in the labor initiated and developed by the prison abolition movement of imagining and generating radically alternative ways of being with each other. In other words, through this study, I link (im)migrant rights activism to the abolitionist agenda and reinforce the notion that taking on the work of political imagining is central to working toward a different social world. I maintain the urgency of engaging such labor because, as the experiences of (im)migrant women demonstrate throughout this study, at stake are consequences that too often materialize through violence.

The dialogue generated in this study between the prison abolition and (im)migrant rights movement contributes to the dismantling of the visionary borders in which the (im)migrant rights movement seems to be fixed. As highlighted with the recent presidential executive action on (im)migration, the deployment of dominant (im)migrant rights narratives is appropriated to implement changes that have dire consequences for many, including increased militarization of the border and interior enforcement (Office of the Press Secretary 2014a). Thus, the struggle for (im)migrant rights continues.

It is important to consider how changes are imagined and to bear in mind their consequences. A significant example to reflect on is the Immigration Reform and Control Act (IRCA) of 1986, the last major (im)migration reform that provided legalization for a considerable number of people. This reform provided almost 3 million undocumented (im)migrants with permanent residency and allowed them to petition for their families. Simultaneously, as discussed in chapter 1, IRCA drastically militarized the border, which contributed to the violence and mounting number of deaths there. The focus of the (im)migrant rights movement on a path to legalization is limited by the hegemonic good/bad (im)migrant dichotomy. This binary valorizes hard work and innocence—categories that are gendered, racialized, sexualized, and classed—and reinforces the expendability and violability of people who find themselves on the bad (im)migrant side of this dichotomy. A legalization process based on this dichotomy, as the example of IRCA demonstrates, fails to address the root causes of (im)migration. As long as this is the case, undocumented (im)migration will continue to form part of the constitution of the United States, and the violence undergone as a result of nation-building will persist.

The significance of the prison abolition movement is its focus on dismantling binaries that construct recuperable and irrecuperable subjects.

Rather than attempting to find recuperable "criminals," this movement interrogates the state's ability to create criminal subjects and the social, political, and economic implications of such a creation. This movement demonstrates how imprisonment is a central tool used in the classed, gendered, sexualized, and racialized governance and formation of US society. Drawing from this movement's ideological work, this study suggests that if the (im)migrant rights movement seriously wants to engage the work of ending the violence lived by (im)migrants, it has to reengage in the labor of imagining visions of belonging and of freedom that not only deviate from but also dismantle the good/bad (im)migrant dichotomy. I maintain that this movement needs to focus on the state's ability to produce (il)legality and criminality. This move shifts attention from (im)migrant personal responsibility and merit toward the state's involvement in producing "illegal" (im)migrants who assume the status of ideal neoliberal laborers—exploitable, disposable, and violable bodies. It also underscores how the deployment of such binaries participates in the racialized policing of US citizenship.

The analysis centers on the experiences of jailed, imprisoned, detained, and deported Latina (im)migrants. Rather than attempting to locate criminality within (im)migrant women—for example, by asking why Latina (im)migrants engage in crime; to what extent do they engage in crime; how has their engagement in crime changed over time; or how does Latina (im)migrants' engagement in crime compare to other groups—the framing of the research question itself shifts attention away from individual actions. Instead, it centers on destabilizing the objectivity of law and demonstrating that the construction and deployment of crime participates in the racialized, gendered, sexualized, and classed organization of society. The analytic lens turns on systems and statecrafting projects that manifest themselves in the experiences of (im)migrant women. The study discloses how the criminalization of Latina (im)migrants is central to US racialized neoliberal governance. Neoliberal transformations construct this group as ideal neoliberal laborers due to their exploitability, which is secured through their legal existence in or closeness to (il)legality. However, moments arise when their actual physical exclusion is deemed necessary, such as in moments of national "crisis," and measures are employed to secure their removal. This study demonstrates how the criminalization of (im)migrant motherhood, which draws on the histories of Black motherhood, employs notions of state dependency that prove to be productive in constructing (im)migrants in general as dependent and public charges. This production ideologically enables strategies of removal, such as attrition through enforcement policies meant to make (im)migrant life unlivable.

The experiences of criminalized Latina (im)migrants underscore the limitations of the (im)migrant rights movement's strategies of expanding the category of recuperable "good" (im)migrants. One, (im)migration laws privilege (im)migrants who are conceptualized as self-sufficient, which is largely a masculinized construction that has overwhelmingly benefited men over women. Two, (im)migrants deported under the category of "criminal alien" are permanently banned from the United States and thus foreclosed from recuperability. Thus, (im)migrants legally categorized as criminals are permanently barred from US legal and social belonging, rendering them irrecuperable.

Furthermore, this movement's strategies fail to address the ways in which interpersonal violence interconnects with state violence. As the experiences discussed throughout demonstrate, (il)legality is differentially lived, and too often the status of "illegal," which is a social construction, enables interpersonal forms of violence. Examples of such violence include the cases of undocumented (im)migrant women in relationships of domestic violence and people violated by individuals while attempting to cross the border. Additionally, these strategies neglect to account for the role that other nation-states assume in determining (im)migrants' experiences. As the case of Mexico displays, the criminalization of (im)migrants travels with them, and they face additional forms of violence even in their countries of origin. A path to legalization for a select number of people fails to address these structural concerns. Instead, it provides a temporary valve to relieve some of the pressure built up over years, which will continue if the root causes of (im)migration are not addressed. This includes the central role that (il)-legality assumes in providing the United States with exploitable and disposable laborers who generate wealth for the (white) nation.

If, as a society, we decide to seriously take on the labor of ending violence against (im)migrants, the question then becomes, how can we engage in the political labor of imagining radically new ways of conceptualizing social belonging while addressing the immediate concerns of (im)migrants? Once again, the prison abolition movement provides some direction.

Here I draw greatly from the work of prison abolitionist Angela Y. Davis and her conceptualization of abolition democracy. Davis borrows this notion from the work of W. E. B. DuBois and his analysis of the end of slavery. DuBois argues that the end of slavery was insufficient to create democracy. According to Davis:

> DuBois pointed out that in order to fully abolish the oppressive conditions produced by slavery, new democratic institutions would have to be created. Because this did not occur; black people encountered new forms of slavery—from debt peonage and the convict leasing system to segregated and second-class education. (Davis and Mendieta 2005, 75)

Davis draws parallels to the prison system, which is rooted in slavery, and argues that prison "has become a receptacle for all of those human beings who bear the inheritance of the failure to create abolition democracy in the aftermath of slavery" (75). Thus, abolition democracy is about the unfinished project of ending slavery. More than destructive, in the sense of the physical elimination of prisons and other carceral sites, the goals of prison abolition, according to Davis, should be to create "an array of social institutions that would begin to solve the social problems that set people on the track to prison, thereby helping to render the prison obsolete" (97). Put differently, "the creation of new institutions that lay claims to the space now occupied by the prison can eventually start to crowd out the prison so that it would inhabit increasingly smaller areas of our social and psychic landscape" (Davis 2003, 108). The following discussion highlights some of the prison abolitionist work that centers on creating spaces that lead to crowding out prisons.

Some years ago I was fortunate to be invited to form part of Leadership, Education, Action, and Dialogue (LEAD), which is a project of the Los Angeles chapter of the prison abolitionist organization Critical Resistance. The purpose of LEAD is to provide educational workshops for women who recently left prison and are housed at A New Way of Life (ANWOL), a reentry project located in Watts, California. I was involved for several months during 2008 and rejoined the efforts in early 2012. Participating with LEAD allowed me to witness prison abolition on the ground. Taking from these experiences and the project's own narrative located on its official website, the following provides a schematic discussion of the visionary *and* practical work of ANWOL to promote social reentry for women leaving prison.

Susan Burton, a formerly incarcerated woman, created ANWOL. It is important to provide some of her history and what led to the creation of the project. Susan's initial incarceration was in great part prompted by the loss of her five-year-old son, who died after a police officer accidentally ran over him when he was playing outside his home. At that point, Susan began to self-medicate with alcohol and drugs to deal with the pain of her loss. This led to her cycling through prisons for approximately fifteen years. These experiences guided her decision to establish ANWOL in 1998 to support women in similar circumstances.

Susan's story reflects Joy James's critique of emancipation versus freedom. In chapter 5, I discuss James's critique of advocacy abolitionism, where she argues that this form of prison abolition work can only grant emancipation, which she maintains is "*given* by the dominant, it being a legal, contractual, and social agreement" (James 2005, xxii–xxiii, emphasis in original). In contrast to emancipation, James presents a definition of freedom, which, she argues, is "*taken* and created. It exists as a right against the captor and/or enslaver and a practice shared in community by the subordinate captives. . . . Freedom is an ontological status—only the individual or collective—and perhaps a god—can create freedom" (xxiii). In the example of Susan and the creation of ANWOL, it is evident that emancipation is not enough. Susan was *emancipated* from prison, but, as a formerly incarcerated woman, she partakes in the process of performing freedom by working against racial, economic, and gender oppression and creating a space for recently released women to also perform and work toward freedom.

The goal of the organization is to provide a living environment for formerly imprisoned women that is conducive to their ability to not only be reintegrated, but also to thrive in society. This is evident in the values promoted by the project:

> We believe all people, including former prisoners, are valuable and should be treated with dignity and respect.
>
> We believe that prisons and punishment are not effective tools for positive change and that treatment better serves the individual and society.
>
> We believe everyone who is given a chance, regardless of the past, can excel with support and community intervention.
>
> We believe in the power of mentoring to help people achieve their dreams. By motivating, supporting, and creating opportunities for others to excel, mentors are valuable role models that build confidence and self-esteem.
>
> We believe in the ability to empower people by educating them

about systems of societal dysfunction, thereby transforming their beliefs. (A New Way of Life 2010)

The values espoused by the organization highlight its visionary work. According to the statement, every member of society is indispensable. In other words, there are no expendable bodies; everyone has something to contribute if offered the opportunity.

In addition to providing a vision of social belonging in which everyone, regardless of past actions, is considered a valuable member of society, ANWOL engages in the practicality of implementing such a vision and contributes to creating a world where imprisonment is not our response to acts constructed as deviant.

The project provides services in three stages: getting started, getting established, and getting independent. The first stage, getting started, includes:

pick ups from prison and jail; clothing and toiletries; assistance in obtaining government documents, including California identification card, Social Security card, and Birth Certificates; weekly 12-step meeting onsite; assistance in obtaining health and mental health services; opportunity to participate in day treatment; assistance in meeting conditions of parole-probation; and transportation assistance.

The second stage provides:

assistance with family reunification, including court advocacy, mother-child activities, educational resources for children, child support, and parenting workshops; referrals to career and educational counseling; and educational programming on topics such as financial literacy, the criminal justice system, recovery and personal growth, health and nutrition.

Finally, the third stage offers "assistance in searching for permanent housing; support in developing a drug-free lifestyle; and advocacy and leadership training." These services provide necessary support for the social reintegration of formerly imprisoned women. Simultaneously, the project promotes "alternative sentencing, reduced reliance on incarceration, and more resources for reentry." In other words, the organization is productively constructive as it strives to meet the immediate needs of women leaving prison, and it is simultaneously productively destructive by working against the expansion of the criminal legal system that absorbs so many members of our communities.

Central to ANWOL's goals are leadership development and political education that de-naturalizes imprisonment. Rather than engaging in neoliberal narratives of personal responsibility, the project incorporates political consciousness as a goal and a means for self- and social transformation.

> It has been our experience that the process of developing a critical analysis of the social, political, and economic circumstances that contributed to one's incarceration can be a powerful tool in healing from the trauma of imprisonment, addiction, and violence. Further, becoming a participant in efforts to change those conditions for better, can contribute to a process of self-discovery, understanding, and empowerment.

The educational and leadership development offered by ANWOL is coordinated in partnership with Critical Resistance. The LEAD Project encourages participants to contextualize their experiences of imprisonment within larger processes of social organization that contributed to their situations. In other words, rather than asking them for confessions, rather than trying to understand "why they did what they did," the project destabilizes the common sense of criminalization and imprisonment. It offers political education and leadership development so that "not only do project participants better understand the connection between the prison system and the many issues that confront them upon release, but they are also provided opportunities to gather necessary skills to become effective change agents in their own communities."

The example of ANWOL provides cues for strategies that social movements can engage to move beyond dominant dichotomies of recuperable and irrecuperable members of society. The project engages the labor of imagining every member of society as indispensable: everybody matters and everyone has something to contribute. Furthermore, the project also takes into account the immediate needs of formerly imprisoned women. While endeavoring to address these needs, it also attempts to one, provide the necessary skills and opportunities to ensure that the participants are able to independently meet their needs in the future, and two, work toward transforming society so that the experiences of participants do not replicate themselves in the lives of other women.

What insight can ANWOL offer the (im)migrant rights movement? A central argument made throughout this study is the need to move away from dichotomies that work to pass judgment over "deserving" and "undeserving" bodies. Instead, this movement needs to account for the ways that the state differentially structures experiences for people through ideas of race, gender, class, sexuality, and nation. In terms of the (im)migrant rights movement, this raises the question of (im)migrants who fall on the "bad" side of the dichotomy. How can organizing take place without passing judgment on "deserving" and "undeserving" (im)migrants? If, as ANWOL argues, no one is expendable, then what does this mean in terms of (im)migrant rights organizing?

From this study, two main interconnected concepts that help to racially police US belonging can be identified: state dependency and criminality. Part of the work that the (im)migrant rights movement needs to emphasize in its strategies is deconstructing these ideas by shifting from the message that "(im)migrants are not criminals, (im)migrants are hard workers" toward marking state dependency and criminality as social and state productions used in the racialized, gendered, classed, and sexualized organization of society.

Just as significant as developing strategies that do not reinforce dichotomies that designate bodies as deserving and undeserving is addressing the immediate needs of (im)migrant communities. However, this labor needs to incorporate an abolitionist agenda that radically addresses the causes of (im)migration and the significant role that the United States has in generating (im)migration through statecrafting projects that further neoliberal capitalist interests. (Im)migrations should be real choices rather than movements shaped by structural forces, such as neoliberal capitalism. This may seem idealistic, but how are we to practically create a different social world if we do not engage in the important labor of imagining other ways of being with each other and perform radical freedom?

Susan Burton and ANWOL provide guidance for those of us concerned with ending violence against women of color and our communities. Performing freedom entails developing a critique of the state as a perpetrator of violence, which shifts attention away from individuals' merit. Susan and ANWOL work precisely with individuals who are considered socially undeserving; they do not only attempt to address individual needs, but they also seek to contribute to women's understanding of racial, economic, and gendered oppression so that they create change for themselves. Susan's story demonstrates how the lived experience of captivity informs how she collectively performs freedom, not only for herself, but also for others. Her story provides insight for those of us concerned with social justice, and it directs us to potential approaches that we can use and, in the process, perform radical freedom.

# Notes

## Introduction

1. Gonzales (2014) argues that this movement had been developing for a long time prior to H.R. 4437. However, this legislation served as a catalyst for the massive mobilizations (50).

2. For discussions on the ways in which (im)migration policies and enforcement participate in racially designing the nation, see Daniels 2004, López 2006, Ngai 2004, Hing 2003 and 2009, Moloney 2012, and Zolberg 2006. For analyses that also take into consideration gender and sexuality, see Canaday 2011, Collins 1999, Fujiwara 2008, Luibhéid 2002, and Park 2011.

3. I draw the notion of unmaking legality from historian Mae Ngai (2004). Ngai demonstrates how the Immigration Act of 1924 initially created the legal category of "illegal alien," which continues to shape (im)migration policies in the United States. For additional discussions on the social construction of (il)legalities, see in general Dowling and Inda 2013 and Menjívar and Kanstroom 2013.

4. Rather than place responsibility on the (im)migrant rights movement and advocates, I intend with this discussion to note the limitations of the ideological framework available for advancing justice for (im)migrants. I continue this discussion in chapter 2.

5. See Calavita 1992, Guerin-Gonzales 1994, Gonzalez 2001, Gonzalez and Fernandez 2002, Sassen 1992, 14–19 and 1996 for discussions on how the United States participates in creating and maintaining (im)migration patterns.

6. Obama's executive action does several things. First, it expands the Deferred Action for Childhood Arrivals (DACA) enacted June 15, 2012. DACA required individuals to be under thirty-one years of age and physically present on the date the policy was enacted; to be younger than sixteen before they entered the United States; to have maintained continuous residence in the United States since June 15, 2007; to be "currently in school, have graduated or obtained a general education development (GED) certificate, or (be) an honorably discharged veteran of the Coast Guard or Armed Forces of the United States"; and to have no serious criminal record or pose "a potential threat to

national security or public safety" (US Citizenship and Immigration Services 2012). Obama's 2014 executive action removes DACA's age requirements and moves the residency requirement to January 1, 2010. These changes increase the number of people eligible for relief under DACA. Second, it grants deferred action and the ability to work legally to parents of US citizens and legal permanent residents who have lived in the United States since January 1, 2014, and who are not priorities for removal, which includes individuals who are considered to pose a threat to national security, border security, or public safety. For an extended list of the various priorities, see US Citizenship and Immigration Services 2014b.

For the purpose of this study, it is important to highlight that individuals with criminal records are considered priorities for detention and removal. There are three levels of priority (Johnson 2014a). Level one includes individuals caught attempting to enter the country unlawfully, individuals involved in gang activities, and individuals with felony convictions. Level two includes individuals convicted of three or more misdemeanor offenses from separate incidents; individuals convicted of a "significant misdemeanor," which is defined as "an offense of domestic violence, sexual abuse or exploitation, burglary, unlawful possession or use of a firearm, drug distribution or trafficking, or driving under the influence; or if not an offense listed above, one for which the individual was sentenced to time in custody of 90 days or more"; individuals who entered the country undocumented after January 1, 2014; and individuals who are considered to have abused their visa or visa waiver programs. The final level, priority three, is for individuals who were issued a final order of removal on or after January 1, 2014. These priorities in Obama's executive order highlight the continued use of criminality to maintain levels of (im)migrant detention and deportation.

7. Alexander (2010) makes the argument that being marked as a criminal enables discrimination similar to that historically lived by Blacks. She writes:

> Today it is perfectly legal to discriminate against criminals in nearly all the ways that it was once legal to discriminate against African Americans. Once you're labeled a felon, the old forms of discrimination—employment discrimination, housing discrimination, denial of the right to vote, denial of educational opportunities, denial of food stamps and other public benefits, and exclusion from jury service—are suddenly legal. As a criminal, you have scarcely more rights, and arguably less respect, than a black man living in Alabama at the height of Jim Crow. (2)

8. While I draw from the framework presented by the prison abolition movement, I recognize that on the ground, abolition efforts, similar to the (im)migrant rights movement, often engage in politics of inclusion to advocate for people in prison. This practice can reproduce hierarchies of deservingness. I engage this conversation in depth in chapter 5. However, I maintain that the difference is the ideological vision of the world that each movement affords. While the dominant framework within (im)migrant rights organizing centers on inclusion into existing social relations, such as granting legalization to undocumented (im)migrants, prison abolition advances radical transforma-

tion, such as creating the institutions necessary to provide everyone opportunities to thrive.

9. Some of the interests furthered by mass criminalization and incarceration include efforts to maintain hierarchical racial structures without explicitly employing racial language; politicians' attempts to appear "hard on crime" to garner political power; corporate interests in the privatization, and thus increased profitability, of corrections; and state efforts to advance the construction of carceral sites as a way to address poverty and unemployment.

10. The invention of the term "illegal aliens" has its origins in the 1882 Chinese Exclusion Act, which was designed to bar Chinese from entering the United States (Ngai 2004, 202).

11. The racialized social construction of the "illegal alien" is exemplified in Ngai's discussion of the production of Asians as "racially ineligible for citizenship" and evidenced in the 1882 Chinese Exclusion Act. It was also evidenced in the "barred Asiatic zone" created in 1917 by Congress to exclude most Asians from migrating to the United States. Ngai notes that the 1870 Nationality Act extended citizenship to former slaves, thus limiting citizenship to Blacks and whites and disallowing those who did not fit these categories from obtaining citizenship (Ngai 2004, 37–38).

12. Espiritu (2003) presents a similar argument through her notion of "differential inclusion." She maintains that rather than simply excluding (im)migrants racially constructed as undesirable, the United States includes them under particular conditions that benefit the nation.

13. Exemplary to this shift is the 1996 Welfare Reform Act, which was intended to move recipients from welfare rolls to the labor market. The state attempted to accomplish this by requiring them to begin working after two years of receiving assistance and placing a five-year limit for people to access welfare benefits throughout their life (Fujiwara 2008, 35).

14. The 2008 presidential election of Barack Obama and his 2012 reelection served to consolidate the image of the United States as a post-racial society.

15. Fujiwara (2008) provides a critique of the Welfare Reform Act of 1996 and the welfare-to-work programs it created. She notes that mothers who accessed welfare were forced to leave the home to make ends meet and citizenship was essentially re-defined. Fujiwara writes, "Wage earning came to define one's standing as a responsible citizen—which means that one is a citizen only if one 'earns'" (35).

16. Some scholars may argue that neoliberal capitalist transformations are global phenomena, and thus, focusing on race in the way that I do is not accurate. My argument largely centers on the ways the United States deployed racial ideologies to promote neoliberal capitalist policies and practices and how mass criminalization became a central tool in this process. My contention is that, from its very foundation, capitalist accumulation in what came to be the United States is a racial project made possible through the subjection of indigenous and Black bodies.

17. See Welch 2000 and 2002, Hernández 2008, and Rodríguez 2008.

18. H.R. 4437 exemplifies the blurring between civil and criminalized activities. The Border Protection, Antiterrorism, and Illegal Immigrant Control Act not only attempted to categorize undocumented crossings as felonies,

but also sought to classify any aid offered to undocumented (im)migrants as a crime. However, what pro-(im)migrant voices often neglect is the fact that the blurring between civil and criminal matters to racially organize society has a much longer history in the United States. This is especially evident in the development of Black codes in the post–Civil War era that criminalized Blacks as a means for re-enslavement.

19. The racialization of this project is evident, for example, in Immigration and Customs Enforcement (ICE) raids where non-white citizens are rounded up alongside undocumented (im)migrants (Becker and McDonnell 2009; Hing 2009).

20. This is the case, for example, with "My Brother's Keeper," an initiative of the Obama administration intended to create opportunities for young boys and men of color who are perceived to be disproportionately affected by punitive policies (Office of the Press Secretary 2014b).

21. Cacho (2012), while not engaged in an explicitly abolitionist framework, provides a useful understanding of the limitations of engaging in practices of valuing by demonstrating that attempts to value are relational and violent.

22. The city of Chowchilla based the demographic information on January 2012 figures from the Department of Finance (Chowchilla, 2013).

23. In late 2012, VSPW was transitioned to Valley State Prison (VSP), a men's facility.

24. Key works that developed and advanced feminist standpoint theory include Nancy Hartsock's "The Feminist Standpoint" (1983); Dorothy Smith's *The Conceptual Practices of Power: A Feminist Sociology of Knowledge* (1990); and Sandra Harding's *Whose Science? Whose Knowledge?* (1991) and *The Feminist Standpoint Theory Reader* (2004).

25. Patricia Hill Collins's 2000 *Black Feminist Thought: Knowledge, Consciousness, and the Politics of Empowerment* and Gloria Anzaldúa and Cherríe Moraga's 2002 (first published in 1984) *This Bridge Called My Back* are seminal works that advance feminist standpoint theory to consider how various factors—including race, gender, sexuality, and class—inform an individual's knowledge and understanding of the world.

26. In chapter 2, I expand on the (im)migrant rights movement and interrogate some of its complexities.

27. I owe the insight, which now seems commonsensical, of terming this oppressive entity the "criminal legal system" (rather than the criminal justice system) to Natalie J. Sokoloff and our conversations at the Feminist Perspectives on Incarceration and Detention Workshop, University of Illinois, Chicago, September 3–5, 2014.

28. Casa del Migrante parallels the work that Instituto Madre Assunta performs, but focuses on servicing (im)migrant men.

**Chapter 1**

A previous version of this chapter was published in *Social Justice* 36, no. 2 (2010): 7–20.

1. The 1976 and 2007 numbers represent the first and the last years included in the "Historical Trends" reports provided by the California Department of Corrections and Rehabilitation. However, more recent numbers demonstrate a significant drop in the number of people incarcerated. Women accounted for 6,594, or 4.8 percent, of a prison population of 136,783 during the 2012 calendar year (California Department of Corrections and Rehabilitation 2013). Since 2009, decreases in incarceration rates have been a trend in the United States in general. However, we began to see the numbers increase again in 2013 (Carson 2014).

2. In contrast to women, 19,964 men were incarcerated in California in 1976 and 160,028 in 2007. This represents approximately a 702 percent increase. Thus, women faced incarceration at a higher rate than men.

3. In 1976, Latinas constituted 18 percent of the overall number of imprisoned women in California (California Department of Corrections 1997), which paralleled the representation of Latinas/os in California's overall population (Gibson and Jung 2002). By 2007, they made up 29.2 percent of women in prison (California Department of Corrections and Rehabilitation 2008b), which was actually a smaller percentage than their approximately 34 percent representation in the overall population (California Department of Finance 2013).

4. In comparison to Latinas, Black women constituted 30.3 percent of women incarcerated in California in 1976 (California Department of Corrections 1997) and approximately 7 percent of California's overall population (Gibson and Jung 2002). By 2007, they were 33.5 percent of women in California prisons (California Department of Corrections and Rehabilitation 2008b) and approximately 6 percent of the overall population (California Department of Finance 2013). In other words, despite the fact that between 1976 and 2007, Black women's representation in the overall population slightly decreased, their representation in prisons increased. In contrast, white women were 48.3 percent of women in prison in 1997 (California Department of Corrections 1997) and approximately 50 percent of the overall population (California Department of Finance 2013). In 2007, they were 36.8 percent of women in prison (California Department of Corrections and Rehabilitation 2008b) and approximately 42 percent of women in the overall population (California Department of Finance 2013). Thus, white women are less likely to be imprisoned, particularly in relationship to Black women.

5. *Policing the Crisis: Mugging, the State, and Law and Order* (Hall, et al. 1978) is often credited with demonstrating the malleability of criminality. In this seminal work, the authors argue that the state generated racialized fear of crime. While they address the British context of the early 1970s, their framework has proven extremely productive in the examination of the US context of mass criminalization.

6. See in general Richie 2012 for an extended discussion of these historical changes.

7. I include individuals with actual holds and those identified by the US Immigration and Customs Enforcement as potentially being an (im)migrant and thus deportable.

8. California prisons have been scrutinized over coercive sterilization pro-

cesses against women in prison. This practice clearly exemplifies how prisons serve as sites for reproductive control. I elaborate on this discussion of sterilizations in California prisons below in note 21.

9. "Latinidad" refers to the development of a pan-Latina/o identity that recognizes that there are common histories that bind Latinas/os, including European colonization. While similarities exist, Latinidad also acknowledges the differences among Latinas/os and resists essentialization.

10. Fujiwara (2008) contends that foreignness performs as a proxy for race. Thus, it is not (im)migrants' foreignness that is at the heart of nativist and anti-(im)migrant ideologies and practices, but rather their non-white racialization (xix–xxiii). See also Hing 2009.

11. Elena R. Gutierrez's 2008 *Fertile Matters: The Politics of Mexican-Origin Women's Reproduction* is a book-length study that examines the construction of Latinas, particularly Mexican-origin women, as racial threats to the nation.

12. The deportation of individuals classified as criminal aliens exemplifies Gilmore's argument (1998 and 2007) that prisons become a *fix* for *excess* produced by neoliberal policies and practices. In this case, (im)migrant women who assume the status of mothers become racialized neoliberal *excess* and their criminalization, particularly their incarceration, enables their deportation.

13. A significant number of scholars examine historical and contemporary Chicana/o/Latina/o experiences of criminalization and state violence. These include the role of the state in the extralegal lynchings of Mexican Americans (Carrigan and Webb 2013; Guidotti-Hernández 2011); the Zoot Suit "riots" and the Sleepy Lagoon murder case (Alvarez 2009; Pagan 2003; Ramírez 2009; Weitz 2010); the particular relationship of police departments to people of Mexican origin (Escobar 1993, 1999, and 2003); the criminalization of the 1960s Chicano Movement activists (López 2003); and particular experiences of Chicanas (Diaz-Cotto 2006). For a discussion of the global criminalization of Latinas, see Diaz-Cotto 2005. See in general Mirandé 1990, Oboler 2009, Olguín 2010, and Romero 2001.

14. For additional discussions on slavery's centrality to the development of early capitalism, see Baptist 2014, Krishnaswami 1992, Wallerstein 2011, and Williams 1994.

15. Parenti (2002) argues that California prisons are part of the political economy of the city of Los Angeles. Prisons have a direct impact on Los Angeles, and the pain and deviance produced in prisons "excrete" into the city (49). As part of his analysis, Parenti provides the example of California's Corcoran prison where the prison guards and administration intentionally created confrontational situations, termed "gladiator fights," primarily between different racial groups. Guards violently responded to these situations, often with lethal force. Parenti cites that between 1989 and 1998, 187 imprisoned men were shot by Corcoran prison guards, resulting in thirty-nine deaths (50). He goes on to discuss other forms of violence carried out by guards, including sexual abuse as a form of torture.

16. Michelle Brown (2005) discusses the spectacle of violence at the Abu Ghraib prison in Iraq, which was made public when images of US soldiers

physically and sexually abusing Iraqi prisoners were exposed in 2004. She also briefly discusses the Guantanamo military prison, located on a US naval base in Cuba, where prisoners of war are held, many indefinitely and without any criminal charges. They are forced to endure various forms of torture and violence. Brown maintains that spaces such as Abu Ghraib and Guantanamo, outside of the territorial United States, are possible because the ideological and material conditions for their existence were already established within the borders of the United States. She argues that prisons are liminal spaces that are simultaneously "inside and outside the constitutional boundaries of law, belonging to (in fact, invented by) but not of the United States" (974). In other words, prisons are contradictory spaces where ideologies such as freedom and democracy are apparently safeguarded through incapacitation and violence.

Whitehorn and Day (2007) and Pinar (2007) make a similar argument. Whitehorn and Day maintain that torture and abuse are "ordinary" practices in US prisons that have become acceptable "standard operating procedure," which extends abroad in the context of US global captivity. Similarly, Pinar situates the Abu Ghraib incident within US history: "the abuse of Iraqi prisoners in Abu Ghraib becomes more fully intelligible when situated in cultural traditions of racialized torture in the United States, among them lynching, the convict-lease system, and abuse by prison guards" (290).

17. James (2007) maintains that in considering the relationship of Blacks and indigenous people to the United States, "this nation has never known democracy in the absence of some form of institutional captivity—warfare and policing become more dynamic and, hence, more relevant to deciphering and rewriting the dominant political template" (xiv).

18. See also Glenn 2002 for a comprehensive examination of how the rights and privileges of white citizens were constructed by denying these to women, poor people, and people of color.

19. Legal scholar Maria L. Ontiveros (2004 and 2007) makes a similar argument that chattel slavery was central in constructing the US labor market. Chattel slavery epitomized the commodification of human beings into objects that could be bought, sold, used, and disposed of with few ramifications. The process of commodification was made possible through their dehumanization via ideas of racial inferiority.

Ontiveros argues that (im)migration-related policies today serve a similar purpose. She cites the 2002 example of Hoffman Plastic Compounds, Inc. v. National Labor Relations Board, where the Supreme Court ruled that certain remedies available to citizens and documented workers are not available to undocumented workers (2004). In this case, an undocumented (im)migrant was laid off for participating in union organizing. The National Labor Relations Board found that he was terminated wrongfully and awarded him back pay. However, in response, the Supreme Court ruled that since the employee had obtained employment illegally, and the Immigration Reform and Control Act of 1986 made this action criminal, he could not be awarded back pay. Ontiveros notes that this ruling creates a "two-tier system of labor rights in America—one tier for documented workers and one tier for undocumented workers" (652). She makes the case that current state (im)migration policies, and specifically the *Hoffman* decision, participate in commodifying (im)migrants, particularly racially brown bodies, and create a slavery-like system. In this system, undocumented (im)migrants find themselves outside legal protection. See also Perea 2011, who examines the 1935 National Labor Relations Act, which excluded agricultural and domestic workers who were predominantly Black. He argues that these labor relations developed during slavery and demonstrates how these exclusions continue to this day and disproportionately affect Latina/o workers.

20. See Morgan 2004 for an extended discussion of enslaved Black women's experiences as both laboring mothers and laboring workers. Morgan discusses how enslaved Black women were both producers, in the masculinized sense of labor, and reproducers of laborers (their enslaved children). Their commodified bodies represented both immediate available capital as well as hopes for future wealth (83).

21. See Flavin 2007 for further discussion on the legacies of slavery in the regulation of Black women's reproduction.

22. A report produced by the Center for Investigative Reporting (Johnson 2013) addressed the issue of the coerced sterilizations of women in California prisons. The findings show that between 2006 and 2010, 148 women received tubal ligations, and in none of these cases did the doctors obtain the proper state approvals. The logic that led to the sterilization of women of color until the 1970s was similar to that employed to perform these procedures. In response to the state spending $147,460 between 1997 to 2010 on sterilizations, Dr. James Heinrich, one of the doctors involved, is quoted in the report: "Over a 10-year period, that isn't a huge amount of money . . . compared to what you save in welfare paying for these unwanted children—as they procreated more." As Heinrich's reasoning highlights, the criminalization of state dependency provides the logic for preventing incarcerated women from reproducing.

23. Wacquant (2010) further expands on the notion of incarceration as a means to contain Blacks displaced from the neoliberal labor market. He connects slavery, the Jim Crow era, and the production of the "ghetto" and argues that ghettos and prisons are in a symbiotic relationship.

24. The increased role of undocumented (im)migrant labor after the enactment of federal legislation in the 1960s that ended de jure segregation mirrors the period after the end of slavery when Asian (im)migrants, particularly Chinese, were sought to aid in developing the West. What we witness in these two moments is that when the exploitation of Black labor is reduced, (im)migrant labor assumes an increased significance.

25. James (2007) addresses the late 1960s and early 1970s shift toward policing and massive incarceration. She maintains the significance of this moment in shaping US state violence: "conflict between law and order and rebellion frame or disrupt an American prototype for normative state violence" (xiv). See also Alexander 2010.

26. See Blackmon 2009 and Oshinsky 1997 for broader discussions of neo-slavery post-Reconstruction.

27. See Beckett 1997; Burton-Rose, Pens, and Wright 1998; Dyer 2000;

Herivel and Wright 2009; and Selman and Leighton 2010 for further examinations of the profitability of prisons.

28.  In *The First Civil Right: How Liberals Built Prison America* (2014), political scientist Naomi Murakawa disrupts the commonsense understanding that the prison buildup took hold in the 1960s. She argues that civil rights liberalism, beginning in the 1940s, was foundational for prison buildup. Murakawa demonstrates that, in great part, the federal government's attempts to safeguard Blacks from violence (hence the book's title) developed into the federal correctional system that captures and warehouses predominantly people of color. She joins the legacy of critical race theorists who maintain that for people of color, not only is justice not to be found within US liberal democracy, but also the very ideals espoused by liberal democracy erase the ways in which they are subjugated. While cognizant of Murakawa's argument, I still mark the late 1960s as a significant moment because this is when the massive capturing of non-white bodies begins to materialize.

29.  Alexander (2010) provides a critique of the law and criminal legal system as colorblind and demonstrates that race-neutral language, such as law and order, sustains white supremacy and racism.

30.  Here I note nationalist movements that directly addressed and aimed to transform the racial organization of the United States and were marked as particularly dangerous by the state. For example, J. Edgar Hoover, then director of the FBI, termed the Black Panthers "public enemy number one" and developed the Counter Intelligence Program (COINTELPRO), intended to neutralize the Black Panthers and other Black nationalist organizations. In a memo, Hoover explained that "the purpose of this new counterintelligence endeavor is to expose, disrupt, misdirect, discredit, or otherwise neutralize the activities of black nationalist hate-type organizations and groupings, their leadership, spokesmen, membership, and supporters" (James 2005, xxxiii).

However, this significant moment in US history was shaped by more than nationalist movements. Civil rights, feminist, lesbian and gay, communist, anti-capitalists, and anti-imperialist organizations and movements greatly contributed to the transformations brought about during this period. See also Churchill and Vander Wall 2001; Conway 2007; Conway and Stevenson 2011; and O'Reilly 1989 for further discussions of repression and criminalization faced by reformist and radical groups in the 1960s and 1970s.

31.  Alexander (2010) maintains that mass incarceration is a response to the Civil Rights Movement. She writes that mass incarceration is "the most damaging manifestation of the backlash against the Civil Rights Movement" (11). However, while the gains made through the Civil Rights Movement may have been the target for neoconservative policies, including mass incarceration, the ideological groundwork necessary for such policies was based on the constructed lawlessness of what were perceived to be more radical movements.

32.  Da Silva presents the concept of "the analytics of raciality" and maintains that the creation of *the racial* was central to Western modernity. Producing the racial "fuses particular bodily traits, social configurations, and global regions, in which human difference is reproduced as irreducible and unsubla-

table" (xix). In other words, the production of the racial entails ascribing social meaning to particular bodily characteristics and ideologically connecting those bodies to specific global regions. This process marked Europe as modern while simultaneously foreclosing this possibility to Europe's others. Da Silva notes that "the arsenal of raciality secures post-Enlightenment Europe's mind and social configuration in transparency, as it writes the others of Europe in a place not encompassed by transcendentality" (175). According to da Silva, "this same subaltern positioning does not unleash the ethical crisis expected by those who argue that racial subjection contradicts modern ethical principles" (175). Put differently, because racial others are written outside of modernity as irrational, uncivilized, ahistorical, and immoral, their subjection is constructed as warranted. Although racial thinking is socially constructed, according to da Silva it cannot be done away with because it is constitutive of the modern world and essential to the construction of the universal Subject.

33. Hall et al. maintain that the state and other agencies that partake in ideological production, such as the media,

> [a]re active in defining situations, in selecting targets, in initiating "campaigns," in structuring these campaigns, in selectively signifying their actions to the public at large, in legitimating their actions through the accounts of situations which they produce. They do not simply respond to "moral panics." They form part of the circle out of which "moral panics" develop. It is part of the paradox that they also, advertently and inadvertently, *amplify* the deviancy they seem so absolutely committed to controlling (emphasis in original). (52)

34. The example of LEAA in strengthening the relationship between federal and local authorities parallels more recent immigration enforcement programs and policies, including ICE's Secure Communities Program, which I discuss later in this chapter. This further highlights how the criminal legal system informs immigration enforcement.

35. Wacquant published a series of books that specifically address neoliberalism and incarceration and demonstrate that prisons assumed the role of warehousing bodies considered undesirable within neoliberal economic arrangements (2009a, 2009b, and 2010). The most affected group is poor urban Black communities.

36. It is significant to note that while unauthorized (im)migrants marked as "criminal aliens" become racial neoliberal excess and irrecuperable, their value to the neoliberal economy is reinstated once they are deported if they have skills that can contribute to the global economy. For example, the women with whom I worked, who were incarcerated in California and then deported (five total), all found work in jobs connected to the global economy. Some work in communications, where English skills are essential; others in tourism, where English skills are an asset; and yet others found jobs near the border, a space that participates in a tourism industry that caters to US consumers. Despite their deportation, they continue to be connected in very important ways to the United States through their labor. Thus, while they are legally irrecuperable in the United States, they provide important labor from abroad.

37. Ronald Reagan is in part responsible for making the image of the "welfare queen" everlasting with a 1976 presidential campaign speech citing alleged news stories. As Reagan described her, "She has 80 names, 30 addresses, 12 Social Security cards and is collecting veteran's benefits on four non-existing deceased husbands. And she is collecting Social Security on her cards. She's got Medicaid, getting food stamps, and she is collecting welfare under each of her names" (Mann, Zatz, and Rodriguez 2006, 143). Although the story was later discredited, the ideological message lived on.

38. "Anchor baby" is a derogatory term used to mark the citizenship of children born to undocumented (im)migrants as unmerited. The assumption is that these parents decide to have children in the United States so that their children will later facilitate their own legalization and access to public resources.

39. The racialized construction of the children of undocumented (im)migrant parents as undeserving is evidenced in legislative attempts to eliminate birthright citizenship (Oliviero 2013; Roberts 1996). This struggle is significant given that birthright citizenship was created through the enactment of the Fourteenth Amendment of the US Constitution and was intended to incorporate Blacks after the end of slavery. Contemporary attempts to deny children of undocumented parents birthright citizenship speaks to the continued significance of race in defining US citizenship.

40. Gutiérrez also cites Samuel Huntington's 2004 article, "The Hispanic Challenge," as exemplifying concern over Latinas' reproduction and its construction as an imminent social threat. Huntington is cited as noting that "the single most serious challenge to America's traditional identity comes from the immense and continuing immigration from Latin America, especially Mexico, and the fertility rates of these immigrants compared to black and white American 'natives'" (5).

41. The exclusion of individuals marked as "likely to become a public charge" continues in recent debates over (im)migration reform. On June 27, 2013, the US Senate passed S. 744, the Border Security, Economic Opportunity, and Immigration Modernization Act (Library of Congress 2013). Although it did not pass in the House, as of this writing, S. 744 is the closest that Congress has come to (im)migration reform in recent years. Under S. 744, legalization would take approximately twenty years. Also, individuals attempting to legalize their status would have to demonstrate "average income or resources that are not less than 125 percent of the Federal poverty level" throughout the entire time they wait to legalize their status. They would have to demonstrate continuous employment with unemployment periods not exceeding sixty days. Petitioners would also be restricted from accessing federal means-tested public benefits.

Again, while S. 744 was not enacted, it provides insight into the direction of potential (im)migration reform. It demonstrates how the "likely to become a public charge" test remains fundamental to (im)migration policy. To a lesser extent, President Barack Obama's 2014 executive action on (im)migration also speaks to how notions of dependency inform belonging. Central to the administration's desire to maintain (im)migrant accountability is the requirement that eligible (im)migrants pay their "fair share of taxes" (Office of the Press Secretary 2014a). Furthermore, this action maintains a focus on "criminal aliens," but it does not address the effect of poverty and how in many situations it informs an individual's engagement in criminalized activities.

42. Lynn Fujiwara (2008) provides an extensive analysis of 1990s policies, specifically the Welfare Reform Act and Illegal Immigration Reform and Immigrant Responsibility Act, both enacted in 1996, and examines their impact on Asian (im)migrant women, particularly Southeast Asian refugees. She maintains that "new nativist racism" drove much of the policy in relation to (im)-migration. According to Fujiwara, this racism "played off the assumed moral depravity that would follow the loss of white national cultural identity" (10). The 1990s were an important decade wherein white supremacy was reaffirmed against poor (im)migrants of color, particularly Latina and Asian (im)migrant women. While I agree with Fujiwara's overall analysis, I argue that rather than a period of new nativist racism, the 1990s were a re-articulation of existing racial ideologies historically developed in relationship to Blacks and earlier (im)-migrant communities. The strength of Fujiwara's analysis draws largely from her pointed contestation of the Asian model minority myth that complicates the (im)migration debate by inserting the experiences of these overlooked communities.

43. While Proposition 187 was voted into law by California voters and later declared unconstitutional, it reinforced the concept of undeserving (im)migrants abusing the system (Fujiwara 2008, 10), which provided the ideological foundation for the Welfare Reform Act signed into federal law by President Bill Clinton in 1996.

44. See Chavez 2008, Fujiwara 2008, Inda 2007, Lindsley 2002, Ono and Sloop 2002, Park 2011, Roberts 1996, and Wilson 1999 for extended discussions on Proposition 187 as racialized and gendered social policy.

45. Park (2011) further addresses the significance of 1996 policies, including the Welfare Reform Act, IIRIRA, and the Antiterrorism and Effective Death Penalty Act (AEDPA). She maintains that together these policies "isolated low-income (im)migrants as burdensome outsiders by reducing their presence to the sole result of US charitable generosity and therefore contributing nothing to the everyday workings of the nation-state" (3).

46. AEDPA mandated the detainment of non-citizens, both documented and undocumented, convicted of a list of crimes, including minor drug offenses.

47. See Stumpf 2006 on the construction of deportable "criminal aliens." See also Dowling and Inda 2013 and Menjívar and Kanstroom 2013.

48. See also Chacón 2007 and 2009, Kanstroom 2004, Legomsky 2007, and Miller 2003 and 2005 for further examinations of the criminalization of (im)migrants and the blurring of the lines between immigration and criminal law. See in general De Genova and Peutz 2010 for discussions on global practices of making deportable (im)migrants.

49. Removals include deportations and exclusion/inadmissibility.

50. The following year, 2013, ICE removed fewer people, 368,644 (Immigration and Customs Enforcement 2014). However, while in 2012 persons with previous criminal convictions accounted for 55 percent of individuals removed, in 2013 they accounted for 59 percent, or 216,810. This fact signifies the increased use of criminality in (im)migration enforcement.

51. Fujiwara (2008) maintains that the Welfare Reform Act was a struggle over the meaning of citizenship and belonging. This policy enforced formal citizenship as a requirement to access a number of public benefits.

52. Stumpf (2006) makes a similar argument and maintains that within the contemporary moment, public resources are distributed based on social status rather than need. This is grounded on the idea that undocumented (im)migrants "must not deserve to share in the limited pie of public benefits. The safety net of public benefits is only available to those who enjoy full citizenship" (407).

53. See Chavez 2008 for further discussion on the representation of Latina/o (im)migrants as threats to the nation.

54. Kate Doyle is senior analyst at the National Security Archive, a nongovernmental research institute and library located at the George Washington Library. She is the institute's director for the Mexico Project and Guatemala Project, projects which in part are dedicated to the declassification of secret government archives.

55. Increased dangers, such as the threat of violence and incarceration, make it so that fewer people are willing to engage in these acts. Thus, those who are willing to assume these risks often do so when there is a significant profit to be made.

56. Through IRCA, significant resources were allocated to border enforcement in general (Stumpf 2006, 289), and the INS in particular (Chishti 2007, 48).

57. The deadly consequences of the militarization of the border are noted by a 2009 report jointly published by the American Civil Liberties Union of San Diego and Imperial Counties and Mexico's National Commission on Human Rights, *Humanitarian Crisis: Migrant Deaths at the US-Mexico Border.* The report was authored by Maria Jimenez and the findings include the fact that more than five thousand people have died in the US-Mexico borderlands. The report also notes that although attempted border crossings decreased between 2007 and 2009, the number of deaths simultaneously escalated. The report regards the 1994 Operation Gatekeeper as particularly significant in generating this destructive situation. See also Cornelius 2001.

58. It is interesting to note, as does Mexican emigration scholar Cecilia Imaz Bayona (2003), that the beginning of Ernesto Zedillo's administration marks the moment when the Mexican state officially accepted its diaspora as part of the Mexican nation. The National Plan for Development (1995–2000), under the chapter on sovereignty, declared, "The Mexican nation extends beyond the territory that contains its borders. That is why, an essential element of the *Mexican Nation* program will be to promote constitutional and legal reforms so that Mexicans preserve their nationality, regardless of citizenship or residency that they have adopted" (6). Thus, while the Mexican state officially accepted the people of its diaspora, it simultaneously criminalized them through the militarization of the border, highlighting Mexico's contradictory relationship to its emigrants.

59. A similar effect took shape after the 1965 enactment of the Immigration and Nationality Act (INA), which at face value was intended to end ethnic and racial discrimination in (im)migration policies. Since (im)migration re-

strictions up to that time were directed largely at (im)migrants from Asia and the Pacific, the passing of the INA significantly expanded the number of (im)-migrants from these places (Ngai 2004, 227). Thus, the increased presence of (im)migrants after the 1986 enactment of the Immigration Reform and Control Act (IRCA) should have been no surprise since IRCA largely drew from the INA.

60. Contemporary "attrition through enforcement" strategies mirror the racialized repatriations of people of Mexican origin during the Great Depression (Díaz 2011). Mexican (im)migrant labor gained significance with the barring of Asian (im)migrants in the late 1800s and early 1900s (Gutierrez 1995, 44). However, their non-white racialization not only relegated them to the bottom of the labor market, but also enabled their subsequent forced and "voluntary" repatriation during the Great Depression (1929–1939) (Gutierrez 1995, 72; US Citizenship and Immigration Services 2014a). Similar to today, one of the strategies of repatriations was to make life extremely difficult for people of Mexican origin so that they would decide to leave. The racialized impact of these policies is evident in the fact that the majority of repatriated people were US citizens.

61. See endnote 6 of the introduction for an extended discussion of the three priority levels for (im)migrant detention and removal. Briefly, the priorities for removal include individuals caught crossing the border undocumented, people with criminal records, and in general, individuals engaged or suspected of being involved in actions that threaten US national security, border security, or public safety.

## Chapter 2

1. For a discussion of DREAMers as exceptional and their representation as good potential citizen material, see Deverall 2008; Galassi 2003; Lee 2006; Nicholls 2013; Olivas 2004 and 2009; Sharron 2007.

2. The framework used to argue undocumented youths' innocence draws from the 1982 Plyler v. Doe case where the attempt by the state of Texas to deny education to undocumented children was held unconstitutional (Lee 2006, 243–244). In part, the decision relied on the notion that legal status is unfixed. By denying these children an education, the court argued that Texas would be creating a caste-like system where the life opportunities of undocumented children (perceived as potential citizens) would be limited (Deverall 2008, 1265; Motomura 2008, 2041–2042). The ruling also maintained children's innocence in their entrance into the United States and placed this responsibility on their families, particularly their parents.

3. See also Chávez 2013; Gonzales 2014; Lara, Greene, and Bejarano 2009; Lawston and Murillo 2009 for critiques of (im)migrant rights inclusionary politics.

4. In 1903, W. E. B. DuBois theorized the conditions of Blacks in the United States and maintained that, rather than being understood as people with problems, Blacks are constructed as "a problem people" (1995, first pub-

lished in 1903). Thus, Blacks are regarded as inherently deviant, and to this day, Blackness remains the signifier of criminality and deviancy.

5. James (2007) discusses some of the problems with antiracist organizing by "white antiracists" and "people of color." She maintains that these are "amorphous groupings that mask the ethnic chauvinism and anti-black racism that lie within [such organizing]. Such formations can provide a rainbow prism of hatreds and envy solidified by a refusal to 'bow down' to blacks and their demands for recognition based on 'exceptionalism'" (6). James marks a uniqueness of Black bodies as "targets for excessive force and the penal site." She asks "What does it mean when 'people of color' or antiracist whites wear the black body to exercise their grievances and outrage at white supremacy but maintain their distance (and disdain?) for the antithesis of whiteness" (6)?

The (im)migrant rights movement often draws from the legacy of Blacks' struggles. For example, in 2012, (im)migrant rights activists drew from the Freedom Rides of the Civil Rights Movement and carried out the "no papers, no fear" freedom bus ride. They began in Arizona, legislatively an anti-(im)migrant state, and went through many states, including several in the South. The ride ended at the Democratic National Convention in North Carolina. While (im)migrant rights strategies that draw on the experiences of struggle faced by Blacks are often coalition work among Latina/o (im)migrants, (im)migrant rights advocates, and Black activist leaders, it is important to consider how the contemporary conditions of Blacks are addressed through these movements. Are these gestures simply ally "appropriation," as James cautions, or are these genuine attempts to learn about and address the struggles of these various communities? These are important questions to consider in social justice organizing.

6. I note the hardworking (im)migrant identity as masculinized because the ideal (im)migrant worker follows the traditional model of male (im)migrant workers. These were men who (im)migrated and labored during their most productive years, severing domestic ties in the process, and eventually returned to their country of origin. The contemporary ideal neoliberal (im)migrant laborer is structured on this model, and it is applied to men and women alike.

7. Attempts by (im)migrants to demonstrate their deservingness of belonging are as old as the first restrictions on (im)migration that largely targeted Asian (im)migrants. Initially, (im)migration restriction centered on Chinese (im)migrants and then expanded to encompass others. The Page Law of 1875, for example, was the first restrictive federal (im)migration law and part of the restrictions targeted Chinese women who were believed to be entering the United States as prostitutes (Luibhéid 2002, 2, 31–53). Through letters, documents, witnesses, and any other means available, Chinese women attempted to demonstrate that they were of "good moral character" in order to be allowed to enter the United States. Central to the struggles to claim belonging is the socio-historical context in which these struggles are fought. Chinese women explicitly confronted ideas of sexual deviancy, but, for Latina/o (im)migrants today, the neoliberal political economy shapes their social membership experiences. See López 2006 for additional examples of (im)migrants' attempts to demonstrate their worthiness of belonging.

8. De Genova's work relates to Cacho's (2012) argument that processes of human valuing are inherently violent since valuing necessitates the devaluing of (an)other.

9. Cohen demonstrates how early responses from Black community leaders and organizations to individuals identified as HIV positive were to mark them either as "junkies" or "faggots," both stigmatizing identities that resulted in secondary marginalization. As a result, their concerns were rarely made part of Blacks' larger political agenda, and silence on the issue of AIDS became the norm among Black communities' leadership. Attempts to prove Blacks' "legitimacy as full citizens" participated in the secondary marginalization of HIV-positive individuals (9). Other works that address African Americans' efforts to present themselves as good (read: normative) citizens through what Evelyn Brooks Higginbotham first termed "politics of respectability" include Victoria W. Wolcott's *Remaking Respectability: African American Women in Interwar Detroit* (2001) and E. Frances White's *Dark Continent of Our Bodies: Black Feminism and the Politics of Respectability* (2001).

10. The *Los Angeles Times* is a significant contributor to the national debate on (im)migration. It is the largest metropolitan daily newspaper in the United States (*Los Angeles Times* 2013) and is the fourth most widely distributed nationally (BurrellesLuce 2013). Los Angeles is significant because of its central location in the Southwest and because it is the destination of the largest concentration of Latina/o (im)migrants in the country.

11. In the examination, I concentrate on keywords "deportation" and "families" in the citation and abstract. I analyze articles to the end of 2008, which is when I concluded the majority of the research for this part of the study.

12. Esther spent the first three years in the California Rehabilitation Center in Norco and the remaining time in Valley State Prison for Women in Chowchilla, California.

13. I met with Esther in Tijuana during June, July, and August 2008. In August, she attempted to cross the border but was caught. Our work continued while she was in (im)migration detention and prison.

14. There is a significant body of literature that addresses how Latinas, particularly undocumented (im)migrants, are rendered vulnerable to interpersonal, and specifically intimate partner, violence (Menjívar and Salcido 2002; Raj and Silverman 2002; Reina, Lohman, and Maldonado 2014; Salcido and Menjívar 2012; Sokoloff and Dupont 2005; Villalón 2010). These works maintain that structural issues—including racism, poverty, sexism, homophobia, isolation, and legal status—condition how women experience interpersonal violence.

The framework of structural marginalization (Sokoloff and Dupont 2005) is useful to complicate the relationship of culture and intimate violence. Rather than marking patriarchy as emanating from Latina/o culture, this framework maintains that patriarchal violence is context specific. In other words, patriarchy operates differently in different contexts, including cultures. The legal status of undocumented Latina (im)migrants notably restricts their ability to leave violent intimate relationships for a variety of reasons. They may depend on their partners for their legalization; they may fear being detained and deported if they call the police or interact with other agencies; they may also fear that their situation will worsen if their partner is not arrested; they may be left economically and socially vulnerable by an arrest if they are dependent on their partner; they may not be aware of services and institutional protections available to them; and they may be ashamed to share their situation with others. Thus, structurally, undocumented Latina (im)migrants are increasingly rendered vulnerable to intimate violence.

15. Marquez (2012) argues that although the death and violence lived in the borderlands are often interpreted as unintended consequences, there is "much evidence suggesting that the border death toll, in particular, has been pre-meditated, that is, presupposed as a method of better deterring immigrants and enforcing immigration law" (474).

16. Sonia Guinansaca's story, featured in a 2013 *Colorlines* article by Von Diaz, provides an example that highlights some of the tensions. At the age of six, Sonia migrated from Ecuador and entered the United States without proper documentation. She is a student at Hunter College and active in the (im)migrant rights movement. Although eligible, Sonia refused to apply for the Deferred Action for Child Arrivals (DACA), created in 2012 to provide temporary relief for certain individuals, because she contends that this policy does not address the structural issues that generate undocumented (im)migration.

Another example is a disagreement between Congressman Luis Gutiérrez, a long-term supporter of (im)migration reform and (im)migrant rights, and the National Immigration Youth Alliance (NIYA), a grassroots organization. On November 3, 2013, Representative Gutiérrez's office issued a press release, "Activist Released at Request of Rep. Gutiérrez. Escorted Out of Rep. Gutiérrez' Office by Police," that announced that the congressman would no longer work with NIYA and maintained, among many things, that the organization's tactics are not productive toward (im)migration reform and actually serve to limit involved youths' opportunities for future legalization. See Pallares and Flores-González (2010) for further discussion on tensions in (im)migrant rights organizing.

17. Race scholar Claire Jean Kim (1999) notes the disciplining of both Asian Americans and Blacks that occurs through the model minority myth. Kim presents the theory of racial triangulation. The author argues that white dominant society engages in relative valorization, which is the denigration of Blacks in relation to Asian Americans. At the same time, Asian Americans face civic ostracism, which marks them as perpetually foreign and culturally and racially inassimilable. Here I note that this disciplining also extends to Latina/o (im)migrants, who are both socially denigrated and marked as perpetual foreigners.

18. These 2003 news stories foreshadow central strategies employed by (im)migrant rights advocates in later years, particularly by DREAMers. Undocumented youth who are represented as exceptional, largely through their academic achievements, are depicted as the (im)migrant archetype to push for rights and inclusion. The work carried out by DREAMers complicates a simplistic reading of the (im)migrant rights movement since they make use of disciplining narratives, such as those that portray (im)migrants as having a strong

work ethic and contributing to society, while the movement also engages in militant strategies, including civil disobedience, to advocate for (im)migrants rights in general.

19. These figures highlight the number of Latinas/os in federal prisons. Mexican citizens make up a significant portion. In 1995, they represented 9.8 percent (Federal Bureau of Prisons 1995, 3); in 2010, 17.4 percent (Federal Bureau of Prisons 2010, 3).

20. There is a growing body of literature that engages the effort to expand the definition of the ideal mother and include (im)migrant women mothering transnationally. Transnational motherhood scholarship often attempts to re-define "good" mothering by valuing women's attempts to provide for their children economically despite the fact that they cannot be physically present. For examples, see Baldassar and Merla 2013; Hondagneu-Sotelo and Avila 1997; Nicholson 2006; Parreñas 2001; and Zimmerman, Litt, and Bose 2006.

21. At the time, Sonia was collecting signatures against Proposition 9, "Criminal Justice System, Victims' Rights, Parole," which was on the November 2008 ballot in California. According to the Legislative Analysts' Office (2008), Proposition 9, "amends the State Constitution and various state laws to (1) expand the legal rights of crime victims and the payment of restitution by criminal offenders, (2) restrict the early release of inmates, and (3) change the procedures for granting and revoking parole."

22. Throughout this study, unless specific facts of the criminalized activities are directly related to the feminist abolitionist analysis employed, I do not include the actions that resulted in individuals being imprisoned. The main reason for this is that providing such details almost automatically elicits judgment and valuing and works to reduce people to these actions, which this study attempts to challenge.

23. Casa Refugio Elvira was converted to Casa Refugio Micaela in 2013.

24. The following is the text Esther placed on her myspace site:

Lately, I forgot about my friends in prison because I have been sad, but next week I will dedicate myself to them . . . . I was in prison for five years. That place is very difficult and sad. I was in V. S. P. W. in the city of Chowchilla, California. Five thousand women exist in that place, and the majority of them are forgotten by their families and society. Most are there unfairly because of a harsh judge, or because of a bad man. I had the opportunity to leave, but there are a lot of women that are never going to get out. When I left that place, I promised God one thing, to help the women that stayed behind sad, imprisoned . . . some forever. But for God nothing is impossible, and maybe one day they will get out. I want to help them by sending them money, cards, and letters. If you have a good heart or if you have ever had a loved one in prison . . . join me to bring happiness to those that are disposed of because they are not free like you or me. I have communication with them because I got out on July 7, 2008. Communicate with me if you want to help because it is very easy to bring happiness to those that are under a lock that only opens at certain times and who are anxious to hear "open, open the door" and get out and get some air and feel better. They see the color of the sky, and they feel better and thank God for one more day. I am beginning this struggle and hope for success. If you want to join me, I await your e-mail. (author's translation)

25. The DIF is a public institution intended to secure the well-being of Mexican families. DIF's social programs are specifically designed to support women, children, youth, people with disabilities, and the elderly.

26. Friendship Park is located at the San Diego-Tijuana border and serves as a meeting place between people on opposite sides of the border. At the time, a conglomeration of individuals and organizations were struggling against its closure.

27. See Escobar 2011 for a discussion of the impact of federal child welfare policies and the structural limitations they place on imprisoned (im)migrant parents.

28. Border Angels is an (im)migrant rights organization primarily dedicated to providing support for (im)migrants who find themselves in difficult border-crossing areas. For example, they place water in the desert to prevent (im)migrants' dehydration, they search for (im)migrants lost during border crossings, and, overall, they work against border militarization.

29. There are many models that advocate against the state monopolizing notions of justice and that present alternatives. In chapter 5, I briefly discuss restorative and transformative justice. These models move away from a punitive framework and maintain that people who harm have usually been harmed themselves and that long-term change will only come with strategies that attempt to heal all parties involved, including the person who caused harm.

## Chapter 3

1. Here I use the term "borderlands" to refer not only to the neighboring regions of the geopolitical US-Mexico border, but also to the various places where (im)migrants travel and where the ideological and material affectability of the border follows them. The borderlands exist where (im)migrants are present. This definition is largely informed by Gloria Anzaldúa's (1999) concept of borderlands. Anzaldúa differentiates between borders and borderlands: "A border is a dividing line, a narrow strip along a steep edge. A borderland is a vague and undetermined place created by the emotional residue of an unnatural boundary. It is in a constant state of transition" (25). The transitory condition of the borderlands is related to the movement of bodies that carry the meaning of the border with them.

2. "Appropriate" femininity and sexuality in relation to the nation-state are defined as heterosexual and patriarchal (Collins 1998; Luibhéid 2002). Women remain significant to the nation-state through their roles as housewives and as social, cultural, and biological mothers (Collins 1999; Fineman and Karpin 1995; Yuval-Davis 1997). Thus, they remain ideologically bound to hetero-patriarchal domesticity. See Canaday 2011 for an in-depth discussion of the way the modern US nation-state constructed itself as heteronormative.

3. Historian Natalia Molina (2006) provides an example of how social

meanings are constructed and attributed to (im)migrant bodies at different time periods. She addresses the early twentieth-century United States and how the discourse of public health was used to make racial meaning and identities. Concerns centered over what bodies were deemed physically fit for American society and what bodies should be targeted for exclusion. Thus, the public health concerns of the time directly shaped the experiences of belonging/nonbelonging for (im)migrants. See also Jamal and Naber 2008, Wu 2013, and Yeng 2013 for works that address the creation of different racial (im)migrant identities over time and space.

4. Harris (2011) provides an excellent review of some of the literature that makes the critique that the anti-violence against women movement contributes to the criminal legal system buildup. See also Garfield 2005, Richie 2012, Silliman and Bhattacharjee 2002, Sudbury and Okazawa-Rey 2009, and Villalón 2010, for similar critiques of the anti-violence against women movement.

5. Scholars and activists engaged in ending violence against women of color and their communities propose strategies such as transformative justice, which draws from restorative justice in attempts to move away from punitive punishment. These efforts center on the fact that individuals who hurt others have often been hurt themselves and thus move away from a punitive framework to deal with harm and violence. However, transformative justice expands restorative justice because it does not only center on healing interpersonal relationships, but also couches the understanding of "harm" (the term used instead of "crime") within larger systems of power and oppression (Harris 2011, 51–64).

6. See Chavez 2008 and his account of the racialization of (im)migrants in relation to the construction of the nation. For a discussion on the historical racialization of Mexicans as non-whites, see Almaguer 1994. See also Gutiérrez 2008 for a gendered analysis of the racialization of Mexicans and people of Mexican origin.

7. See Inda 2007 for an analysis of Operation Gatekeeper, Proposition 187, the Illegal Immigration Reform and Immigrant Responsibility Act of 1996, and the denial of prenatal care as biopolitical techniques intended to exclude Latina/o (im)migrants from the body politic.

8. See da Silva 2007 for an analysis of the racialized production of the modern universal Subject.

9. Wright (2011) applies the concept of necropolitics to the feminicide (which she terms "femicide") of women in Ciudad Juarez and the violence produced by Mexico's militarized drug wars. Wright provides an analysis of how the Mexican state deploys gendered understandings of the public and private spheres as masculine and feminine, respectively, to provide interpretations of this violence and these deaths. The Mexican state represents the murdered women of Juarez as violating gender norms (not remaining in the domestic sphere) and the individuals involved in the drug trade are portrayed as rational subjects who target only other individuals involved in this business. Thus, "innocent" people need not fear. Through her analysis, Wright demonstrates how gender is central to the ability of the Mexican state to (re)produce and legitimize itself.

10. Glenn (2002) examines the early development of US citizenship and considers how the rights and privileges of white citizens, particularly white

males, were historically developed in relation to the lack of both freedom and opportunities for women and people of color. The citizen and the non-citizen are racialized and gendered interdependent constructions and gained meaning in contrast to one another (20). Glenn demonstrates that the conceptual dichotomies of public-private and independent-dependent were central in the definition of US citizenship and used to determine who obtained national membership. Women and Blacks were marked by the private sphere and constructed as dependent while white men were designated to the public sphere and marked as independent.

11. Meaningfully, while Latina (im)migrants' biological reproduction in the United States is marked as undesirable, their presence is considered necessary to support the ability of white middle- and upper-class families' social reproduction. The negation of Latina (im)migrants' ability to biologically and socially reproduce is directly correlated to the fostering of white middle- and upper-class families (Chang 2000; Hondagneu-Sotelo and Avila 1997).

12. While abuse and neglect are often the rationale used to take children from their families and place them in the care of the state, children taken from families with incarcerated parents do not have to be abused or neglected. The time restrictions applied by ASFA make family separation not only possible, but probable (Day 2005; Escobar 2011; Genty 2008; Greenway 2003; Lee, Genty, and Laver 2005; Smith, Jefferson, and Young 2003; Smith 2006).

13. The Innocence Project is a national organization dedicated to exonerating individuals who are wrongfully convicted. They mostly focus on cases where DNA testing can be evaluated.

14. Scholarship reflects this fact that women are the primary targets of domestic violence. An exception is Villalón (2010), who includes the story of Samuel, a heterosexual (im)migrant Latino who was abused by his wife. Samuel reached out to the organization where Villalón conducted her research in order to obtain support to legalize his status under policies aimed to provide relief for (im)migrant victims of domestic violence. Villalón recounts that Samuel did not fit into the "ideal" client identity desired due to a previous criminal record, so the organization decided to discontinue support for him. Samuel's case speaks to the fact that once marked criminal, an individual is considered irrecuperable.

15. Timothy Dunn (2010) addresses the 1993 Operation Blockade that militarized border areas in Texas. He marks it as a watershed moment in (im)-migration enforcement policies that previously favored detaining (im)migrants once they had crossed the border. Operation Blockade instead centered on "prevention through deterrence," which intended to make crossing the border so difficult that (im)migrants would decide not to cross, which became the dominant paradigm in terms of border enforcement.

## Chapter 4

1. The quotes appear numbered as they appear in the study.

2. I use [she/he] because the gender of the judges is not explicitly stated in the quotes.

3. It is important to note that incarceration as a transnational phenomenon that leads to cross-country collaboration is not specific to the United States and Mexico. It is a relationship that develops between the United States and countries with agreements for repatriation. Latin American countries are especially involved because of the intense criminalization of Latinas/os in the United States that results in their over-representation in deportations. Central American countries with significant refugee communities in the United States are especially affected. Many of the refugee youth affected by the US law-and-order and hard-on-crime policies, especially the war on gangs, have been legally classified as "criminal aliens" and deported to their countries of origin (Coutin 2010; Zilberg 2004 and 2007). Often, the anti-gang discourses and policies are exported to Central American countries and thus follow and continue to shape deportees' lives (Coutin 2010, 353).

4. The third era, "the politics of no politics," is challenged by Cecilia Imaz Bayona (2003). Imaz Bayona notes that traditionally Mexico has exerted a politics of protection to its nationals abroad. Although there were no policies to curtail emigration to the United States, between 1965 and 1976, following the termination of the Bracero Program, the Mexican government developed the border area through assembling plants (maquiladoras) as a way to absorb returning (im)migrant labor (9), to prevent potential emigration, and to give job opportunities to the border area that remained separate from the rest of the country (14).

5. Mexico not only negotiates its relationship with the United States at its northern border, but also with "transit" migration from other Latin American countries and the policing of its southern border. Mexico's increased (im)-migration enforcement policies, principally targeted at Central Americans, is in part informed by its interdependence with the United States. For example, according to Andreas and Biersteker (2003), immediately after the events of September 11, 2001, Mexico attempted to obtain intelligence from possible terrorists. Also as part of these anti-terrorism efforts, US and Israeli "border enforcers" were deployed to Mexico's southern border (12). As Andreas and Biersteker note:

> It seems that Mexico has pragmatically accepted that part of the price of being viewed and treated as an insider, rather than as an outsider, is to police more intensively its southern border. Central American neighbors, in turn, complain that a hardening of Mexico's southern border means Mexico is doing Washington's police work. Indeed, Mexico's border enforcement initiatives may be viewed as a "thickening" of the US border, with Mexico becoming a buffer zone. (13)

The Washington Office on Latin America, a non-governmental organization that examines the impact of US foreign policy on Latin America to further human rights, published an extensive report on Mexico's southern border, "Mexico's Other Border: Security, Migration, and the Humanitarian Crisis at the Line with Central America" (Isacson, Meyer, and Morales 2014). The report addresses the increased presence of Central American migrants in the United States, the increased anxiety this produces for the United States, and some of the collaborative policy responses developed between the United States and Mexico to address this situation. This includes launching the Mexico-Guatemala-Belize Border Region Program, which provides more than $50 million in equipment to patrol this border (5). The examples cited demonstrate Mexico's role in policing and criminalizing Central American (im)migrants as part of its efforts to negotiate its relationship with the United States.

6. Members of the Congregation of the Missionaries of St. Charles, usually referred to as Scalabrinian missionaries, focus their work on providing support and guidance to (im)migrants and refugees.

7. According to staff at Instituto Madre Assunta, there appear to be thirteen (im)migrant shelters in Tijuana (e-mail to author, October 27, 2014). I attempted to verify this information with Mexico's Instituto Nacional de Migración (INM), the government body responsible for managing and governing (im)migration-related issues, including immigration, emigration, and repatriation. The INM's representative in the Tijuana office stated that it is difficult to verify the number of (im)migrant shelters because not all are officially registered and some shelters have been abandoned or moved to other locations (phone conversation, November 1, 2014).

8. (Im)migrant women note that although Casa services men, its greater media visibility leads many to seek this space, rather than Instituto. However, since they are in immediate proximity to each other, (im)migrant women who arrive at Casa are redirected to Instituto.

9. An example of work carried out to provide support for (im)migrants is the Scalabrini network of (im)migrant shelters, which includes Casa and Instituto. This network consists of shelters in the cities of Nuevo Laredo (Tamaulipas), Tijuana (Baja California), and Tapachula (Chiapas), as well as shelters in Guatemala, including Ciudad Guatemala and Tecún Umán (Red Casa del Migrante Scalabrini, 2014).

10. I initially spent six months conducting research at the Instituto and I later returned as a volunteer. While I did not conduct interviews during this time, my volunteer experiences shaped my perspective of this border space.

11. The practice of arresting and forcing to labor without pay is reminiscent of US Black codes that criminalized recently freed Black slaves and their behaviors. When jailed, they could then be put to work in public works or leased to private parties. This practice also parallels the labor carried out by people in US prisons. This includes the everyday labor necessary to operate these institutions, which is usually unpaid, as well as labor done for private companies, which can be paid, but at extremely low wages.

12. According to their website, Grupo Beta de Protección al Migrante, a government agency, was established in 1990 to protect (im)migrants' human rights and to save the lives of (im)migrants crossing the border (www.inm.gob .mx/index.php/page/Grupo_Beta).

13. In discussing Suly's story, I do not apply any moralistic judgment to sex work. Rather, my argument is that options for women in the public sphere are limited, and the use of their female sexual bodies becomes a means to provide for themselves and others. However, there should be more support for individuals, such as Suly, so that sex work is not perceived as the *only* option.

14. On several occasions throughout the time I visited Instituto, I wit-

nessed women covertly place food from their plates into plastic bags and later deliver the bags to their partners and others outside the shelter.

15. As noted by other scholars (Falcón 2007; Luibhéid 2002), sexual violence, including rape, is widespread in the experiences of unauthorized (im)-migrants, particularly women, who have crossed or attempt to cross the border. Most of the women in this study had suffered sexual violence, had witnessed others' violations, or had family members and friends who had experienced this type of violence. In some cases, women reported initiating the use of birth control prior to their journeys in anticipation of this potential violence. In one case, a woman shared a story of a group of (im)migrant women and men who had been raped en masse by a group who abducted them while they were traveling to the United States. She noted that while this type of violence is usually targeted at women, men are also vulnerable. The woman who shared this story had traveled with her mother to Tijuana from the state of Mexico in search of her brothers who had gone missing while attempting to cross the border. They had been abducted and a ransom had been requested. The family waited for a call from the abductors, but the call never came. Her brothers' bodies were eventually found. They had been shot. These stories of sexual violence and death underscore (im)migrants' vulnerability. As Falcón and Luibhéid maintain, these forms of violence are perpetrated not only by civilians, but also official authorities.

16. Since the conclusion of this research, the San Ysidro/Tijuana border crossing has undergone significant construction that dramatically changed the physical design of this space.

## Chapter 5

1. I problematize "unjust" sentences because, following the logic of prison abolition, all sentences are unjust. However, advocacy work often focuses on cases where there is evidence that the individual did not engage in the criminalized activities for which they are imprisoned, or there is evidence that there was some form of discrimination in their case.

2. I use the term "transformative social movements" to differentiate between movements that explicitly seek to challenge and disrupt relationships of power and inequality and movements that intentionally reinforce social inequalities.

3. See also Richie 2012 for a discussion of how the United States's structure as a prison nation shapes interpersonal experiences of violence for Black women. Richie provides a critique similar to those of Garfield and Villalón of the mainstream anti-violence against women movement.

4. See Gilmore 2000 for a discussion of the notion of unfreedom and the connections between slavery and prisons.

5. The death of prison intellectual George Jackson and the Attica rebellion drew international attention to the situation of people in prison in the United States (Davis and Rodriguez 2000, 215). Jackson was sentenced to one year in prison for stealing seventy dollars from a gas station in Los Angeles. In prison,

he gained political consciousness and became active in the Black Panther Party. His sentence was continuously extended as a response to his revolutionary activities. On August 21, 1971, he was shot and killed by prison guards in San Quentin under mysterious circumstances. On September 9, 1971, in part as a response to Jackson's murder and in protest of the conditions of their incarceration, men incarcerated in Attica Prison in New York seized control of the prison. As a response, on September 13, police and soldiers re-took control of Attica, and in the process, more than thirty men, mostly Black and Latino, were massacred. Again, these moments of state repression and violence brought international attention to the situation of people of color in the United States.

6. Punitive juvenile justice reform was primarily driven by the construction of poor, urban youth of color as "superpredators," a term coined in the mid-1990s by right-wing conservatives (Rios 2006, 51). This was the case with Proposition 21, which was in part driven by the fear of highly publicized news stories of youth engaged in school shootings (Taylor 2002, 991). It allowed the state to try youth as young as fourteen as adults and gave this discretion to prosecutors, rather than judges (991). It also increased penalties for various criminalized activities, targeted gang-related activities, and expanded the list of what were considered violent and serious offenses. Cacho (2012) offers an extended and insightful discussion of Proposition 21 and the failed attempt to prosecute a group of seven white suburban teenagers who viciously attacked a group of elderly Latino migrant workers whom the teenagers mistakenly identified as undocumented. She shows how the criminal legal system participates in determining the racialized value of life where the lives of these young white youth are valued against the lives of young men of color, constructed as the targets of punitive policies such as Proposition 21, and the elderly Latino men.

7. In defining radical freedom, prison abolitionists do not maintain one "true" definition. For example, Angela Y. Davis (2012) maintains that freedom is a collective social process, often fixed in difficult dialogues, aimed at creating the social conditions in which everyone is afforded opportunities to thrive. This collective social process can take on many different expressions. However, even though there is not one "true" definition of freedom, prison abolitionists, such as Davis and James, agree that freedom is something that is not granted by the state (or any other external repressive entity). Rather, freedom is defined, created, and brought about by subjugated individuals and communities. Hames-García (2004) makes a similar case and notes that prison intellectuals, such as Assata Shakur, conceptualize freedom as something that is continuously practiced. In other words, it is an action (verb) more than a concrete thing (noun).

8. Cacho (2012) makes a similar critique. She maintains that racialized criminalization serves to render non-white bodies socially dead. The ability to socially live is inherently contingent on the decisions of civil society and the state to grant individuals this "gift" (6–7). Thus, it is a "gift," rather than an inalienable right, and thus, fundamentally coercive.

9. Prison intellectual George Jackson (1990) argued that the capitalist dominant ruling class maintains hegemony, despite serious historical challenges, because it is allowed to engage in economic reform. He defines this as

fascist. Jackson wrote, "But if one were forced for the sake of clarity to define [fascism] in a word simple enough for all to understand, that word would be 'reform'" (118). His analysis applies to the US prison system as maintained and institutionalized through constant reform.

10. Similar to the work of those in prison abolition advocacy organizations, I am also driven by a sense of urgency. For example, in September 2014, I received a letter from one of the Latina (im)migrants I worked with through CCWP. Due to California's Realignment, women at VSPW were transferred to CCWF and California Institution for Women (CIW) in Corona, California. She wrote that since her transfer in October 2013, fourteen people had died at CIW. Several of the deaths were suicides, which she attributed to the conditions at this prison. It is important to note that she initiated her transfer to CIW as part of her effort to reunite with friends who had previously been transferred. Her struggle against isolation resulted in being placed in what she perceived as a more violent carceral space.

11. Justice Now is a nonprofit organization, and CCWP, under Legal Services for Prisoners with Children (LSPC), is also a nonprofit organization. Although funded/supported by the communities affected by mass incarceration, they are not beyond the reach of the nonprofit industrial complex.

12. Adhering to Angela P. Harris's (2011) call to problematize the category of "women in prison," since it erases the fact that not everyone incarcerated in women's prisons identify as women, I attempt throughout this chapter to use gender-neutral language, except when referring to others' perspectives. I use the concept "people in women's prisons."

13. An example of the violence Justice Now and similar organizations attempt to address is evidenced in a recent campaign spearheaded by Justice Now to pass State Bill 1135, which was signed into law by Governor Jerry Brown in September 2014. S.B. 1135 is meant to end forced sterilizations in California prisons. Between 2006 and 2010, the CDCR sterilized at least 148 incarcerated women, many coercively or without proper consent (Johnson 2013).

14. The appropriation of prison abolitionist and reformist critiques is evident in the discourse employed by the CDCR in its response to the Supreme Court's decision. For example, to quote from the CDCR report (2012), "The Future of California Corrections: A Blueprint to Save Billions of Dollars, End Federal Court Oversight, and Improve the Prison System":

> For years, California's prison system has faced costly and seemingly endless challenges. Decades-old class-action lawsuits challenge the adequacy of critical parts of its operations, including its health care system, its parole-revocation process, and its ability to accommodate inmates with disabilities. In one case, a federal court seized control over the prison medical care system and appointed a Receiver to manage its operations. The Receiver remains in place today. The state's difficulty in addressing the prison system's multiple challenges was exacerbated by an inmate population that—until recently—had been growing at an unsustainable pace. (1)

Prison abolition advocacy organizations, including Justice Now, were involved in some of the class-action lawsuits referenced, including Plata v.

Schwarzenegger, where a number of people in prison challenged the constitutionality of California's prison medical care system. The court sided with the plaintiffs and affirmed that "this level of overcrowding causes serious and at times deadly harm to prisoners, prison staff, and the public" (Rappaport and Dansky 2010). The CDCR report goes on to discuss how Realignment would address the challenges stated.

The CDCR statement attests to the ways in which the prison system appropriates the critiques made against it. This occurs through the implementation of reforms, which serves to further entrench prisons in society, without structurally addressing the root causes of mass criminalization and incarceration. This is a typical example of the ways in which the state reorganizes itself by incorporating critiques made against it, particularly by social movements demanding change.

15. The violent conditions endured by people who were transferred from VSPW to CIW noted in note 10, including witnessing fourteen deaths in less than one year, is in part informed by the conversion. I do not mean to argue that the conversion led to these deaths. However, we need to consider that the situation, including increased overcrowding at CCWF and CIW, may have exacerbated the detrimental conditions in these already difficult carceral spaces and indirectly participated in making these deaths probable.

16. It is significant that the greater social isolation that people experience in women's prisons (versus men's prisons) is what makes a women's prison attractive to the city of Chowchilla. In other words, because people in women's prisons tend to be isolated from their family and loved ones to a greater extent than individuals in men's prisons, women's carceral sites are more desirable. In contrast, families and loved ones of people incarcerated in men's prisons tend to remain more connected, making a men's prison undesirable. Furthermore, there are also concerns about men being more prone to violence than women, and this promotes the undesirability of locating a men's prison in or near the city.

17. While imprisoning individuals in county jail does not reduce the overall number of people held in carceral spaces, there are other aspects of Realignment that have had an effect on reducing the number of people incarcerated. For example, fewer people are being incarcerated on drug-related charges. In June 2013, 8.7 percent of people imprisoned in California were incarcerated for drug charges, down from 20 percent in 2005 (Atkinson, Coder, and Weishahn 2013). Several of the individuals with whom I worked through CCWP had previously been denied parole, some on multiple occasions. After the implementation of the Realignment plan, all six people who had hearings were granted parole. While these changes appear to be turning the incarceration tide in California, it is important to observe the capriciousness of these trends. The individuals who received parole had previously presented their cases, some with almost the same exact files, and yet, were denied. Changes in policy, and not their individual behaviors, resulted in their parole. This highlights the subjective nature of incarceration that makes communities vulnerable to sociopolitical developments.

18. Simon (2014) addresses the reduction in levels of incarceration, not just in California, but also in the United States in general. He argues that, despite the apparent reduction in people being imprisoned, the racialized logic

of violence and criminality remains and will more than likely participate in re-stabilizing and legitimating what he terms the "strong state." In considering the apparent waning of the war on crime, Frampton, López, and Simon (2008) and various contributors to their anthology also caution against claiming victory and urge us to consider the long-lasting impact on various institutions and society in general. This work calls for a new reconstruction (in reference to post-slavery Reconstruction) to begin to address the long-lasting damages created by the war on crime.

19. Rafter (1985) notes that the critique of prisons being modeled after men and not meeting women's needs was first developed in the nineteenth century by middle-class reform movements. This critique led to the creation of reformatories, which highlights how reform serves to expand the criminal legal system. Rafter demonstrates that notions of who was considered redeemable were racialized so that white women tended to be sent to reformatories, to be instilled with "proper" gender norms, while Black women were often incarcerated in men's prisons and made vulnerable to the lease system where they were forced to work (149–152).

20. During the transition, most were transferred to CCWF, and I continued the visits there.

21. I state "allegedly" because, in reality, the severity of an individual's criminal conviction is often cited by the board in their decisions.

22. Joana was approved for parole in February 2014 and was deported to Mexico in July 2014. While Joana submitted a very similar file in previous hearings, it appears that what made a difference in being awarded parole is not necessarily additional evidence of her rehabilitation, but rather, changes in the CDCR's policies and procedures. Particularly relevant is CDCR's priority to reduce overcrowding as mandated by the courts.

23. I problematize "encouraged" because, although they cannot legally require (im)migrants to have two parole hearings, boards often cite the lack of support, evidenced by not having a parole plan for either the United States or their country of origin, for decisions to deny (im)migrants parole.

# Bibliography

A New Way of Life. 2010. "About Us." Last accessed April 2, 2010. www
.anewwayoflife.org/about-us.

Abramowitz, Mimi. 1988. *Regulating the Lives of Women: Social Welfare Policy
from Colonial Times to the Present.* Cambridge: South End Press.

Alexander, Michelle. 2010. *The New Jim Crow: Mass Incarceration in the Age of
Colorblindness.* New York: New Press.

Almaguer, Tomás. 1994. *Racial Faultlines: The Historical Origins of White Supremacy in California.* Berkeley: University of California Press.

Alvarez, Luis. 2009. *The Power of the Zoot: Youth Culture and Resistance during World War II.* Berkeley: University of California Press.

American Civil Liberties Union. "The Immigration Detention Boom." Last
accessed November 1, 2014. www.aclu.org/immigrants-rights/frontline
-map-us-immigration-detention-boom.

Andreas, Peter. 2000. *Border Games: Policing the US-Mexico Divide.* Ithaca:
Cornell University Press.

Andreas, Peter, and Thomas J. Biersteker, eds. 2003. *The Rebordering of North
America.* New York: Routledge.

Andreas, Peter, and Richard Price. 2001. "From War Fighting to Crime Fighting: Transforming the American National Security State." *International
Studies Review* 3, no. 3 (Fall): 31–52. doi: 10.1111/1521-9488.00243.

Anzaldúa, Gloria. 1999. *Borderlands/La Frontera: The New Mestiza.* San Francisco: Aunt Lute Books.

Anzaldúa, Gloria, and Cherrie Moraga. 2002. *This Bridge Called My Back:
Writings by Radical Women of Color.* San Antonio: Third Woman Press.

Atkinson, Jay, Jacqui Coder, and David Weishahn. 2013. "Prison Census
Data as of June 30, 2013." Sacramento: Department of Corrections and
Rehabilitation.

Baker, Bryan, and Nancy Rytina. 2013. "Estimates of the Unauthorized Immigrant Population Residing in the United States: January 2012." Washington, DC: Office of Immigration Statistics. Last accessed November 5, 2014.
www.dhs.gov/sites/default/files/publications/ois_ill_pe_2012_2.pdf.

Baldassar, Loretta, and Laura Merla, eds. 2013. *Transnational Families, Mi-*

*gration and the Circulation of Care: Understanding Mobility and Absence in Family Life.* New York: Routledge.

Baptist, Edward E. 2014. *The Half Has Never Been Told: Slavery and the Making of American Capitalism.* New York: Basic Books.

Beckett, Katherine. 1997. *Making Crime Pay: Law and Order in Contemporary American Politics.* New York: Oxford University Press.

Bell, Derrick. 1992. "Racial Realism." *Connecticut Law Review* 24, no. 2: 363–379.

Blackmon, Douglas A. 2009. *Slavery by Another Name: The Re-Enslavement of Black Americans from the Civil War to World War II.* New York: Anchor Books.

Blackstock, Nelson. 2000. *COINTELPRO: The FBI's Secret War on Political Freedom.* New York: Pathfinder.

Bonilla-Silva, Eduardo. 2001. *White Supremacy and Racism in the Post-Civil Rights Era.* Boulder: Lynne Rienner Publishers.

———. 2003. *Racism Without Racists: Color-blind Racism and the Persistence of Racial Inequality in the United States.* Lanham: Rowman & Littlefield.

Bortner, Margaret A. 2002. "Controlled and Excluded: Reproduction and Motherhood among Poor and Imprisoned Women." In *Women at the Margins: Neglect, Punishment, and Resistance,* edited by Josefina Figueira-McDonough and Mary C. Sarri, 255–270. New York: Hawthorn.

Braz, Rose. 2006. "Kinder, Gentler, More Gender Responsive Cages: Prison Expansion Is Not Prison Reform." *Women, Girls and Criminal Justice* (Fall): 87–91. Last accessed May 3, 2015. www.againstequality.org/wp-content/uploads/2009/10/gender_responsive_cages.pdf.

Brown, Michelle. 2005. "Setting the Conditions for Abu Ghraib: The Prison Nation Abroad." *American Quarterly* 57, no. 3: 973–997. doi:10.1353/aq.2005.0039.

Brownell, Peter B. 2001. "Border Militarization and the Reproduction of Mexican Migrant Labor." *Social Justice* 28, no. 2 (Summer): 69–92.

BurrellesLuce. 2013. "Top Media Outlets: Newspapers, Blogs, Consumer Magazines, Broadcasters, Websites & Social Networks." Last accessed November 23, 2014. www.burrellesluce.com/sites/default/files/Top_Media_June_2013_FNL%281%29.pdf.

Burton-Rose, Daniel, Dan Pens, and Paul Wright. 1998. *The Celling of America: An Inside Look at the US Prison Industry.* Monroe: Common Courage Press.

Bush-Baskette, Stephanie. 1998. "The War on Drugs as a War Against Black Women." In *Crime Control and Women: Feminist Implications of Criminal Justice Policy,* edited by Stephanie Miller, 113–129. Thousand Oaks: Sage.

Cacho, Lisa Marie. 2012. *Social Death: Racialized Rightlessness and the Criminalization of the Unprotected.* New York: New York University Press.

Calavita, Kitty. 1992. *Inside the State: The Bracero Program, Immigration, and the I.N.S.* New York: Routledge.

California. 1994. "California Voter Information: Proposition 187. Text of Proposed Law." Last accessed June 18, 2008. www.americanpatrol.com/REFERENCE/prop187text.html.

California Department of Corrections. 1997. "Historical Trends: Institution and Parole Population, 1976–1996." Last accessed November 5, 2013. www.cdcr.ca.gov/reports_research/offender_information_services_branch /Annual/HIST2/HIST2d1996.pdf.

California Department of Corrections and Rehabilitation (CDCR). 2008a. "Fourth Quarter 2008 Facts and Figures." Last accessed January 17, 2009. www.cdcr.ca.gov/Adult_Operations/docs/Fourth_Quarter_2009_Facts _and_Figures.pdf.

———. 2008b. "Historical Trends: 1987–2007." Sacramento: Offender Information Services Branch. Last accessed February 8, 2009. www.cdcr.ca.gov /Reports_Research/Offender_Information_Services_Branch/Annual /HIST2/HIST2d2007.pdf.

———. 2011. "Lifer Parole Process." Last accessed January 10, 2013. www .cdcr.ca.gov/Parole/Life_Parole_Process/Index.html.

———. 2012. "The Future of California Corrections: A Blueprint to Save Billions of Dollars, End Federal Oversight, and Improve the Prison System." Last accessed October 2, 2013. www.cdcr.ca.gov/2012plan.

———. 2013. "Number of Inmates in the Institution Population Who Have a USICE Hold, Have a Potential USICE Hold or Do Not Have an Actual or Potential USICE Hold By Country of Birth and Hold Status as of April 30, 2013." Sacramento: Offender Information Services Branch.

California Department of Finance. 2013. "State and County Female Population Projections by Race/Ethnicity and Detailed Age, 2010–2060 (as of July 1)." Sacramento: Demographic Research Unit. Last accessed October 14, 2014. www.dof.ca.gov/research/demographic/reports/projections/P-3/.

Canaday, Margot. 2011. *The Straight State: Sexuality and Citizenship in Twentieth-Century America.* Princeton: Princeton University Press.

Cantú, Lionel. 2009. *The Sexuality of Migration: Border Crossings and Mexican Immigrant Men.* Edited by Nancy Naples and Salvador Vidal-Ortiz. New York: New York University Press.

Carrigan, William D., and Clive Webb. 2013. *Forgotten Dead: Mob Violence against Mexicans in the United States, 1848–1928.* New York: Oxford University Press.

Carson, Ann E. 2014. "Prisoners in 2013." In *Prisoners Series*, 32: US Department of Justice.

Chabat, Jorge. 2002. "Mexico's War on Drugs: No Margins for Maneuver." *Annals of the American Academy of Political and Social Science* 582, no. 1 (July): 134–148. doi:10.1177/000271620258200110.

Chacón, Jennifer M. 2007. "Unsecured Borders: Immigration Restrictions, Crime Control and National Security." *Connecticut Law Review* 39: 1827–1891.

———. 2009. "Managing Migration Through Crime." *Columbia Law Review* 109: 135–148.

Chang, Grace. 2000. *Disposable Domestics: Immigrant Women Workers in the Global Economy.* Cambridge: South End Press.

Chávez, Karma R. 2013. *Queer Migration Politics: Activist Rhetoric and Coalitional Possibilities.* Urbana: University of Illinois Press.

Chavez, Leo. 2001. *Covering Immigration: Popular Images and the Politics of the Nation.* Berkeley: University of California Press.

———. 2007. "The Condition of Illegality." *International Migration* 45: 192–196.

———. 2008. *The Latino Threat: Constructing Immigrants, Citizens, and the Nation.* Stanford: Stanford University Press.

Child Welfare Information Gateway. 2011. "Home Study Requirements for Prospective Foster Parents." Washington, DC: Department of Health and Human Services, Children's Bureau. Last accessed May 3, 2015. www .childwelfare.gov/systemwide/laws_policies/statutes/homestudyreqs.pdf.

Chishti, Muzaffar A. 2007. "Testimony of Muzaffar A. Chishti Before the US House of Representatives Committee on the Judiciary Subcommittee on Immigration, Citizenship, Refugees, Border Security, and International Law, April 19, 2007." Washington, DC: US Government Printing Office.

Churchill, Ward, and Jim Vander Wall. 2001. *Agents of Repression: The FBI's Secret Wars Against the Black Panther Party and the American Indian Movement.* Boston: South End Press.

City of Chowchilla, California. 2013. "City of Chowchilla, California, Demographics." Last accessed November 22, 2013. www.ci.chowchilla.ca.us /city%20facts/demographics.htm.

Clark-Alfaro, Victor. 2008. "Migrantes Repatriados: Arresto y Detenciones Arbitrarias: Derechos Humanos: Derechos Violados" (report). Tijuana, Mexico: Centro Binacional de Derechos Humanos.

Cohen, Cathy J. 1999. *The Boundaries of Blackness: AIDS and the Breakdown of Black Politics.* Chicago: University of Chicago Press.

Collins, Patricia Hill. 1998. "It's All in the Family: Intersections of Gender, Race, and Nation." *Hypatia* 13, no. 3: 62–82.

———. 1999. "Producing the Mothers of the Nation: Race, Class and Contemporary US Population Policies." In *Women, Citizenship and Difference*, edited by Nira Yuval-Davis, 118–129. London: Zed Books.

———. 2000. *Black Feminist Thought: Knowledge, Consciousness, and the Politics of Empowerment.* New York: Routledge.

Congressman Luis Gutiérrez Office. 2013. "Activist Released at Request of Rep. Gutiérrez. Escorted Out of Rep. Gutiérrez's Office by Police." Press release, November 3, 2013. Last accessed November 5, 2013. http:// gutierrez.house.gov/press-release/statement-niya.

Conway, Marshall Eddie. 2007. "Domestic Warfare: A Dialogue." In *Warfare in the American Homeland: Policing and Prison in a Penal Democracy*, edited by Joy James, 98–119. Durham, NC: Duke University Press.

Conway, Marshall Eddie, and Dominique Stevenson. 2011. *Marshall Law: The Life & Times of a Baltimore Black Panther.* Edinburgh: AK Press.

Cornelius, Wayne. 1989. "Impacts of the 1986 US Immigration Law on Emigration from Rural Mexican Sending Communities." *Population and Development Review* 15, no. 4 (December): 689–705.

———. 2001. "Death at the Border: The Efficacy and 'Unintended' Consequences of US Immigration Control Policy 1993–2000." San Diego: Center for Comparative Immigration Studies. Last accessed February 14, 2012. http://escholarship.org/uc/item/7mx516pr.

Cornelius, Wayne A., and Jorge A. Bustamante, eds. 1989. *Mexican Migration to the United States: Origins, Consequences, and Policy Options.* La Jolla: Center for US-Mexican Studies, University of California, San Diego.

*Correctional News.* 2013. "Valley State Prison Makes Full Transition to Male Facility," March 6. Last accessed October 15, 2014. www.correctionalnews.com /articles/2013/03/6/valley-state-prison-makes-full-transition-male-facility.

Coutin, Susan Bibler. 2013. "Exiled by Law: Deportation and Inviability of Life." In *Governing Immigration Through Crime: A Reader*, edited by Julie A. Dowling and Jonathan Xavier Inda, 233-251. Stanford: Stanford University Press.

Critical Resistance. "History." Last accessed September 2, 2013. http:// criticalresistance.org/about/history/.

Daniels, Roger. 2004. *Guarding the Golden Door: American Immigration Policy and Immigrants Since 1882.* New York: Hill and Wang.

Das Gupta, Monisha. 2006. *Unruly Immigrants: Rights, Activism, and Transnational South Asian Politics in the United States.* Durham, NC: Duke University Press.

da Silva, Denise Ferreira. 2007. *Toward a Global Idea of Race.* Minneapolis: University of Minnesota Press.

Davis, Angela Y. 1981. "Reflections on the Black Woman's Role in the Community of Slaves." *Black Scholar* 12, no. 6: 2–15.

———. 2003. *Are Prisons Obsolete?* New York: Seven Stories.

Davis, Angela Y., and Robin Kelly. 2012. *The Meaning of Freedom: and Other Difficult Dialogues.* San Francisco: City Lights Publishers.

Davis, Angela Y., and Eduardo Mendieta. 2005. *Abolition Democracy: Beyond Empire, Prisons, and Torture.* New York: Seven Stories Press.

Davis, Angela Y., and Dylan Rodriguez. 2000. "The Challenge of Prison Abolition: A Conversation." *Social Justice* 27, no. 3: 212–218.

Day, Sally. 2005. "Mothers in Prison: How the Adoption and Safe Families Act of 1997 Threatens Parental Rights." *Wisconsin Journal of Law, Gender and Society* 20, no. 2: 217–243.

De Genova, Nicholas P. 2002. "Migrant 'Illegality' and Deportability in Everyday Life." *Annual Review of Anthropology* 31: 419–447. doi:10.1146/ annurev.anthro.31.040402.085432.

———. 2005. *Working the Boundaries: Race, Space, and "Illegality" in Mexican Chicago.* Durham, NC: Duke University Press.

———. 2013a. "Immigration 'Reform' and the Production of Migrant 'Illegality.'" In *Constructing Immigration "Illegality": Critiques, Experiences, and Responses*, edited by Cecilia Menjívar and Daniel Kanstroom, 37–62. New York: Cambridge University Press.

———. 2013b. "The Legal Production of Mexican/Migrant 'Illegality.'" In *Governing Immigration Through Crime: A Reader*, edited by Julie A. Dowling and Jonathan Xavier Inda, 41–57. Stanford: Stanford University Press.

De Genova, Nicholas, and Nathalie Peutz, eds. 2010. *The Deportation Regime: Sovereignty, Space, and the Freedom Movement.* Durham, NC: Duke University Press.

Delgado Wise, Raúl, and Humberto Márquez Covarrubias. 2005. "Migración, Políticas Pública Desarrollo: Reflexiones en Torno al Caso de México." Red Internacional de Migración y Desarrollo. Last accessed February 20, 2009. http://meme.phpwebhosting.com/~migracion/modules/seminarioe /delgadoraul.pdf.

Detention Watch Network. "About the US Detention and Deportation System." Last accessed November 1, 2014. www.detentionwatchnetwork.org /resources.

Deverall, Aimee. 2008. "Make the Dream Reality: Why Passing the Dream Act is the Logical First Step in Achieving Comprehensive Immigration Reform." *John Marshall Law Review* 41 (Summer): 1251–1279.

Díaz, Jesse. 2011. "Immigration Policy, Criminalization and the Growth of the Immigration Industrial Complex: Restriction, Expulsion, and Eradication of Undocumented in the US." *Western Criminology Review* 12, no. 2: 35–54. http://wcr.sonoma.edu/v12n2/Díaz.pdf.

Diaz, Von. 2013. "Three Faces of DACA." *Colorlines*, September 17. Last accessed November 14, 2013. http://colorlines.com/archives/2013/09 /undacamented_received_declined_and_denied_1.html.

Diaz-Cotto, Juanita. 2005. "Latinas and the War on Drugs in the United States, Latin America, and Europe." In *Global Lockdown: Race, Gender, and the Prison-Industrial Complex*, edited by Julia Sudbury, 137–154. New York: Routledge.

———. 2006. *Chicana Lives and Criminal Justice: Voices from el Barrio*. Austin: University of Texas Press.

Diaz-Strong, Daysi, Christina Gomez, Maria E. Luna-Duarte, Erica R. Meiners, and Luvia Valentin. 2009. "Commentary: Organizing Tensions—From the Prison to the Military Industrial Complex." *Social Justice* 36, no. 2: 73–84.

Dowling, Julie A., and Jonathan Xavier Inda. 2013. *Governing Immigration Through Crime: A Reader*. Stanford: Stanford University Press.

Doyle, Kate. 2003. "Operation Intercept: The Perils of Unilateralism." National Security Archive. Last accessed March 17, 2009. www2.gwu.edu /~nsarchiv/NSAEBB/NSAEBB86/#article.

Dreher, Sabine. 2007. *Neoliberalism and Migration: An Inquiry into the Politics of Globalization*. Piscataway, NJ: Transaction.

DuBois, W. E. B. 1969. *The Souls of Black Folk*. New York: New American Library.

———. 1995. *Black Reconstruction in America 1860–1880*. New York: Touchstone.

Dunn, Timothy. 1996. *The Militarization of the US-Mexico Border, 1978–1992: Low Intensity Conflict Doctrine Comes Home*. Austin: University of Texas Press.

———. 2010. *Blockading the Border and Human Rights: The El Paso Operation that Remade Immigration Enforcement*. Austin: University of Texas Press.

Dunn, Timothy J., and José Palafox. 2000. "Border Militarization and Beyond: The Widening War on Drugs." *Borderlines* 8, no. 4: 14–16.

Dyer, Joel. 2000. *The Perpetual Prisoner Machine: How America Profits from Crime*. Boulder: Westview.

Enos, Sandra. 1998. "Managing Motherhood in Prison: The Impact of Race and Ethnicity on Child Placements." *Women and Therapy* 20, no. 4: 57–73.

———. 2001. *Mothering from the Inside: Parenting in a Women's Prison*. Albany: State University of New York Press.

Epstein, Edward Jay. 1977. *Agency of Fear: Opiates and Political Power in America*. New York: Putnam.

Escobar, Edward J. 1993. "The Dialectics of Repression: The Los Angeles Police Department and the Chicano Movement, 1968–1971." *Journal of American History* 79, no. 4: 1483–1514.

———. 1999. *Race, Police, and the Making of a Political Identity: Mexican Americans and the Los Angeles Police Department, 1900–1945*. Berkeley: University of California Press.

———. 2003. "Bloody Christmas and the Irony of Police Professionalism: The Los Angeles Police Department, Mexican Americans, and Police Reform in the 1950s." *Pacific Historical Review* 72, no. 2: 171–199.

Escobar, Martha D. 2011. "ASFA and the Impact on Imprisoned Migrant Women and Their Children." In *Razor Wire Women: Prisoners, Scholars, Activists, and Artists*, edited by Jodie Lawston and Ashley Lucas, 75–91. Albany: State University of New York Press.

Espiritu, Yen Le. 2003. *Homebound: Filipino American Lives Across Cultures, Communities, and Countries*. Berkeley: University of California Press.

Falcón, Sylvanna. 2001. "Rape as a Weapon of War: Advancing Human Rights for Women at the US-Mexico Border." *Social Justice* 28, no. 2: 31-50.

Federal Bureau of Prisons. 1995. "State of the Bureau." Washington, DC: Bureau of Prisons. Last accessed August 13, 2013. www.bop.gov/news/PDFs/sob95.pdf.

———. 2007. "State of the Bureau." Washington, DC: Bureau of Prisons. Last accessed August 13, 2013. www.bop.gov/news/PDFs/sob07.pdf

———. 2010. "State of the Bureau." Washington, DC: Bureau of Prisons. Last accessed August 13, 2013. www.bop.gov/news/PDFs/sob10.pdf.

Feldman, Allen. 1991. *Formations of Violence: The Narrative of the Body and Political Terror in Northern Ireland*. Chicago: University of Chicago Press.

Fernández-Kelly, Patricia, and Douglas S. Massey. 2007. "Borders for Whom? The Role of NAFTA in Mexico-US Migration." *ANNALS of the American Academy of Political and Social Science* 610, no. 1: 98–118. doi: 10.1177/0002716206297449

Fineman, Martha Albertson, and Isabel Karpin. 1995. *Mothers in Law: Feminist Theory and Legal Regulation of Motherhood*. New York: Columbia University Press.

Fitzsimmons, Emma G. 2014. "Nebraska City Votes to Keep Rule Aimed at Illegal Immigrants." *New York Times*, February 12. Last accessed October 10, 2014. www.nytimes.com/2014/02/12/us/nebraska-city-votes-to-keep-rule-aimed-at-illegal-immigrants.html?_r=0.

Flavin, Jeanne. 2007. "Slavery's Legacy in Contemporary Attempts to Regulate Black Women's Reproduction." In *Race, Gender, and Punishment*, edited by Mary Bosworth and Jeanne Flavin, 95-114. New Brunswick: Rutgers University Press.

Florido, Adrian. 2013. "Deported Migrants Cope After Tijuana Police Destroy Their Homes." KPBS News, August 9. Last accessed November 10, 2013. www.kpbs.org/news/2013/aug/09/deported-migrants-cope-after-tijuana -police-destro/.

Foucault, Michel. 1972. *Power/Knowledge: Selected Interviews and Other Writings 1972–1977.* Edited by Colin Gordon. New York: Pantheon Books.

———. 1978. *The History of Sexuality, Vol. 1: An Introduction.* New York: Random House.

———. 1995. *Discipline and Punish: The Birth of the Prison.* New York: Vintage.

———. 2008. *The Birth of Biopolitics: Lectures at the Collège De France, 1978– 1979.* Edited by Michel Senellart and translated by Graham Burchell. New York: Picador.

Frampton, Mary Louise, Ian Haney López, and Jonathan Simon, eds. 2008. *After the War on Crime: Race, Democracy, and a New Reconstruction.* New York: New York University Press.

Fregoso, Rosa-Linda. 2007. "Toward a Planetary Civil Society." In *Women and Migration in the US-Mexico Borderlands: A Reader,* edited by Denise A. Segura and Patricia Zavella, 35–66. Durham, NC: Duke University Press.

Fregoso, Rosa-Linda, and Cynthia Bejarano. 2010. *Terrorizing Women: Feminicide in the Americas.* Durham, NC: Duke University Press Books.

Fujiwara, Lynn. 2008. *Mothers Without Citizenship: Asian Immigrant Families and the Consequences of Welfare Reform.* Minneapolis: University of Minnesota Press.

Gabel, Katherine, and Denise Johnston, eds. 1995. *Children of Incarcerated Parents.* New York: Lexington Books.

Galassi, Jennifer. 2003. "Dare to Dream? A Review of the Development, Relief, and Education for Alien Minors (DREAM) Act." *Chicano-Latino Law Review* 24: 79–94.

Gardner, Andrew M. 2010. "Engulfed: Indian Guest Workers, Bahraini Citizens, and the Structural Violence of the Kafala System." In *The Deportation Regime: Sovereignty, Space, and the Freedom of Movement,* edited by Nicholas De Genova and Nathalie Peutz, 196–223. Durham, NC: Duke University Press.

Gardner, Martha Mabie. 2005. *The Qualities of a Citizen: Women, Immigration, and Citizenship, 1870–1965.* Princeton: Princeton University Press.

Garfield, Gail. 2005. *Knowing What We Know: African American Women's Experiences of Violence and Violation.* New Brunswick: Rutgers University Press.

Gavett, Gretchen. 2001. "Map: The US Immigration Detention Boom." *Frontline,* October 18. Last accessed May 3, 2015. www.pbs.org/wgbh/pages /frontline/race-multicultural/lost-in-detention/map-the-u-s-immigration -detention-boom/.

Genty, Philip M. 2008. "The Inflexibility of the Adoption and Safe Families Act and Its Unintended Impact upon the Children of Incarcerated Parents and Their Families." In *CW360°: A Comprehensive Look at a Prevalent Child Welfare Issue.* Minnesota: Center for Advanced Studies in Child

Welfare. Last accessed June 20, 2014. http://academy.extensiondlc.net/file
.php/1/resources/CIP-CW360.pdf.

Gibson, Campbell, and Kay Jung. 2002. "Historical Census Statistics on Population Totals by Race, 1790 to 1990, and by Hispanic Origin, 1970 to 1990, for the United States, Regions, Divisions, and States." Washington, DC: US Census Bureau. Last accessed October 14, 2014. www.census.gov /population/www/documentation/twps0056/twps0056.html.

Gilens, Martin. 2000. *Why Americans Hate Welfare: Race, Media, and the Politics of Antipoverty Policy.* Chicago: University of Chicago Press.

Gilmore, Kim. 2000. "Slavery and Prison—Understanding the Connections." *Social Justice* 27, no. 3: 195–205. Last accessed May 3, 2015. www .jstor.org.libproxy.csun.edu/stable/29767242?pq-origsite=summon&seq =1#page_scan_tab_contents.

Gilmore Wilson, Ruth. 1998. "Globalisation and US Prison Growth: From Military Keynesianism to Post-Keynesian Militarism." *Race and Class* 40, no. 2–3: 171–188. doi:10.1177/030639689904000212.

———. 2007. *Golden Gulag: Prisons, Surplus, Crisis, and Opposition in Globalizing California.* Berkeley: University of California Press.

Glenn, Evelyn Nakano. 2002. *Unequal Freedom: How Race and Gender Shaped American Citizenship and Labor.* Cambridge: Harvard University Press.

Golden, Renny. 2005. *War on the Family: Mothers in Prison and the Children They Leave Behind.* New York: Routledge.

Gonzales, Alfonso. 2014. *Reform Without Justice: Latino Migrant Politics and the Homeland Security State.* New York: Oxford University Press.

Gonzalez, Juan. 2001. *Harvest of Empire: A History of Latinos in America.* New York: Penguin.

González, Omar Millán. 2008a. "Quiero que Me Escuchen: Hija de Madre Deportada Hablará Durante la Convención." *Enlace*, August 22.

———. 2008b. "US Teen Whose Mom was Deported to Tell Story at Convention." *San Diego Union-Tribune*, August 25. Last accessed September 9, 2008. www.utsandiego.com/uniontrib/20080825/news_1m25elisa.html.

González Gutiérrez, Carlos. 2006. *Relaciones Estado–Diáspora: Aproximaciones Desde Cuatro Continentes.* México: Miguel Ángel Porrúa/Secretaría de Relaciones Exteriores/Universidad Autónoma de Zacatecas.

González Ortiz, Felipe, and Liliana Rivera Sánchez. 2004. "Migrantes y Políticas Públicas: Apuntes Desde la Expereiencia del Programa 'Iiciativa Ciudadana Tres por Uno' en Los Estados de México y Puebla." Zinacantepec, Mexico: El Colegio Mexiquense.

Gorman, Anna. 2007. "A Family's Painful Split Decision: Deported to Tijuana, Conflicted Parents Decide Their 3 US-Born Children Should Stay in San Diego." *Los Angeles Times*, April 27. Last accessed May 3, 2015. http:// articles.latimes.com/2007/apr/27/local/me-kids27.

Greenaway, Antoinette. 2003. "When Neutral Policies Aren't So Neutral: Increasing Incarceration Rates and the Effect of the Adoption and Safe Families Act of 1997 on the Parental Rights of African-American Women." *National Black Law Journal* 17: 247–255.

Guerin-Gonzales, Camille. 1994. *Mexican Workers and American Dreams:*

*Immigration, Repatriation, and California Farm Labor, 1900–1939.* New Brunswick: Rutgers University Press.

Guidotti-Hernández, Nicole Marie. 2011. *Unspeakable Violence: Remapping US and Mexican National Imaginaries.* Durham, NC: Duke University Press.

Gutiérrez, Elena R. 2008. *Fertile Matters: The Politics of Mexican-Origin Women's Reproduction.* Austin: University of Texas Press.

Hahamovitch, Cindy. 2003. "Creating Perfect Immigrants: Guestworkers of the World in Historical Perspective." *Labor History* 44, no. 1: 69–94.

Hall, Stuart, Charles Critcher, Tony Jefferson, John Clarke, and Brian Roberts. 1978. *Policing the Crisis: Mugging, the State, and Law and Order.* London: Macmillan.

Hames-García, Michael. 2004. *Fugitive Thought: Prison Movements, Race, and the Meaning of Justice.* Minneapolis: University of Minnesota Press.

Handler, Joel F. 2002. "Welfare Reform: Tightening the Screws." In *Women at the Margins: Neglect, Punishment, and Resistance,* edited by Josefina Figueira-McDonough and Rosemary C. Sarri, 33–45. New York: Haworth Press.

Harding, Sandra G. 1991. *Whose Science? Whose Knowledge? Thinking From Women's Lives.* Ithaca: Cornell University Press.

———. ed. 2004. *The Feminist Standpoint Theory Reader: Intellectual and Political Controversies.* New York: Routledge.

Harris, Angela P. 2011. "Heteropatriarchy Kills: Challenging Gender Violence in a Prison Nation." *Washington University Journal of Law & Policy* 37, no. 3: 13–65.

Hartman, Saidiya. 1997. *Scenes of Subjection: Terror, Slavery and Self-Making in Nineteenth-Century America.* New York: Oxford University Press.

Hartsock, Nancy. 1983. "The Feminist Standpoint." In *Discovering Reality: Feminist Perspectives on Epistemology, Metaphysics, Methodology, and Philosophy of Science,* edited by Sandra Harding and Merrill B. Hintikka, 283–310. Dordrecht and Boston: D. Riedel.

Harvey, David. 2005. *A Brief History of Neoliberalism.* New York: Oxford University Press.

Herivel, Tara, and Paul Wright, eds. 2009. *Prison Profiteers: Who Makes Money from Mass Incarceration.* New York: New Press.

Hernández, David Manuel. 2008. "Pursuant to Deportation: Latinos and Immigrant Detention." *Latino Studies* 6: 35–63. doi:10.1057/lst.2008.2.

Hing, Bill Ong. 2003. *Defining America through Immigration Policy.* Philadelphia: Temple University Press.

———. 2009. "Institutional Racism, ICE Raids, and Immigration Reform." *University of San Francisco Law Review* 44 (December): 1–49. Last accessed May 3, 2015. http://papers.ssrn.com/abstract=1525578.

Hoefer, Michael D. 2009. "2008 Yearbook of Immigration Statistics." Washington, DC: US Department of Homeland Security. Last accessed June 2009. www.dol.gov/oasam/programs/history/webid-meynihan.htm.

Hondagneu-Sotelo, Pierrette. 1994. *Gendered Transitions: Mexican Experiences of Immigration.* Berkeley: University of California Press.

———. 1995. "Women and Children First: New Directions in Anti-Immigrant Politics." *Socialist Review* 25, no. 1: 169–190.

Hondagneu-Sotelo, Pierrette, and Ernestine Avila. 1997. "I'm Here, but I'm There: The Meaning of Latina Transnational Motherhood." *Gender and Society* 11, no. 2: 548–571.

Huebner, Beth M., and Timothy S. Bynum. 2008. "The Role of Race and Ethnicity in Parole Decisions." *Criminology* 46, no. 4 (November): 907–938. doi:10.1111/j.1745-9125.2008.00130.x.

Imaz Bayona, Cecilia. 2003. "La Relación Política del Estado Mexicano Con Su Diáspora en Estados Unidos." *Migración y Desarrollo: Transnacionalismo y Perspectivas de Integración*. Last accessed October 4, 2009. http://meme.phpwebhosting.com/~migracion/ponencias/15_1.pdf.

INCITE! Women of Color Against Violence, ed. 2006. *The Color of Violence: The Incite! Anthology*. Cambridge: South End Press.

———, ed. 2009. *The Revolution Will Not Be Televised: Beyond the Non-Profit Industrial Complex*. Cambridge: South End Press.

Inda, Jonathan Xavier. 2007. "The Value of Life." In *Women and Migration in the US-Mexico Borderlands: A Reader*, edited by Denise A. Segura and Patricia Zavella, 134–157. Durham, NC: Duke University Press.

Instituto Nacional de Migración. "Grupos Beta del INM." Last accessed May 3, 2015. www.inm.gob.mx/index.php/page/Grupo_Beta.

———. "Acerca del INM." Last accessed May 3, 2015. www.inm.gob.mx/index.php/page/Mision_Vision_Objetivos.

Isacson, Adam, Maureen Meyer, and Gabriela Morales. 2014. "Mexico's Other Border: Security, Migration, and the Humanitarian Crisis at the Line with Central America." Washington, DC: Washington Office on Latin America. Last accessed November 15, 2014. www.wola.org/files/mxgt/report/.

Jackson, George. 1990. *Blood in My Eye*. Baltimore: Black Classic Press.

Jamal, Amaney, and Nadine Naber, eds. 2008. *Race and Arab Americans Before and After 9/11: From Invisible Citizens to Visible Subjects*. Syracuse, NY: Syracuse University Press.

James, Joy, ed. 2000. *States of Confinement: Policing, Detention and Prison*. New York: St. Martin's Press.

———, ed. 2005. *The New Abolitionists: (Neo)Slave Narratives and Contemporary Prison Writings*. Albany: State University of New York Press.

———, ed. 2007. *Warfare in the American Homeland: Policing and Prisons in a Penal Democracy*. Durham, NC: Duke University Press.

Jayasuriya, Kanishka. 2006. *Statecraft, Welfare, and the Politics of Inclusion*. New York: Palgrave Macmillan.

Jimenez, Maria. 2009. "Humanitarian Crisis: Migrant Deaths at the US-Mexico Border." ACLU of San Diego & Imperial Counties and Mexico's National Commission of Human Rights. Last accessed March 13, 2012. www.aclu.org/files/pdfs/immigrants/humanitariancrisisreport.pdf.

Johnson, Corey G. 2013. "Female Inmates Sterilized in California Prisons without Approval." Center for Investigative Reporting, July 7. Last accessed September 9, 2014. http://cironline.org/reports/female-inmates-sterilized-california-prisons-without-approval-4917.

Johnson, Elizabeth I., and Jane Waldfogel. 2002. "Parental Incarceration: Recent Trends and Implications for Child Welfare." *Social Service Review* 76, no. 3: 460–479.

Johnson, Jeh Charles. 2014a. "Policies for the Apprehension, Detention and Removal of Undocumented Immigrants Memorandum." Washington, DC: Department of Homeland Security. Last accessed December 9, 2014. www .dhs.gov/sites/default/files/publications/14_1120_memo_prosecutorial _discretion.pdf.

———. 2014b. "Secure Communities Memorandum." Washington, DC: Department of Homeland Security. Last accessed December 9, 2014. www .dhs.gov/sites/default/files/publications/14_1120_memo_secure_commu nities.pdf.

Jordan-Zachery, Julia Sheron. 2009. *Black Women, Cultural Images, and Social Policy.* New York: Routledge.

Kanstroom, Daniel. 2004. "Criminalizing the Undocumented: Ironic Boundaries of the Post-September 11th 'Pale of Law'." *North Carolina Journal of International Law and Commercial Regulation* 29 (Summer): 639–670.

Kaplan, Sara Clarke. 2007. "Love and Violence/Maternity and Death: Black Feminism and the Politics of Reading (Un)representability." *Black Women, Gender, and Families* 1, no. 1 (Spring): 94–124.

Katz, Michael B. 1989. *The Undeserving Poor: From the War on Poverty to the War on Welfare.* New York: Pantheon.

Kim, Claire Jean. 1999. "The Racial Triangulation of Asian Americans." *Politics & Society* 27 (March): 105–138.

Krishnaswami, Shreeram. 1992. "Colonial Foundations of Western Capitalism." *Economic and Political Weekly* 27, no. 30: 81–89.

Lara, Dulcinea, Dana Greene, and Cynthia Bejarano. 2009. "A Critical Analysis of Immigrant Advocacy Tropes: How Popular Discourse Weakens Solidarity and Prevents Broad, Sustainable Justice." *Social Justice* 36, no. 2: 21–37.

Law, Victoria. 2014. "Against Carceral Feminism: Relying on State Violence to Curb Domestic Violence Only Ends up Harming the Most Marginalized Women." *Jacobin*, October 17. Last accessed November 24, 2014. www .jacobinmag.com/2014/10/against-carceral-feminism/.

Lawston, Jodie M., and Ruben Murillo. 2009. "The Discursive Figuration of US Supremacy in Narratives Sympathetic to Undocumented Immigrants." *Social Justice* 36, no. 2: 38–53.

Lee, Arlene F., Philip M. Genty, and Mimi Laver. 2005. *The Impact of the Adoption and Safe Families Act on Children of Incarcerated Parents.* Washington, DC: Child Welfare League of America.

Lee, Youngro. 2006. "To Dream or Not to Dream: A Cost-Benefit Analysis of the Development, Relief, and Education for Alien Minors (DREAM) Act." *Cornell Journal of Law and Public Policy* 16: 231–262.

Legislative Analyst's Office. 2008. "Proposition 9: Criminal Justice System, Victims' Rights, Parole. Constitutional Amendment and Statute." Last accessed May 15, 2009. www.lao.ca.gov/ballot/2008/9_11_2008.aspx.

Legomsky, Stephen H. 2007. "The New Path of Immigration Law: Asymmetric Incorporation of Criminal Justice Norms." *Washington & Lee Law Review* 64: 469–528.

Lewis, Oscar. 1959. *Five Mexican Families: Mexican Case Studies in the Culture of Poverty*. New York: Basic Books.

Library of Congress. 1996. "Bill Summary & Status 104th Congress (1995–1996) S.735." Last accessed November 22, 2014. http://thomas.loc.gov /cgi-bin/bdquery/z?d104:SN00735:@@@L&summ2=m&.

———. 2013. "Bill Text 113th Congress (2013–2014) S. 744." Last accessed July 15, 2013. http://thomas.loc.gov/cgi-bin/query/D?c113:3:. /temp/~c113hifa2z::.

Lichtenstein, Alex. 1996. *Twice the Work of Free Labor: The Political Economy of Convict Labor in the New South*. London and New York: Verso.

Light, Michael T., Mark Hugo Lopez, and Ana Gonzalez-Barrera. 2013. "The Rise of Federal Immigration Crimes: Unlawful Reentry Drives Growth." Washington, DC: Pew Research Center. Last accessed November 21, 2014. www.pewhispanic.org/2014/03/18/the -rise-of-federal-immigration-crimes/.

Lindsley, Syd. 2002. "The Gendered Assault on Immigrants." In *Policing the National Body: Race, Gender, and Criminalization*, edited by Jael Silliman and Anannya Bhattacharjee, 175–196. Cambridge: South End Press.

López, Ian Haney. 2003. *Racism on Trial: The Chicano Fight for Justice*. Cambridge: Belknap Press.

———. 2006. *White by Law: The Legal Construction of Race*. New York: New York University Press.

Lopez, Mark Hugo, and Michael T. Light. 2009. "A Rising Share: Hispanics and Federal Crime." Washington, DC: Pew Hispanic Center. Last accessed April 9, 2010. http://pewhispanic.org/reports/report.php?ReportID=104.

*Los Angeles Times*. 2013. "About Us." Last accessed November 30, 2013. www .latimes.com/about/mediagroup/#axzz2m9XGqr00.

Lowe, Lisa. 1996. *Immigrant Acts: On Asian American Cultural Politics*. Durham, NC: Duke University Press.

Lubiano, Wahneema. 1992. "Black Ladies, Welfare Queens, and State Minstrels: Ideological War by Narrative Means." In *Race-ing Justice, Engendering Power: Essays on Anita Hill, Clarence Thomas, and the Construction of Social Reality*, edited by Toni Morrison, 323–363. New York: Pantheon Books.

Luibhéid, Eithne. 2002. *Entry Denied: Controlling Sexuality at the Border*. Minneapolis: University of Minnesota Press.

Luibhéid, Eithne, and Lionel Jr. Cantú, eds. 2005. *Queer Migrations: Sexuality, US Citizenship, and Border Crossings*. Minneapolis: University of Minnesota Press.

Lusane, Clarence. 1991. *Pipe Dream Blues: Racism and the War on Drugs*. Boston: South End Press.

Lytle-Hernández, Kelly. 2006. "The Crimes and Consequences of Illegal Immigration: A Cross-Border Examination of Operation Wetback, 1943 to 1954." *Western Historical Quarterly* 37, no. 4 (Winter): 421–444. Last accessed May 3, 2015. www.jstor.org/stable/25443415.

———. 2010. *Migra! A History of the US Border Patrol.* Berkeley: University of California Press.

Macek, Steve. 2006. *Urban Nightmares: The Media, The Rights, and the Moral Panic Over the City.* Minneapolis: University of Minnesota Press.

Magee, Rhonda V. 2009. "Slavery as Immigration?" *University of San Francisco Law Review* 44, no. 2: 273–306. http://ssrn.com/abstract=1671763.

Mann, Coramae Richey, Marjorie S. Zatz, and Nancy Rodriguez, eds. *Images of Color, Images of Crimes: Readings.* New York: Oxford University Press, 2006.

Manza, Jeff, and Chris Uggen. 2006. *Locked Out: Felon Disenfranchisement and American Democracy.* New York: Oxford University Press.

Marable, Manning. 1999. *How Capitalism Underdeveloped Black America: Problems in Race, Political Economy, and Society.* Cambridge: South End Press.

Marquez, John. 2012. "Latinos as the 'Living Dead': Raciality, Expendability, and Border Militarization." *Latino Studies* 10: 473–498. doi:10.1057/1st.2012.39.

Massey, Douglas S., Jorge Durand, and Nolan J. Malone. 2002. *Beyond Smoke and Mirrors: Mexican Immigration in an Era of Economic Integration.* New York: Russell Sage Foundation.

Mattingly, Doreen J. 1997. "Working Men and Dependent Wives: Gender, Race, and the Regulation of Migration from Mexico." In *Women Transforming Politics*, edited by Kathy Jones, Joan Toronto, and Cathy Cohen, 47–61. New York: New York University Press.

Mauer, Marc. 1999. *Race to Incarcerate.* New York: New Press.

Mbembe, Achille. 2003. "Necropolitics." *Public Culture* 15, no. 1: 11–40.

McDonnell, Patrick J. 1997. "Criminal Past Comes Back to Haunt Some Immigrants. Law: Legal Residents Now Face Deportation for Crimes in US, No Matter How Old. Many Insist They've Reformed." *Los Angeles Times*, January 20.

McKanders, Karla Mari. 2007. "Welcome to Hazelton! 'Illegal' Immigrants Beware: Local Immigration Ordinances and What the Federal Government Must Do About It." *Loyola University Chicago Law Journal* 39, no. 1: 6–13.

Melamed, Jodi. 2006. "From Racial Liberalism to Neoliberal Multiculturalism." *Social Text* 89, no. 4 (Winter): 1–24.

Menjívar, Cecilia, and Daniel Kanstroom, eds. 2013. *Constructing Immigrant "Illegality": Critiques, Experiences, and Responses.* New York: Cambridge University Press.

Menjívar, Cecilia, and Olivia Salcido. 2002. "Immigrant Women and Domestic Violence: Common Experiences in Different Countries." *Gender and Society* 16, no. 6: 898–920.

Miller, Jerome. 1996. *Search and Destroy: African-American Males in the Criminal Justice System.* Cambridge: Cambridge University Press.

Miller, Teresa A. 2003. "Citizenship & Severity: Recent Immigration Reforms and the New Penology." *Georgetown Immigration Law Journal* 17, no. 4: 611–666.

———. 2005. "Blurring the Boundaries Between Immigration and Crime

Control After September 11th." *Boston College Third World Law Journal* 25, no. 1: 81–123.

Mills, Charles W. 1999. *The Racial Contract.* Ithaca, NY: Cornell University Press.

Mink, Gwendolyn. 1990. "Lady and the Tramp: Gender, Race, and the Origins of the American Welfare State." In *Women, the State, and Welfare,* edited by Linda Gordon, 92–122. Madison: University of Wisconsin Press.

Mirandé, Alfredo. 1990. *Gringo Justice.* Notre Dame: University of Notre Dame Press.

Molina, Natalia. 2006. *Fit to Be Citizens? Public Health and Race in Los Angeles, 1879–1939.* Berkeley: University of California Press.

———. 2014. *How Race Is Made in America: Immigration, Citizenship, and the Historical Power of Racial Scripts.* Berkeley: University of California Press.

Moloney, Deirdre. 2012. *National Insecurities: Immigrants and US Deportation Policy since 1882.* Chapel Hill: University of North Carolina Press.

Morgan, Jennifer L. 2004. *Labor Women: Reproduction and Gender in New World Slavery.* Philadelphia: University of Pennsylvania Press.

Motomura, Hiroshi. 2008. "Immigration Outside the Law." *Columbia Law Review* 108, no. 8: 2037–2097.

Moynihan, Daniel Patrick. 1965. "The Negro Family: The Case for National Action." Washington, DC: Department of Labor. Last accessed November 12, 2009. www.dol.gov/dol/aboutdol/history/webid-meynihan.htm.

Muhammad, Khalil Gibran. 2011. *The Condemnation of Blackness: Race, Crime, and the Making of Modern Urban America.* Cambridge: Harvard University Press.

Murakawa, Naomi. 2014. *The First Civil Right: How Liberals Built Prison America.* New York: Oxford University Press.

Neubeck, Kenneth J., and Noel A. Cazenave. 2001. *Welfare Racism: Playing the Race Card Against America's Poor.* New York: Routledge.

Nevins, Joseph. 2002. *Operation Gatekeeper: The Rise of the "Illegal Alien" and the Remaking of the US-Mexico Boundary.* New York: Routledge.

New York Lawyers for the Public Interest. 2012. "Discharge, Deportation, and Dangerous Journeys: A Study on the Practice of Medical Repatriation." Last accessed February 15, 2014. www.nylpi.org/images/FE /chain234siteType8/site203/client/FINAL%20MED%20REPAT%20RE PORT%20FOR%20WEBSITE.pdf.

Ngai, Mae M. 2004. *Impossible Subjects: Illegal Aliens and the Making of Modern America.* Princeton, NJ: Princeton University Press.

Nicholls, Walter. 2013. *The Dreamers: How the Undocumented Youth Movement Transformed the Immigrant Rights Debate.* Stanford: Stanford University Press.

Nicholson, Melanie. 2006. "Without Their Children: Rethinking Motherhood among Transnational Migrant Women." *Social Text* 24, no. 88: 13–33.

Oboler, Suzanne, ed. 2009. *Behind Bars: Latino/as and Prison in the United States.* New York: Palgrave Macmillan.

Office of Immigration Statistics. 2006. "2004 Yearbook of Immigration Statistics." Washington, DC: US Department of Homeland Security. Last accessed November 1, 2014. www.dhs.gov/xlibrary/assets/statistics/year book/2004/Yearbook2004.pdf.

———. 2008. "2007 Yearbook of Immigration Statistics." Washington, DC: US Department of Homeland Security. Last accessed November 1, 2014. www.dhs.gov/xlibrary/assets/statistics/yearbook/2007/ois_2007_year book.pdf.

Office of the Press Secretary. 2014a. "FACT SHEET: Immigration Accountability Executive Action." Washington, DC: White House. Last accessed November 27, 2014. www.whitehouse.gov/the-press-office/2014/11/20/fact-sheet-immigration-accountability-executive-action.

———. 2014b. "Opportunity for All: President Obama Launches My Brother's Keeper Initiative to Build Ladders of Opportunity for Boys and Young Men of Color." Washington, DC: White House. Last accessed March 15, 2014. www.whitehouse.gov/the-press-office/2014/02/27/fact-sheet-opportunity-all-president-obama-launches-my-brother-s-keeper-.

O'Leary, Anna Ochoa, and Azucena Sanchez. 2011. "Anti-Immigrant Arizona: Ripple Effects and Mixed Immigration Status Households Under 'Policies of Attrition' Considered." *Journal of Borderland Studies* 26: 1–19.

Olguín, B. V. 2010. *La Pinta: Chicana/o Prisoner Literature, Culture, and Politics.* Austin: University of Texas Press.

Olivas, Michael. A. 2004. "IIRIRA, the DREAM Act, and Undocumented College Student Residency." *Journal of College and University Law* 30, no. 2: 435–464.

———. 2009. "The Political Economy of the DREAM Act and the Legislative Process: A Case Study of Comprehensive Immigration Reform." *Wayne Law Review* 55: 1757–1785.

Oliviero, Katie E. 2013. "The Immigration State of Emergency: Racializing and Gendering National Vulnerability in Twenty-First-Century Citizenship and Deportation Regimes." *Feminist Formations* 25, no. 2 (Summer): 1–29.

Omi, Michael, and Howard Winant. 1994. *Racial Formation in the United States: From the 1960s to the 1990s.* New York: Routledge.

Ono, Kent A., and John M. Sloop. 2002. *Shifting Borders: Rhetoric, Immigration, and California's Proposition 187.* Philadelphia: Temple University Press.

Ontiveros, Maria L. 2004. "Immigrant Workers' Rights in a Post-Hoffman World: Organizing Around the Thirteenth Amendment." *Georgetown Immigration Law Journal* 18: 651–672.

———. 2007. "Noncitizen Immigrant Labor and the Thirteenth Amendment: Challenging Guest Worker Programs." *University of Toledo Law Review* 38, no. 2: 923–940. http://ssrn.com/abstract=1017092.

O'Reilly, Kenneth. 1989. *Racial Matters: The FBI's Secret File on Black America, 1960–1972.* New York: Free Press.

Orozco, Samuel. 2008. *The Repatriated.* RB Network, Radio Bilingüe, July 31. Fresno: KSJV. Last accessed August 20, 2008. http://archivosderb.org/?q=en/node/793.

Oshinsky, David. 1997. *Worse than Slavery: Parchman Farm and the Ordeal of Jim Crow Justice.* New York: Free Press.

Pagan, Eduardo Obregon. 2003. *Murder at the Sleepy Lagoon: Zoot Suits, Race, and Riot in Wartime L.A.* Chapel Hill: University of North Carolina Press.

Palafox, Jose. 1996. "Militarizing the Border." *Covert Action Quarterly* 56 (Spring): 14–19.

———. 2000. "Opening Up Borderland Studies: A Review of US-Mexico Border Militarization Discourse." *Social Justice* 27: 56–72.

Pallares, Amalia, and Nilda Flores-González, eds. 2010. ¡*Marcha! Latino Chicago and the Immigrant Rights Movement.* Champaign: University of Illinois Press.

Parenti, Christian. 1999. *Lockdown America: Police and Prisons in the Age of Crisis.* New York: Verso.

———. 2002. "Satellites of Sorrow: Los Angeles, Prison, and Circuits of Control." In *Unmasking L.A.: Third World and the City*, edited by Deepak Narang Sawhney, 47–62. New York: Palgrave.

Park, Lisa Sun-Hee. 2001. "Perpetuation of Poverty Through 'Public Charge'." *Denver University Law Review* 78, no. 4: 1161–1177.

———. 2005. *Consuming Citizenship: Children of Asian Immigrant Entrepreneurs.* Stanford: Stanford University Press.

———. 2011. *Entitled to Nothing: The Struggle for Immigrant Health Care in the Age of Welfare Reform.* New York: New York University Press.

Parreñas, Rhacel Salazar. 2001. *Servants of Globalization: Women, Migration, and Domestic Work.* Stanford: Stanford University Press.

Pateman, Carole. 1988. *The Sexual Contract.* Cambridge: Polity Press.

Payán, Tony. 2006. *The Three US-Mexico Border Wars: Drugs, Immigration, and Homeland Security.* Westport: Praeger Security International.

Perea, Juan F. 2011. "The Echoes of Slavery: Recognizing the Racist Origins of the Agricultural and Domestic Worker Exclusion from the National Labor Relations Act." *Ohio State Law Journal* 72: 95–138.

Perez, William. 2009. *We Are Americans: Undocumented Students Pursuing the American Dream.* Sterling: Stylus Publishing.

Pew Research Hispanic Trends Project. 2009. "Fact Sheet: Mexican Immigrants in the United States, 2008." Washington, DC: Pew Research Center. Last accessed October 10, 2014. http://pewhispanic.org/files/factsheets/47.pdf.

Pinar, William F. 2007. "Cultures of Torture." In *Warfare in the American Homeland: Policing and Prison in a Penal Democracy*, edited by Joy James, 290–304. Durham, NC: Duke University Press.

Raeder, Myrna S. 2003. "Gendered Implications of Sentencing and Correctional Practices: A Legal Perspective." In *Gendered Justice: Addressing Female Offenders*, edited by Barbara E. Bloom, 173–207. Durham, NC: Carolina Academic Press.

Rafter, Nicole Hahn. 1985. *Partial Justice: Women in State Prisons, 1800–1935.* Boston: Northeastern University Press.

Raj, Anita, and Jay Silverman. 2002. "Violence Against Immigrant Women: The Roles of Culture, Context, and Legal Immigrant Status on Intimate Partner Violence." *Violence Against Women* 8: 367–398.

Ramírez, Catherine S. 2009. *The Woman in the Zoot Suit: Gender, Nationalism, and the Cultural Politics of Memory*. Durham, NC: Duke University Press.

Ramirez, Christian. 2008. "Vigil to Save Friendship Park." YouTube video, 9:37, posted by "VronRN2." Last accessed August 20, 2008. www.youtube .com/watch?v=kozK5yYJIRg&noredirect=1.

Rappaport, Aaron, and Kara Dansky. 2010. "State of Emergency: California's Correctional Crisis." *Federal Sentencing Reporter* 22, no. 3 (February): 133–143.

Red Casas del Migrante Scalabrini. 2014. "Ciudades." Last accessed November 20, 2014. www.migrante.com.mx/Ciudades.htm.

Rediker, Marcus. 2008. *The Slave Ship: A Human History*. New York: Penguin.

Reina, Angelica S., Brenda J. Lohman, and Marta Maria Maldonado. 2014. "'He Said They'd Deport Me': Factors Influencing Domestic Violence Help-Seeking Practices Among Latina Immigrants." *Journal of Interpersonal Violence* 29, no. 4: 593–615.

Richie, Beth E. 1995. *Compelled to Crime: The Gender Entrapment of Battered Black Women*. New York: Routledge & Kegan Paul.

———. 2012. *Arrested Justice: Black Women, Violence, and America's Prison Nation*. New York: New York University Press.

Rios, Victor M. 2006. "The Hyper-Criminalization of Black and Latino Male Youth in the Era of Mass Incarceration." *Souls: A Critical Journal of Black Politics, Culture, and Society* 8, no. 2: 40–54.

Roberts, Dorothy. 1995. "Racism and Patriarchy in the Meaning of Motherhood." In *Mothers in Law: Feminist Theory and Legal Regulation of Motherhood*, edited by Martha Albertson Fineman and Isabel Karpin, 224–249. New York: Columbia University Press.

———. 1996. "Who May Give Birth to Citizens? Reproduction, Eugenics, and Immigration." In *Immigrants Out! The New Nativism and the Anti-Immigrant Impulse in the United States*, edited by Juan F. Perea, 205–243. New York: New York University Press.

———. 1997. *Killing the Black Body: Race, Reproduction, and the Meaning of Liberty*. New York: Random House.

———. 2002. *Shattered Bonds: The Color of Child Welfare*. New York: Basic Books.

Rodríguez, Dylan. 2006. *Forced Passages: Imprisoned Radical Intellectuals and the US Prison Regime*. Minneapolis: University of Minnesota Press.

———. 2008. "'I Would Wish Death on You . . .' Race, Gender, and Immigration in the Globality of the US Prison Regime." *Scholar and Feminist Online* 6, no. 3 (Summer). Last accessed June 2, 2014. www.ethnicstudies .ucr.edu/publications_media/rodriguez/SCHOLAR_AND_FEMINIST _ONLINE.pdf.

Rodriguez, Nestor, and Cristian Paredes. 2013. "Coercive Immigration Enforcement and Bureaucratic Ideology." In *Constructing Immigrant "Illegality": Critiques, Experiences, and Responses*, edited by Cecilia Menjívar and Daniel Kanstroom, 63–83. New York: Cambridge University Press.

Romero, Mary. 2001. "State Violence, and the Social and Legal Construction of Latino Criminality: From El Bandido to Gang Member." *Denver University Law Review* 78: 1081–1118.

Rudrappa, Sharmila. 2004. *Ethnic Routes to Becoming American: Indian Immigrants and the Cultures of Citizenship.* Brunswick: Rutgers University Press.

Salcido, Olivia, and Cecilia Menjívar. 2012. "Gendered Paths to Legal Citizenship: The Case of Latin-American Immigrants in Phoenix, Arizona." *Law & Society* 46, no. 2: 335–368.

Santa Ana, Otto. 2002. *Brown Tide Rising: Metaphors of Latinos in Contemporary American Public Discourse.* Austin: University of Texas Press.

Sassen, Saskia. 1992. "Why Migration?" *NACLA Report on the Americas* 26, no. 1: 14–19.

———. 1996. *Losing Control? Sovereignty in an Age of Globalization.* New York: Columbia University Press.

Schmidt Camacho, Alicia R. 2008. *Migrant Imaginaries: Latino Cultural Politics in the US-Mexico Borderlands.* New York: NYU Press.

Seccombe, Karen. 2010. *So You Think I Drive a Cadillac? Welfare Recipients' Perspectives on the System and Its Reform.* New York: Pearson.

Selman, Donna, and Paul Leighton. 2010. *Punishment for Sale: Private Prisons, Big Business, and the Incarceration Binge.* Lanham: Rowman & Littlefield Publishers.

Sharp, Susan F., and M. Elaine Eriksen. 2003. "Imprisoned Mothers and Their Children." In *Women in Prison: Gender and Social Control,* edited by Barbara H. Zaitzow and Jim Thomas, 119–136. Boulder: Lynne Rienner Publishers.

Sharron, Jessica. 2007. "Passing the DREAM Act: Opportunities for Undocumented Americans." *Santa Clara Law Review* 47: 599–645.

Silliman, Jael, and Anannya Bhattacharjee, eds. 2002. *Policing the National Body: Race, Gender, and Criminalization.* Cambridge, MA: South End Press.

Simanski, John F. 2014. "Immigration Enforcement Actions: 2013." Washington, DC: DHS Office of Immigration Statistics. Last accessed November 10, 2014. www.dhs.gov/sites/default/files/publications/ois_enforcement_ar_2013.pdf.

Simanski, John, and Lesley M. Sapp. 2012. "Immigration Enforcement Actions: 2011." DHS Office of Immigration Statistics. Last accessed November 24, 2013. www.dhs.gov/sites/default/files/publications/immigration-statistics/enforcement_ar_2011.pdf.

Simmons, Ann M. 2004. "Deportation May Cut Short an Immigrant Success Story. Couple in US for 20 Years, Must Leave Unless They Are Given a Last-Minute Reprieve." *Los Angeles Times,* September 29. http://articles.latimes.com/2004/sep/29/local/me-deport29.

———. 2005. "Q&A/Immigrants and Deportations. Broad Range of Offenses Can Lead to Removal." *Los Angeles Times,* September 7. http://articles.latimes.com/2005/sep/07/local/me-explainer7.

Simmons, Charlene Wear. 2000. *Children of Incarcerated Parents.* Sacramento: California Research Bureau. Last accessed November 24, 2014. www.library.ca.gov/crb/00/notes/v7n2.pdf.

Simon, Jonathan. 2014. *Mass Incarceration on Trial: A Remarkable Court Decision and the Future of Prisons in America*. New York: New Press, 2014.

Smith, Carrie Jefferson, and Diane S. Young. 2003. "The Multiple Impacts TANF, ASFA, and Mandatory Drug Sentencing for Families Affected by Maternal Incarceration." In *Children and Youth Services Review* 25, no. 7: 535–552.

Smith, Dorothy E. 1990. *The Conceptual Practices of Power: A Feminist Sociology of Knowledge*. Boston: Northeastern University Press.

Smith, Gail T. 2006. "The Adoption and Safe Families Act of 1997: Its Impact on Prisoner Mothers and Their Children." In *Women and Girls in the Criminal Justice System: Policy Issues and Practices*, edited by Russell Immarigeon. Kingston, NJ: Civic Research Institute.

Sokoloff, Natalie J., and Ida Dupont. 2005. "Domestic Violence at the Intersections of Race, Class, and Gender: Challenges and Contributions to Understanding Violence Against Marginalized Women in Diverse Communities." *Violence Against Women* 11: 38–64.

Stern, Alexandra Minna. 2005. "Sterilized in the Name of Public Health: Race, Immigration, and Reproductive Control in Modern California." *American Journal of Public Health* 95, no. 7: 1128–1138.

Stumpf, Juliet. 2006. "The Crimmigration Crisis: Immigrants, Crime, and Sovereign Power." *American University Law Review* 56: 367–419.

Sudbury, Julia, ed. 2005. *Global Lockdown: Race, Gender, and the Prison-Industrial Complex*. New York: Routledge.

Sudbury, Julia, and Margo Okazawa-Rey, eds. 2009. *Activist Scholarship: Anti-racism, Feminism, and Social Change*. Transnational Feminist Studies. Boulder: Paradigm Publishers.

Taylor, Jennifer. 2002. "California's Proposition 21: A Case of Juvenile Injustice." *Southern California Law Review* 75: 983–1020.

Tonry, Michael. 1995. *Malign Neglect: Race, Crime and Punishment in America*. New York: Oxford University Press.

US Bureau of Labor Statistics. 2014. "Labor Force Characteristics by Race and Ethnicity, 2013." Last accessed November 1, 2014. www.bls.gov/cps/cpsrace2013.pdf.

US Citizenship and Immigration Services (USCIS). 2012. "Consideration of Deferred Action for Childhood Arrivals (DACA). Washington, DC: DHS Immigration and Customs Enforcement. Last updated December 4, 2014. www.uscis.gov/humanitarian/consideration-deferred-action-childhood-arrivals-daca.

———. 2014a. "INS Records for 1930s Mexican Repatriations." Washington, DC: DHS Immigration and Customs Enforcement. Last updated November 3, 2014. www.uscis.gov/history-and-genealogy/our-history/historians-mailbox/ins-records-1930s-mexican-repatriations.

———. 2014b. "Executive Actions on Immigration." Washington, DC: DHS Immigration and Customs Enforcement. Last updated December 5, 2014. www.uscis.gov/immigrationaction#2.

US Department of Justice. 2007. "Corrections Statistics." Washington, DC: Bureau of Justice Statistics. Last accessed February 9, 2009. http://bjs.ojp.usdoj.gov/.

———. 2012. "Correctional Populations in the United States, 2011." Washington, DC: Bureau of Justice Statistics. Last accessed November 9, 2013. www.bjs.gov/content/pub/pdf/cpus11.pdf.

US Immigration and Customs Enforcement. 2011. "Fact Sheet: Detention Management." US Department of Homeland Security. Last accessed November 10, 2013. www.ice.gov/news/library/factsheets/detention-mgmt .htm.

———. 2012. "FY 2012: ICE Announces Year-End Removal Numbers, Highlights Focuses on Key Priorities and Issues New National Detainer Guidance to Further Focus Resources." Washington, DC: Department of Homeland Security. Last accessed November 10, 2013. www.ice.gov/news/releases /fy-2012-ice-announces-year-end-removal-numbers-highlights-focus-key -priorities-and.

———. 2013a. "FY 2013 ICE Immigration Removals." Washington, DC: Department of Homeland Security. Last accessed November 10, 2013. www .ice.gov/removal-statistics.

———. 2013b. "Removal Statistics." Washington, DC: Immigration and Customs Enforcement. Last accessed November 10, 2013. www.ice.gov /removal-statistics/.

———. 2014. "FY 2013 ICE Immigration Removals." *ERO Annual Report*. Washington, DC: Department of Homeland Security. Last accessed November 5, 2014. www.ice.gov/doclib/about/offices/ero/pdf/2013-ice -immigration-removals.pdf.

———. "Delegation of Immigration Authority Section 287(g) Immigration and Nationality Act." Washington, DC: Department of Homeland Security. Last accessed November 20, 2014. www.ice.gov/287g/.

———. "Secure Communities." Washington, DC: Department of Homeland Security. Last accessed November 22, 2014. www.ice.gov/secure _communities/.

US Immigration and Naturalization Services. 1997. "Illegal Immigration Reform and Immigrant Responsibility Act of September 30, 1996." Washington, DC: Department of Justice, March.

Venn, Couze. 2009. "Neoliberal Political Economy, Biopolitics and Colonialism: A Transcolonial Genealogy of Inequality," *Theory, Culture & Society* 26, no. 6: 206–233.

Vila Freyer, Ana. 2007. "Las Políticas de Atención a Migrantes en los Estados de México: Acción, Reacción y Gestión." In *¿Invisibles? Migrantes Internacionales en la Escena Política*, edited by Cecilia Imaz, 77–105. México: Facultad de Ciencias Sociales y Políticas/Universidad Nacional Autónoma de México/Sitesa.

Villalón, Roberta. 2010. *Violence Against Latina Immigrants: Citizenship, Inequality, and Community*. New York: New York University Press.

Wacquant, Loïc. 2009a. *Punishing the Poor: The Neoliberal Government of Social Insecurity*. Durham, NC: Duke University Press.

———. 2009b. *Prisons of Poverty*. Minneapolis: University of Minnesota Press.

———. 2010. *Deadly Symbiosis: Race and the Rise of the Penal State*. Cambridge: Polity Press.

Wallerstein, Immanuel. 2011. *The Modern World-System III: The Second Era of Great Expansion of the Capitalist World-Economy, 1730s–1840s.* Berkeley: University of California Press.

Walsh, James P. 2014. "Watchful Citizens: Immigration Control, Surveillance, and Societal Participation." *Social and Legal Studies* 32, no. 2: 237–259.

Watanabe, Teresa. 2003a. "Federal Policy Becomes Family Matter: US Orders Couple's Deportation, Though Judge Ruled It Would Hurt Their Gifted Child." *Los Angeles Times,* October 27.

———. 2003b. "Parents Who Feared Deportation Granted Temporary Reprieve: Lawmakers Introduce Legislation to Try to Keep Family of Gifted Bell Gardens Girl Together." *Los Angeles Times,* December 12.

Weitz, Mark A. 2010. *The Sleepy Lagoon Murder Case: Race Discrimination and Mexican-American Rights.* Lawrence: University Press of Kansas.

Welch, Michael. 2000. "The Role of the Immigration and Naturalization Service in the Prison-Industrial Complex." *Social Justice* 27, no. 3: 73–89.

———. 2002. *Detained: Immigration Laws and the Expanding INS Jail Complex.* Philadelphia: Temple University Press.

Wessler, Seth Freed. 2012. "Supreme Court Upholds 'Show Me Your Papers' in Arizona's SB 1070." *Colorlines,* June 25. http://colorlines.com /archives/2012/06/supreme_court_upholds_show_me_your_papers_in _sb_1070_blocks_other_provisions.html.

White, E. Frances. 2001. *Dark Continent of Our Bodies: Black Feminism and the Politics of Respectability.* Philadelphia: Temple University Press.

Whitehorn, Laura, and Susie Day. 2007. "Resisting the Ordinary." In *Warfare in the American Homeland: Policing and Prison in a Penal Democracy,* edited by Joy James, 273–289. Durham, NC: Duke University Press.

Willen, Sarah S. 2010. "Citizens, 'Real' Others, and 'Other' Others: The Biopolitics of Otherness and the Deportation of Unauthorized Migrant Workers from Tel Aviv, Israel." In *The Deportation Regime: Sovereignty, Space, and the Freedom of Movement,* edited by Nicholas De Genova and Nathalie Peutz, 262–294. Durham, NC: Duke University Press, 2010.

Williams, Eric. 1994. *Capitalism and Slavery.* Chapel Hill: University of North Carolina Press.

Williams, India. 2011. "Arizona Senate Bill 1070: State Sanctioned Racial Profiling?" *Journal of the Legal Profession* 36: 269–284.

Wilson, Tamar Diana. 1999. "Anti-Immigrant Sentiment and the Process of Settlement among Mexican Immigrants to the United States: Reflections on the Current Wave of Mexican Immigrant Bashing." *Review of Radical Political Economics* 31, no. 2 (Spring): 1–26.

———. 2000. "Anti-immigrant Sentiment and the Problem of Reproduction/ Maintenance in Mexican Immigration to the United States." *Critique of Anthropology* 20, no. 2: 192–213. doi:10.1177/0308275X0002000206.

Wolcott, Victoria W. 2001. *Remaking Respectability: African American Women in Interwar Detroit.* Chapel Hill: University of North Carolina Press.

Woldenberg, Laura. 2013. *Deportee Purgatory.* Documentary. Vice News. Last accessed October 30, 2014. http://www.vice.com/video/deportee -purgatory-video.

Wright, Melissa. 2011. "Necropolitics, Narcopolitics, and Femicide: Gendered

Violence on the Mexico-US Border." *Signs: Journal of Women in Culture and Society* 36, no. 3: 707–731.

Wu, Ellen D. 2013. *The Color of Success: Asian Americans and the Origins of the Model Minority*. Princeton: Princeton University Press, 2013.

XIX Ayuntamiento en Tijuana. 2008. "Comunicado Numero '1' del Dia: Visita Presidenta de DIF Tijuana 'Casa Refugio Elvira'." Last accessed September 20, 2008. www.tijuana.gob.mx/webpanel/comunicado/comunicado Completo.aspx?iIdComunicado=1917.

Yeng, Sokthan. 2013. *The Biopolitics of Race: State Racism and US Immigration*. Lanham: Lexington Books.

Yuval-Davis, Nira. 1997. *Gender and the Nation*. Thousand Oaks: Sage Publications.

Zilberg, Elana. 2004. "Fools Banished from the Kingdom: Remapping Geographies of Gang Violence between the Americas (Los Angeles and San Salvador)." *American Quarterly* 56, no. 3: 759–779.

———. 2007. "Gangster in Guerilla Face: A Transnational Mirror of Production between the USA and El Salvador." *Anthropological Theory* 7: 37–57.

Zimmerman, Mary K., Jacquelyn S. Litt, and Christine E. Bose. 2006. *Global Dimensions of Gender and Carework*. Stanford: Stanford University Press.

Zolberg, Aristide R. 2006. *A Nation by Design: Immigration Policy in the Fashioning of America*. New York: Russell Sage Foundation Press.

# Index